KISS TOMORROW
HELLO

DOUBLEDAY NEW YORK LONDON TORONTO SYDNEY AUCKLAND

KISS TOMORROW
HELLO

NOTES FROM THE
MIDLIFE UNDERGROUND BY
TWENTY-FIVE WOMEN OVER FORTY

edited by
KIM BARNES and
CLAIRE DAVIS

PUBLISHED BY DOUBLEDAY
a division of Random House, Inc.

DOUBLEDAY and the portrayal of an anchor with a dolphin
are registered trademarks of Random House, Inc.

Book design by Chris Welch
Interior photography @www.csaimages.com

Library of Congress Cataloging-in-Publication Data

ISBN 0-385-51541-3

PRINTED IN THE UNITED STATES OF AMERICA

March 2006

First Edition

1   3   5   7   9   10   8   6   4   2

WITH LOVE AND GRATITUDE TO OUR MOTHERS:
CLAUDETTE BARNES AND CLARA DAVIS

AND FOR ALL THE WOMEN—MOTHERS, SISTERS,
AUNTS, FRIENDS—THE ONES WHO SPOKE, AS WELL AS
THE ONES WHO NEVER FOUND WORDS

Probably the happiest period in life most frequently is in middle age, when the eager passions of youth are cooled, and the infirmities of age not yet begun; as we see that the shadows, which are at morning and evening so large, almost entirely disappear at midday.

— ELEANOR ROOSEVELT

The really frightening thing about middle age is the knowledge that you'll grow out of it.

— DORIS DAY

How did it get so late so soon?

— THEODORE GEISEL

CONTENTS

III

I HAVE A CRUSH ON TED GEISEL

IV

WHAT WE KEEP

KISS TOMORROW
HELLO

INTRODUCTION

Are you one of us?

Daughter. Mother. Sister. Lover. Friend.

Yes?

Are you a woman of a *certain age*?

Your aliases, then: Auntie. Elder. Spinster. Ex. Mrs. Robinson, aka the older woman. Mom. Grandma. Wise woman. Crone. Primary caregiver. Friend to the end.

Your password?

Time.

And experience.

Of course. All that water under the bridge you yourself might have floated away on, and sometimes wanted to. Those Terrible Twenties, awash in desire, decisions, despair. The Thirties Without a Thought in Your Head because all of your intellectual and emotional energy seemed already committed: that career, those children, the lover who waited so hopefully for scraps from the burgeoning table of your life. Or didn't.

Are you one of us? Part of the generation that embodies the very definition of change and transition. From the Pointer Sisters to Sister Sledge; from a schoolgirl's love of Jim Morrison to the sexily maternal adoration of Andrea Bocelli; from Diane Keaton in *Annie Hall* to Diane Keaton in *Something's Gotta Give.*

Perhaps you've been a nice girl, bad girl, party girl, Girl Friday. You've read *Fear of Flying, The Women's Room, The Second Sex, The Story of O, Our Bodies, Ourselves, First Edition,* gone braless as an act of subversion, only to find yourself, all these years later, searching Lingerie for greater *support,* dependent upon salesclerks half your age who have never heard the word *foundations* in reference to undergarments.

Are you one of us?

You look around and see that the world has changed somehow. The first husband, gone. Perhaps the second has followed like a penny thrown after one already lost. The exciting career you sacrificed so much for has lost some of its luster. Should you give it all up, shift gears, try something new? At *your* age? You've begun to count the years until retirement. In the mirror, a reflection you hardly recognize: those marks at the corners of the eyes, that drifting chin, the hair disappearing in one place and then sprouting in places you never dreamed it could. One day, you awaken into a new body, just when you were growing fond of the old one.

Here you are: midway, midlife, on the cusp, resting from the uphill climb, ready to coast. You've made it this far, haven't you? You've learned some things. You've earned a rest.

But, then, the parents are aging. They need a little more of your time, perhaps to move them into a smaller home (what is *in* all those boxes in the basement?), or to help them fill out their living wills. And those unused eggs you've guarded so carefully against accidental conception (all those years of pills, condoms, diaphragms, and jittery mornings after)— well, those eggs are aging, too. Instead of kicking back, you find yourself kicking in, finding another hour before bed to arrange for your mother's care, another hour before dawn to exercise, another hour come Sunday to make love, do the laundry, pay the bills, finish the novel, and, perhaps, take a walk, take a deep breath, appreciate the life you have made for yourself.

You circle the block, the neighborhood, the lake. You end up right back where you began.

Are you lost? Are you found?

Here we are, others like you, who have grown weary of anger, tired to angst, fed up with despair. We've discovered we can step through the looking glass of our own lives and still exist. Did you miss out on the psychedelic-mushroom trip when you were twenty? Try the mind-altering experience of a midnight hot flash. That guilt that kept you nailed to the floor of the playroom, your children needy at your knees as you daydreamed of a tropical beach or, more likely, a dark closet where you might sit in singular silence, just for a while? That's been replaced with the solitude and wide-open spaces left by teenagers departing on the Next Shuttle to Adulthood.

But it's not all shits and giggles, is it? Our forties, our fifties, our sixties. Things go right more often than we're willing to believe. Things go wrong.

Maybe it seems that you are living your life in reverse, like Antonya Nelson, say, who was born to worry, ". . . burdened with that paradoxical combination of a hyperactive imagination for catastrophe coupled with a physically exhausted affect"—her definition of middle age. Or perhaps you've *waited,* chosen your partner so carefully, picked *just the right time* in such a mature and responsible manner . . . only to discover, as Lolly Winston did, that your body—and your ovaries—have continued on down the road without you. "How could 'old age' be a medical diagnosis," Lolly asks, "when I wasn't even forty?"

Your body—giver of pleasure, of life. And pain. Judy Blunt contemplates the summer of fire—the forests all around her hometown of Missoula burning—as a season of change: "I arrived at this new place: middle-aged, my three children beautifully grown, even as the part of me that grew them threatened mutiny, my medical charts a growing litany of unusual bleeding and bad Pap smears." Julia Glass quells the mutiny of her body—breast cancer—with surgery but decides against chemotherapy so that she might yet conceive the child she longs for, only to undergo a new uprising after the birth of her son. As she struggles with the too-early onset of chemically induced menopause, she finds comfort, if not resolution, in the books of Dr. Seuss that she reads to her young son: "If once upon a time the rhythms of my life felt like those of a square dance, now they feel a lot like the dear doctor's madcap poetry. . . ."

When you look in the mirror, who is it you see? The girl you were at twenty, or the woman you've become? In "She Who Once Was," Rebecca McClanahan explores the desire we feel to retain youth and give ourselves over to the cosmetic knife: ". . . .if aging is difficult for those who were only sometimes cute," she says, "just imagine how hard it must be for the aging knockouts, the living dolls." Lauren Slater, self-described "frowzer," wonders at the debutante-come-lately she miraculously becomes when fitted with a new and expensive suit. Brenda Miller observes from a distance her once-unencumbered self, when, at nineteen, she hitchhiked solo to Grateful Dead concerts and danced with a body unaware of its inevitable cessation: "[That girl] has no doubts, no worry, no fear: Those clumsy emotions will belong to her older self, a middle-aged woman who watches from her post in the future, amused but also a little annoyed, a bit peeved with that girl's careless beauty, her naïveté, a faith that holds solid as an acolyte's."

But this body—it is still good, isn't it? What discomforts it visits upon us are often matched by our heightened awareness of its capacity for pleasure and transcendence. The Older Woman (OW) in us might envy Karen Karbo and the humorous satisfaction she finds with J. (her YM—younger man). "For it's common knowledge," she states, "that by virtue of being the OW, I've been miraculously transformed into the modern-day equivalent of the sexually ravenous French courtesan who knows all the moves and when to expertly apply them, and J., by virtue of being the YM, is as well endowed as a porn star, eager to learn, and indefatigable."

Tell us what you have survived. We know. We've been there, too. Illness. Childbirth. Violence. Fear. Share with us your victories. In her essay "Tearing Up the Sheets," Ellen Sussman, having suffered a rape as a young woman, revels in her recaptured sexuality: "I love sex. I love middle-age sex. I love married sex. I'm almost fifty and I've never felt sexier. But damn, it took a long time to get here." And "In My Red Dress Voice," Joy Passanante describes the delight she has always taken in her body's erotic promise and mourns the unfettered laugh she has lost to dysphonia, even as she celebrates her new, more sustainable voice, "silken, delicate as a cream-colored orchid."

Like you, we are of the age when we know—please!—that we cannot have it all. We know just *how she does it* (and we have invented a few *new* ways, which we may or may not share). We have come to accept that the world will survive without our constant attention, and so we turn our gaze outward, feel that road before us begin to open. And if it's not all downhill, so much the better. We've got some climbing to do— we need that strength in our legs, the air filling our lungs. Because we intend to keep moving forward along the path. Upward. Inward.

Along the way, we make discoveries. Joyce Maynard, in her quest for midlife companionship, realizes that on-line dating (who could resist LoveMeDo, HaveAHeart, ZenWhat?) will never be a sure thing and that her female friendships may be what will sustain her. In "Coffee Dates with a Beefcake," Pam Houston, married to a man who shares her dedication to "the notion that no one person can provide all things for any other," discovers that she is infatuated with another seemingly perfect male, "Monsieur Gâteau du Boeuf." *"Whose idea was it,"* she wonders, *"to give the average woman forty years, say, to figure out that she has a sex drive, that she has sexual power, that her longings are valid, that her curves are sexy, that her breasts are the right shape, that there are at least three different kinds of orgasm and she can have all of them?"*

You know, as we do, that the road to self-discovery is not paved with gold, is never straight, and sometimes leads into dark forests and deep jungles. We awaken from the dream of our lives to find ourselves in another country, our lover gone, our children grown, the house silent around us. In the throes of her second divorce, Lisa Norris finds herself lost in the fun house of identity: "High-desert summer but not hot enough for hallucinations: That guy outside the Bittercreek Alehouse in his baseball cap, T-shirt, jeans, and shell necklace really could be twenty-nine-year-old movie star Ben Affleck . . . And who is that woman who looks just like me in the mirror behind the bar? Could she be some evil twin, sitting in a place I'd never go alone, acting like a hanger-on, a groupie?"

Lynn Freed, contemplating her fiftieth birthday, relates her aversion to so much attention being paid to aging and the "celebrating—twin to that other horror of modern parlance, honoring—[that] attaches itself like a weed to every damp spot along the female path, birth to death." In "Sources of Pleasure," Joan Silber finds that the sense of loss she feels after her fiftieth birthday is not remedied by her trip to Provence. Not until she volunteers as a Buddy for AIDS patients does she understand that "in time of extremity, you need human love." When Annick Smith's adult son tells her that she has a teenage granddaughter—a precious secret he has kept from her—she questions her perception of the honesty she believes she has always shared with her children: "I felt betrayed. The trust I expected . . . had been broken. But trust is a tricky concept, and even past sixty (perhaps especially past sixty), women like me feel impelled to stick to the myths we have invented for ourselves."

Finally, after decades of hoarding and purging our emotional baggage, of surrendering too much and, sometimes, not enough of ourselves, what we come to realize is this: There are some things that we keep for reasons that matter. We keep what we have learned from our elders along the way, as Bharti Kirchner does in "Lipstick and Bindi": "Slow down. Don't be so frenetic. Contemplate on the insights you have gained. Listen to the silence within." We learn that our desire to travel, to escape, to remain still may be as genetically encoded as the color of our eyes and hair: Diana Abu-Jaber recognizes her father's Bedouin spirit in her own impulse to move from the very place she might call home; Beverly Lowry defines her tendency toward wanderlust in the context of her parents'—Moo and Big's—nomadic life. And in "Moving My Mother," Andrea Chapin is startled to discover that her elderly mother's memory is chock-full of life-shattering secrets that the ailing woman has kept silent for years.

And *your* mother? Did she pass on her secrets? Did she whisper the truths of her own transformation, or speak of it not at all? As though the honest details of the body's progression through time were an immodest proposal, an act of espionage. So often, if you're a woman, simply growing old is enough to bring on shame, to necessitate euphemisms and coded snippets of intimate information. You've heard them, haven't you? The women speaking in low voices as though there has been a crime— your mother and aunts, in the kitchen, with the pot roast: *female trouble, that time of life, the Change.*

Their collected trinkets and treasures pass into our hands, and we wonder what we might keep of the women who birthed us—those strange familiars. As Mary Clearman Blew surveys the abandoned ranch house in which she was raised and considers what to take away before the house is sold, she remembers how her mother had little use for sentimentality or keepsakes of any kind. Mary remembers, too, her mother's anger and resentment and realizes that what her mother wanted was the "absence of reminders" of her own past. Toi Derricotte finds the terrain of her mother's death complicated more by relief than by grief. And Meredith Hall, as she observes herself in the mirror, remembers not only her own young body but the body of her dying mother, whose arms and legs were withered by multiple sclerosis. Only in death is the mother's body renewed, not euphemistically, but literally . . . "a great and mysterious transformation. The devastation from the illness receded, as if time were in rapid reverse. Her skin smoothed. Her arms and legs and hands thinned, as if muscle again held flesh to bone. Her paunchy belly flattened. The etchings of courage against such fear, of effort and grit, left her face . . . And then she was gone." What Meredith comes to understand is that, finally, what we keep is carried in the narrative of the mind as well as the body: "The young woman's body I live inside still, that unforgotten home, is a text. It is engraved with memory . . ."

Your body. Our body. Our various selves. We are in this together, joined by circumstance, and by choice. We share our stories over coffee, over wine, over the phone, in letters, on-line. In the past, our *time* was a time to whisper, but things have *changed,* haven't they?

These are our stories. Our secrets written out loud.

Listen.

We are your Sibyl. Your gender-bended Dante. We know things.

Follow us into the underground.

We will show you the way.

PART I

SHE WHO
ONCE WAS

Since it is the Other within us who is old, it is natural that the
revelation of our age should come to us from outside—from
others. We do not accept it willingly.
— SIMONE DE BEAUVOIR

•

I've never understood why people consider youth a time of
freedom and joy. It's probably because they have
forgotten their own.
— MARGARET ATWOOD

•

These days, [I] don't sit there going, "Oh my God, she's getting
wrinkles." I think, "Oh my God, look what she just did
on that trapeze!"
— SUSAN SARANDON

She Who Once Was

REBECCA McCLANAHAN

We were standing at the kitchen sink, chopping vegetables for a salad, when Martha announced her plan. She'd thought about it for months, she said. Maybe years. I regretted my response immediately, and to this day still regret it. Just listen to me. I am telling my friend that she does not need a face-lift, that she is one of the most beautiful women I know.

"I knew you'd say that," she says, as if I've insulted her. In this kitchen moment, Martha is fifty-three, the age I am now, seven years later, as I write these words. She is trim and fit, a marathon runner with classic good looks, a dazzling smile, and the angular facial structure of a photographer's model. The kind of woman who turns heads when she enters a room.

"The person in the mirror is older than the person I am inside," she continues, her chiseled features sharpening.

"The world needs beautiful older women," I say.

She flinches as though I've slapped her. "I'm not ready to be an older woman."

Something scratches at the edge of consciousness. A memory, jagged, fleeting: a few months before, Christmas breakfast at my brother's table. We are on vacation, my husband and I, still wearing our robes and luxuriating in our laziness, the California sun pouring through the tall windows onto our faces. My brother takes a seat across the table. "Hmm," he says, staring at my face, then turning his gaze to Donald. "The wife looks a little different in this light, doesn't she?" End of Christmas morning, end of sunlight on my face.

"When I look in the mirror," Martha is saying. "I don't know who that person is."

"Then don't look in the mirror," I snap. I study her face—the strong, taut jaw, the high cheekbones, the smooth brow. What could she possibly want to change?

Martha takes a sip of wine. "I just thought you should know that I'll be out of commission for a while, until everything heals. I won't be going out. Some friends"—and here she hesitates, as if considering whether to include me in this group—"plan to come by. To bring a movie, a meal." A few years before, I had visited Martha in the hospital, bringing flowers and candy, steadying her as she shuffled down the corridor. But that was for a hysterectomy. Something to save her life, to prolong it. This hardly fits in the same category, does it?

This is when I should start backpedaling. After all, it's her face, her decision. But I can't let it go. The arguments stack up in my mind; some form into sentences. I am morally opposed to plastic surgery. And what about the expense? You could send a kid to college for what it would cost. And what about the messages this sends to young women, to our own nieces? I know I should get off my high horse, try another ploy, but I am suddenly desperate to make my point. I ask her if she's seen the PBS series, the British one with the older woman and her much younger lover. "She's very sexy," I say. "Age can be very sexy."

Martha clenches her jaw, but still I don't stop, though I have long since depleted my arsenal of logic and must resort to dumb repetition. "You need to get your vision checked. You are one of the most beautiful women I know." I mention the plaque that hangs over the bureau in my friend Suzanne's guest room, where most people would hang a mirror: THE BEST MIRROR IS AN OLD FRIEND. Until this moment, I'd assumed that "old" referred to the longevity of the friendship. Now it occurs to me that the plaque carries another meaning altogether. Okay, how far am I willing to go with this? "If you look old to yourself," I begin, "then your friends must look old, too." I don't know what I expect her to say other than the truth, which is the last thing I want to hear.

"You're right," she says. "They do."

THE FIRST AND only time I saw Aunt Bessie cry was the night I played Lottie Moon. It was 1965 and the production was *Her Lengthened Shadow*, a sentimental playlet about a woman missionary who died nearly a century ago. I was fifteen, the same age Lottie Moon is when the play opens, and in the hour it took to perform the play, I aged fifty-seven years. Great-Aunt Bessie, a fixture in my parents' home for many years and my sometime roommate, had gone to church with the rest of the family to see the play. My mother had sewn the costumes and someone else's mother had applied the pancake makeup and, during scene changes, penciled in lines between my eyes and on the sides of my mouth. I remember frowning mightily to create forehead furrows and smiling crazily, unnaturally, to form craters around my mouth so that she could guide the eyebrow pencil into the depressions. In the last scene, when a special lightbulb cast a shadow across the stage, signifying my death at the unthinkably old age of seventy-two, I heard gasps in the audience and knew I had played my part well.

After changing back into my clothes and cold-creaming the years from my face, I walked out to the family's station wagon, parked at the edge of the church parking lot. My parents and siblings were waiting with almost universal praise, but Bessie was uncharacteristically silent, facing straight ahead, her hands clasped tightly in her lap. I climbed into the backseat beside her. Though I was a petite teenager, I sat higher in the seat than Bessie, who, try as she might, could never quite keep herself erect; her crooked hip tilted her body to the side. Bessie was smaller than any grown-up I knew, but her hands were disproportionately large, marbled by dark, prominent veins and mottled with age spots. Did I mention that Bessie was old? Always, always, from my first knowledge of her, old. And now, smack-dab in the middle of the Lottie Moon memory, I am stopping to do the math. Nineteen sixty-five. Bessie was eighty-five years old. Tears were sliding down her ancient face. Tears? I had known Bessie all my life, had slept in the same room with her, the same bed, had, I now realize, even loved her in my selfish, adolescent way. But I had never seen her cry.

I tapped my mother on the shoulder. "What's wrong?" I asked. I often talked around Aunt Bessie as if she weren't there, as if she were a piece of furniture that had been in the house so long, you no longer saw it—may the universe forgive me for this. My mother turned from the front seat and calmly shook her head as if to silence the question. But Aunt Bessie had heard, and she turned to me, her eyes rimmed with red, brimming. "You looked so old," she said. "It hurt to see you look so old."

EARLY PHOTOGRAPHS OF my mother bear witness to my father's frequent remark: "She was a living doll." Sometimes I correct him, joking that if he's looking to make point, he shouldn't use the past tense. But usually I don't make a federal case about it, partly because the remark doesn't seem to bother my mother, but mostly because his affection for her is so obvious and steadfast, so daily. Let's say she's getting up from her chair, where she's been piecing a quilt or arranging photographs in an album or writing a note to one of their fifteen grandchildren. As she moves across the room, without fail my father's gaze will follow her with all the admiration of a newlywed, for, if we are to believe his eyes, she is all news to him, this woman to whom he has been married sixty years. Sometimes, out of the blue, he will say to me, "Juanita is a wonderful woman. You have an amazing mother. Do you know that?" This is a rare gift, I realize, for a daughter—of any age, let alone a daughter as old as I am—to witness a father's love for her mother, and hers for him. And I mark it here, so I will not forget. If beauty resides in the beholder's eyes, my mother is still beautiful to her beholder. Yet even so, there remains that troublesome past tense: My mother *was* a living doll.

AS I MENTIONED earlier, on the afternoon in which she announced her plans, Martha was a beautiful woman. Two weeks ago, a few days past her sixtieth birthday, I visited her in her southern city and I can attest that she is still a beautiful woman. I hesitate to phrase it that way. To say that a woman is *still* beautiful suggests a remove from what went before. It hints at time, change and loss, placing the receiver of the compliment in a fragile holding pattern. *Still* beautiful. Still holding. I don't like the implications, but it is difficult to compliment an aging woman, even one as attractive as Martha, without employing some syntactic time marker. She looks so *youthful,* we say. Or: She is *aging* well. Recently, a young colleague, after seeing my age reported in a magazine, said, "If I hadn't seen this in print, I wouldn't believe it. I mean, you look good." As if it were some minor miracle, at my advanced age, to look presentable. I shushed her with thanks before she could say more, before I could say more. No need to confuse her with details that are no one's business but my own: that, on the advice of my older sister, I touch up my hair color every six weeks or so. That, to be honest, I have been doing this for over a decade now, long before Martha had her face-lift. "Nothing ages a woman faster than gray hair," my sister had said, though there was no need to convince me. The first wiry gray coils had sprouted shortly after my fortieth birthday. No way, I thought. No way is the woman in the mirror going to be older than the woman I am inside. I'm too young to be old.

LAST MONTH, ONE of my nieces gave birth to a daughter, and I am happy to report that little Addison Kate is aging quite well. She came into this world already nine months old and, if the universe permits, she will continue to age until she dies. If Addie keeps growing old, perhaps one day a century from now some young sculptor will cast her likeness in bronze as Rodin did the old woman we now call the Helmet-Maker's Wife. Actually, the full title I read in the museum beneath Rodin's arresting sculpture was *She Who Was Once the Helmet-Maker's Beautiful Wife.* Art critics make a big fuss about the sculpture's content—the withered naked figure, her sagging flesh and shriveled breasts—but it is the work's title that breaks something loose inside me. To be named not by what you are now, in this moment, but by what you once were. As if everything that matters is already gone. The old women pass by on the streets of my city, and I imagine captions floating over their heads: "She

Who Was Once the College Professor's Brilliant Daughter." "She Who Was Once the City Ballet's Principal Dancer." "She Who Was Once a Living Doll."

Aunt Bessie's caption might have read, "She Who Was Once the Young Woman Beneath the Flowering Tree, Holding a Guitar Close to Her Face and Leaning Visibly into the Music." This is one of the few early photographs in which Bessie is not looking away from the camera, or tilting her head down. For even in the eye of the most sympathetic beholder—her husband, for instance, who died long before I was born—Bessie could hardly have been seen as beautiful, even in her youth. Tiny at birth, weighing only four pounds, she never grew into the voluptuous form of her mother or of her sister, my grandmother Sylvia, who stands always directly in front of the camera's lens. Bessie's body remained, throughout her life, scrawny and tough, her crooked hip hitched at a cubist angle. And her face offered little comfort. One eye wandered to the left, and a deep scar across her nose, the result of a childhood encounter with boiling lye, was a burden she carried, not always without bitterness and shame, until her death.

Yet even so, Bessie aged well. Released early on from the expectation of beauty, she could turn her gaze outward to all that caught her wandering eye—farming, reading, bird-watching, traveling, mothering the tribe of great-nieces and -nephews—and away from the woman in the mirror, her fading, if imperfect, glory.

I DON'T REMEMBER when I first suspected that beauty was not my strongest suit. I do remember a contest that some girls in my sixth-grade class organized. During lunch one day in September, probably about the time the Miss America pageant was due to air, they passed out ballots listing the names of all the girls in our class, and beside each name, four possible boxes that you could check: "Beautiful," "Pretty," "Lovely," and "Cute." You were allowed four votes, one girl for each category. By the time the dismissal bell rang, Marilyn Stacklo had been declared "Beautiful," Christy Schutz was "Pretty," and two girls whose names I cannot recall were "Lovely" and "Cute." There were no check marks beside my name, but Marilyn informed me that I did get one write-in vote. On the bottom of a ballot, someone had neatly penciled my name, proclaiming me "Sometimes Cute."

The universe offered other clues, and by the time I turned fourteen, I had concluded that though in a pinch I might pass for pretty, I was definitely not a "knockout," the word I'd heard people use when describing my sisters. My skin was pale at a time when pale wasn't fashionable; my sisters tanned easily and evenly. Plus, they had our mother's dark, expressive eyes. I'd inherited our father's blues, which, according to all the songs in the sixties, were what every American girl wanted. But who among us wants what we already possess? Desire is measured by what we lack.

At any rate, I believe I am being truthful in saying I am grateful for being eased out of the beauty race and into the whirl of school and clubs and plays and writing. For if aging is difficult for those who were only sometimes cute, just imagine how hard it must be for the aging knockouts, the living dolls. Especially those who knew the power of early beauty. My friend Gail, who knew such power, powerfully, and who has openly mourned its passing over the past few years, has begun making alternate plans. "I've decided if I can't be beautiful anymore," she says, "I will make beautiful things." The things she plans to make—or, rather, to continue making, for she has been making them for decades now—are poems. Other women make other beautiful things: gardens, homes, businesses, paintings, symphonies. My mother made children. Then grandchildren. Then a church nursery school. Along the way, the homes she and my father made housed not only their children but also her elderly parents, Great-Aunt Bessie, and assorted lost souls for whom the home served as halfway house: a mentally ill niece, a young woman studying at a nearby college, a Chinese immigrant who had no other place to go.

When the house finally emptied, my mother returned to an early passion, hand quilting. Twice a month, she gathers around quilt frames with dozens of other women and makes beautiful things to give away. Five of the quilters are in their nineties. One is nearly a century old, and as I watch Gertie bent intently over her work, the intricately carved face and hands seem to me works of art. I do not know if they seem so to Gertie. Perhaps not. But if she mourns lost youth, she gives no hint of it. Gertie appears to live her days, as my grandmothers lived, as Aunt Bessie lived and as my mother lives, from the inside out. This is not to say that Gertie does not see herself as an object for adornment. Her lust for color and texture is legendary, and she always wears cheerfully bright outfits with coordinated accessories. The bureau in her bedroom, with its wide, tall mirror, holds a collector's cache of colorful lipsticks along with earrings and pins that she dons whenever she goes out, which is often. And who knows? Perhaps she wears them at home, too, so that when she passes by the mirror, she will be pleased, will nod at the woman reflected there, dressed in everyday finery and looking, well, if she does say so herself, not a day over eighty.

LAST NIGHT, I dreamed the scaffolding dream. More accurately, I redreamed it. I have been dreaming it, on and off, for years, and once even published a poem about it, so powerfully had its images captured me. In the dream, a tiny workman is perched on scaffolding that has been erected around a woman's face. He wears a hard hat and a tool belt, from which dangles an array of chisels, axes, hammers, and knives. Stepping gingerly from platform to platform, he hammers a bit there, a bit here, putties in cracks, sands down her rough edges. From the tool belt he extracts a tiny knife and begins to slice around the eyes, the nose, the sagging jowls. The huge woman is silent and unmoving. She does not even blink.

This is where a different writer, one who lives more sagely from the inside out, would interrupt with wisdom, New Age or old. Wisdom older than the stars. She would speak comfort, telling of earth mothers and Gaea, cosmic wombs and the mysteries of the Kula flower. In my thirties, I tried hard to be this kind of woman, and I haven't completely shaken my awe for the well-aging crone. Think of the freedom these women must feel, the ones I see at literary conferences, on yoga mats at the Y, on the jacket covers of thick books. Look, this one is standing defiantly in front of the camera, barefoot in a field of wheat, her large breasts loose under a cotton tent dress, her gray hair tangling in the wind. This is who I am, her weathered face says. Take me or leave me.

I have earned the years. Count them on my ringless hands, in the flesh around my middle.

I have studied such women from afar and have been blessed to know others who could teach me how to do this natural, terrifying thing called aging. If I wish to learn, I can stand at the edge of my mother's life, or my aunts' lives, or the life of Suzanne, the friend who keeps the plaque about old friends above her guest room dresser. Suzanne writes books, reads voraciously, teaches children and adults, sings in choirs, plays the piano, travels to see her grandchildren and elderly mother. Taking visible delight in whatever life throws her way, she gleefully anticipates each birthday and laughs about the years ahead, when her children will put her in "the home." "I can't wait," she says, running her hands through a no-nonsense cap of thick white hair. "I'll finally be able to catch up on all those movies I missed." Thin and wiry since childhood, as she enters her seventh decade she openly welcomes the first hints of fleshy padding. "In case I get sick," she says. "Old women lose weight when they get sick. I want some extra, just in case." And her black eyes glisten.

I THINK OF it as my Diane von Furstenberg moment. It was a cold but sunny March day, snow melting on city streets and me with a sense of *young* again because it was almost spring and I had a few hours between adult appointments, so when I saw the blue warp dress in the store window, I stopped. I am not usually a happy shopper—it is hard work for me—but something about the dress filled me with possibility. I'd had one just like it, decades before, a von Furstenberg wrap dress I'd worn forever, worn to threads, so perfectly it accented my narrow waist and camouflaged what I imagined, in those days, to be overly abundant thighs. Look, I thought, pulling the dress from the rack. It's the same dress! The same size, too. Oh fabulous joy, my lucky day!

You can guess the rest. The dressing room crisis, the shock when the wrap didn't come close to wrapping, the clerk bringing the next-largest size, and the next, and the years flashing through me in a blur. How could this be? Is this how it happens? You're going along just fine, living inside yourself, looking out at the world and feeling as young as you've always felt. Then, smack, you're hit with some objective measure, brought up short. How swiftly and unexpectedly it happens, and what a violent surprise! My younger sister, one of the former knockouts, swears that for her it happened overnight. She went to bed with one chin and woke up with two. My latest rude awakening took a different form but was no less violent. One morning not too long ago, I opened my eyes to a world where everyone with any power over me—my boss, doctor, lawyer, accountant, editor, agent—was younger than I was. Lately, I've had to force myself not to scan the Library of Congress birth dates of writers before I read their new books.

How did this happen? And where will it end? Why can't I gleefully accept that I have not only entered but am firmly planted in—and here I must take a deep breath—my *sixth* decade. Yes, sixth. I've done the math. If little Addie Kate has entered her first decade, and my niece, Addie's thirty-year-old mother, has entered her fourth, and Aunt Bessie died at the end of her tenth, then I must be in my sixth. There is no other way around it.

Time for a paragraph break. A glass of wine. A walk in Central Park. Time to step back into myself and look at the world from the inside out.

HOW GLORIOUS a natural aging would be. I love the idea of it. The further away I stand, the more attractive the idea becomes. And I welcome its incarnation—in other women. I like how age looks on others. But when it gets too close for comfort, well, there I am, peering into my husband's digital camera, which contains the candid shots he's been taking all day. "Delete," I tell him. And again, "Delete." "Bad angle on that one," I say. Or "Bad lighting." "Bad day." My gracefully aging husband shakes his head, not even bothering with his usual tack—that I look great, that he enjoys taking my picture. He just shrugs, clicks the delete key, and the evidence is erased, easy as that. If I asked, he could digitally alter the photographs; he has the technology. He could lift those drooping jowls, x out the crow's-feet around my eyes. But I'm not about to stoop that low.

Later, as I lie in bed beside this man in whose eyes I am beautiful, the arguments rage inside my head. What kind of woman am I becoming? Didn't I lecture Martha? And what were my reasons? What did I say? Oh yes, that age is sexy. That women like Faye Dunaway are cheating the world out of the chance to see a beautiful woman age. Liv Ullman had it right, I said. We need to listen to Liv. Remember what she said to the reporter, explaining why she is leaving her face alone: She is curious to see what time will do to her. Is that not a fine gift to her beholders, to allow us to see what time will do to a face as magnificent as hers? And an even finer gift to her child, her grandchildren. To let time have its way with her, to clear a space for her daughter, then her granddaughter, so that the natural order can continue.

What is the alternative? The world I glimpsed yesterday while waiting in line at the drugstore? Two young women flipping through magazines, and one pointing to a photograph of the comedienne whose multiple face-lifts are legendary. "She looks amazing," she said. "Yeah," said the other. "Amazing." And then, without a hint of irony: "She looks younger than her daughter." What kind of a science-fiction movie are we living, that mothers look younger than daughters? I am trying to imagine my mother, freshly reconditioned after a face-lift or tummy tuck or liposuction. The images, thankfully, will not come. So I scroll back a generation, imagining my grandmothers refusing to look like grandmothers, or, more devastating to my memories, refusing to *feel* like grandmothers. In her last decades, Grandma Goldie would shake her head side to side until her jowls wobbled, then laugh aloud and say, "Silly old grandmother with the chicken neck." She let us grandchildren—and later the great-grandchildren—touch the silky folds that hung beneath her once-taut jaw. And when I sat on Grandma Sylvia's generous lap, I leaned into her round belly and stroked the loose, soft underside of her upper arms. She never pulled away or asked me to stop. Even scrawny Aunt Bessie allowed me access to her oldness, anticipating what I wanted when I reached for her hand. Without complaint, she would turn her hand palm side down, then offer it to me so that I could do what I always did: pinch the thin spotted skin, then count the seconds before it finally settled back into shape.

Did my grandmothers ever lie in bed, as I do, and wonder where the years had gone, what manner of woman they were becoming? Did they touch their soft bellies, their fallen skin, and mourn the changes? Maybe I have been wrong all along about their easy acceptance of all that time did to them. I may be wrong about Gertie and Suzanne, too. And my mother? "Oh, no," she answered recently when I related my brother's proud assessment that *our mother is totally without ego.* "Oh, no," she said. "That is not true. I am too vain. I always have been." My mother, vain? My mother, She Who Was Once the Living Doll? Is she trying to tell me this isn't easy for her, either, this loss of what has been?

And what of the Helmet-Maker's Wife? Living inside herself, did she feel the shift from still beautiful to once beautiful? If so, when did the holding pattern break? It is often said of a woman, "She is in her prime," but I have never known a woman who recognized her prime when she was in the midst of it. It seems we can only identify that time when we are looking back on it from a distance. And how long does a prime last? To say that the Helmet-Maker's Wife was *once* beautiful suggests a single occurrence. Only once could she be that beautiful thing. In the next moment, the next year, the next decade—depending on how long the *once* lasts—she would become something else entirely. Some other form of beautiful thing, perhaps. Or so she might conclude, years later, looking back.

During a recent family reunion, when the clan was gathered to celebrate two of my nieces' eighteenth birthdays and to watch home movies of a family wedding held the summer before, one of the nieces called out, "Look how young I was, how skinny. How skinny all of us were!" The tone of her voice made it clear that skinny was good, that young was good, that her prime, that *our* prime, was already past. It is hard to describe how sad this makes me.

ON AND OFF over the years, I have wondered at the source of Bessie's tears: "It hurt to see you look so old." Older, perhaps, than she herself felt? This is not the way things should be. Nieces should not be older than their great-aunts. Watching me onstage, she must have suddenly seen herself, the ancient self that others had been seeing all along but which she had never fully recognized, living, as she did, from the inside out. Was she caught up short? Maybe she was hurt because she thought I was mimicking her. I didn't intend this, but perhaps I unconsciously borrowed her gestures, my performance a kind of rehearsal for the old woman she was teaching me to be. *Is* teaching me to be. In those moments, Bessie must have glimpsed the old woman I would become, and this glimpse threw her headlong into a future she was not prepared for, a future is which she would be no more. She Who Once Was would be no more. Like the child Margaret in Hopkins's poem, who appears to be grieving for the fallen leaves, the "Goldengrove unleaving," when she is actually grieving for herself, Bessie was mourning what would not be. The autumns she would not see, the nieces who would grow old without her.

If little Addie continues growing *old,* and one day some young sculptor casts her image . . .

Wait, let me try that again, this time with the emphasis on *growing* rather than on *old.* To remind myself of flowers, plants, grasses and trees and all living things, for *growing* is a living word with forward motion, even if one is growing old. As opposed to *staying,* which has no motion, which is a dying word, even if one is staying young. Stay is a refusal to go farther, and thus an alternate form of death, the death of progress toward time's proper movement. Though I will not be alive to see Addie's progress into old age, I hope she lasts a long, long time. As Great-Aunt Bessie lasted, as my grandmothers, Goldie and Sylvia, lasted. As the array of old women I see in my city each day are lasting. Just yesterday, on my afternoon walk through Central Park, I came upon a woman—ninety if a day—at the edge of the Sheep Meadow. She had positioned her cane between two benches as if it were a barre, and she was performing, excruciatingly slowly but with classic precision, each of the five ballet positions, gesturing gracefully with one thin arm, the other grasping the cane for balance.

I am not yet ready to be an older woman, but it's time I began preparing. According to He Who Was Once the Beautiful Woman's Husband and Director, Liv Ullman's face is remarkable because it is "a face which can lend itself to an immense number of roles." Perhaps there is a role I can grow into: She Who Was Once Sometimes Cute? Or, when I gain the courage to move boldly forward, She Who Once Loved All That Was Given to Her Without Looking Back. If I squint into the mirror, I can almost imagine that time, can throw myself into the prime of my future, when that time comes. As it must come, as it will. There I am on the stage of one niece's house or another, the children tumbling on the floor around me. If a great-niece reaches to touch my neck, she will be rewarded with a handful of extraordinary folds. And if she wants to pinch my hand, I will offer it to her. "Here," I will say, patting my lap. And we will sit, the Child I Once Was and the Old Woman She Will Become, our moments together so swift and sweet, we will barely feel them pass.

The Suit

LAUREN SLATER

've never been good at fashion. Some people have the knack; even a scarf flung casually about the neck looks somehow silken and august. I, on the other hand, am a rumpled person, both literally and philosophically. I see the universe as messy, black cloth crumpled with pins and rips. My view is fundamentally pessimistic. I have never understood the expression "freak accident." Given the existence of black holes and burst blood vessels, it astounds me that anyone really has the courage to get dressed up in the morning. Accidents are not the exception. They are the rule. Therefore, one should outfit oneself accordingly. The truly paranoid should wear yellow hard hats and carry candles. The others, like me, who live on the perpetual edge of an overprocessed ironic worry, should just be frumpy. And that is what I am.

One of my earliest memories involves clothes. I was six years old. I had a great future in front of me. I wanted to be a zoologist, a chemist, a teacher, and a tailor. Mrs. Pichonio, the old widow who lived down the street from us and had a magnificent high hump in her bent back, owned a sewing machine. It was stored in a golden-wood cabinet with iron scrollwork legs and many miniature drawers. The machine itself had SINGER written on it, each letter red and formed from tiny painted flowers. The needle nosed in, nosed out, with a chattering sound. Once she let me try it, and it amazed me, that cloth could come together, that the open-ended could be so easily seamed, that you could cuff and button and hem.

Back at home, I set to work with a plain old needle and thread, the only supplies I could find, plus a large swatch of pink fabric from my mother's rag basket. Within a few days, I had fashioned for myself a skirt, a lopsided article of clothing, sticky with glue and snarled with knots. I proudly wore it to school. Having become frustrated with the process of fastening silver snaps, I simply clasped it at my back with masking tape. I was not the kind of kid one laughed at; people simply stared.

Thus began my clothing career, or, what I should more accurately term my anticlothing career. I looked like a frowzer and I loved it. After awhile, the love went away and it became my habit, a manifestation of who I essentially was, something snarled. I lost my interest in sewing, no surprise, but the tendency toward clothes that did not fit, ugly clothes, sloppy clothes—that became ingrained. For the past twenty or thirty years, almost every day, I have rolled out of bed, grabbed for the raveled sweater, the paint-splattered pants. I never understood why people bothered to change their outfit *every day*. I have always worn the same outfit, minus the underwear, for one week at a time. It cuts down on laundry and so simplifies things. During the darkest parts of my life, I have even slept in my clothes, thereby avoiding the tiring task of getting dressed in the morning.

That I am a writer, a freelancer, with no office to go to, has, of course, only more deeply ingrained my tendency. But, as occasionally happens to writers, a few weeks ago, someone read my work and liked it and asked me to go on TV for two minutes. That didn't excite me. I have been on TV for two minutes before and I've long lost the illusion it will make me famous. And it probably doesn't help that I have almost always refused the makeup, with the exception of Oprah, who insisted.

The publishing company, however, the one that has consented to print my work continuously despite obvious profit loss, that company did not share my attitude. For the publicist, this was a great opportunity—it was CNN—and she instructed me to dress accordingly. She knew me. She knew that without firm direction and tutelage, I would probably not look good. She told me to go to Ann Taylor and buy a suit. A suit! "Expense it to us," she said, sounding a little desperate. Ann Taylor! I only shop at Target, and before Target came to the East Coast, I shopped at Bradlees, whose bankruptcy I am still in the process of mourning.

The publicist was so insistent upon the suit, and so worried I wouldn't obey, that in the end she traveled from New York to Boston, where I live and where the filming was, in order to supervise my shopping. She wanted to go with me to Ann Taylor to pick out my clothes. This I knew I could not do. One does not show one's publicist the unpublic places, the bulges and lumps. I said I would go on my own.

Of course, I didn't. I went straight to Target and found a red suit for thirty dollars. I thought it looked fine. It didn't entirely fit; the sleeves of the jacket were too long and the skirt was a little loose, but these were minor details, and besides, they usually film only from the neck up. I liked this suit. The red made me look happy; it underscored the flush in my face. It lit up my skin.

I went home and tried it on for my husband. "You look," he said, "like you're about to go trick-or-treating."

I returned the suit. I did not want to get the publicist mad. I knew she was not after a style with any witch in it. I thought my husband was wrong, but I wasn't going to risk it.

The next day, a Sunday, I conceded. I went to Ann Taylor. The store was in a mall, and I try to avoid malls as much as possible, due to potential terrorist attacks. I figured, however, it was Sunday, I was there first thing, the mall was relatively empty, and it was not prime time in terms of bombs or aerosolized chemicals. I thought as soon as I stepped foot in the mall I would get sweaty, but, in fact, that didn't happen. The mall was nice. It smelled of coffee and had booths selling wind chimes and wigs and glass cats. It was almost whimsical.

Ann Taylor itself had a charmed hush to it. There were a few woman there, and they drifted among the racks of clothes like wraiths—like angels or ghosts. I collided with cashmere. There was a white sweater and a matching white scarf and it was as soft as snow to touch, but warm. I studied some velvet. It was satisfyingly raspy. These clothes were gorgeous; anyone could see that. They called attention not so much to themselves as to the way the light fell around their forms, suggesting the body beneath, at once sheathed and open.

A saleslady drifted up to me; I told her my situation, that I needed a suit and I needed it fast. She was so gracious. She flicked through the racks of soft things and stylish things and held them up to me with complete confidence. If I seemed strange to her in my big rubber boots with old overalls tucked in, she didn't show it, not a bit. I was another customer, her charge, her mission for the moment. She brought me back to a dressing room and handed me jackets and skirts and shirts. The clothing felt cool against my skin, and it all looked good. I am not accustomed to having clothes that truly fit. I have always been content with an approximate fit, tending toward the too large. These jackets enclosed my waist, and had whalebone buttons. The skirts were straight and slit. I was, she informed me, a petite. I thought of Hans Christian Andersen's wonderful tale "Thumbelina" and the big pink flower and the river and the bee. Petite! In fact, I was extra petite. Size six petite didn't fit me; size four, still too large; size two, close but not quite; size zero, perfect. On the one hand, I was truly proud. For what woman would size zero not be an actual accomplishment? On the other hand, was I zero, zilch, nothing? Was I really here? Was I basically a good soul? Zero. It was, for sure, a mixed message.

But here's what really mattered. In the size zero suit, I looked great. I looked serious and sexy. I looked like a lawyer, like someone in a sky rise, a woman with extra influence. The transformation was total, in part because of the fit. The suit at once concealed and revealed my shape. I had a shape! I had a little waist. I had a collarbone that gave me an appropriately gaunt look. My throat was white and long.

I bought the suit—several hundred bucks, and on sale, too. She gave it to me in a bag with velvet handles. She asked me if I'd like shoes to go with the outfit, but I was overcome, overwhelmed, and out of money. I told her no one the shoes. I said I already had some. Then, on my way out of the mall, I snuck into Payless and got a fourteen-dollar pair of pumps.

At home, I tried the suit on in front of my full-length mirror. I was wondering whether the mirrors at Anne Taylor were rigged in some way, and now, face-to-face with the glass on the back of my closet door, I would see the truth. And I did see the truth. The truth was I still looked good. My waist was still small. My collarbone flared. I had a charming freckle on my chest.

The next morning, when I woke up, I didn't reach for the raveled sweater and paint-splattered leggings. I put on the suit. It was slightly itchy but immensely gratifying. I went to work, which for me amounts to traveling from my bedroom to my study, across the hall. Usually, I work in some version of my pajamas, but this day was different; I decided to get all dressed up, as though to meet my characters. My writing was sharper because of that suit. My characters all said witty things, and my overwrought lyricism gave way to a kind of muscular minimalism. I started to think the suit was magic.

I went on TV the next day and I was very articulate. My publicist, who herself was wearing a suit and mauve lipstick and sling-back shoes, was impressed. Huge white lights shone down on me and behind me stood a man with a silver disk. Then it was over. I went home. The house seemed oddly quiet, in a way both creepy and peaceful. The sheer curtains billowed with sunshine. The cat wreathed around my legs. I stripped, and hung the suit way in the back of my peeling closet.

But something was different. Even with the suit off, I still felt like it was a little bit on. My walk was more purposeful. I felt *aloft*. I felt pretty and I liked it. I began to wonder about Botox. I pinched my lips to plump them out and, sure enough, that made me prettier still. Suddenly, there were so many possibilities. Perhaps I should get a perm, some smart, springy, sexy curls to accompany and enhance my new image. I bought a fashion magazine and went to see a stylist at Lords and Ladies. She grabbed a hunk of my hair and said, "Perm, no way. You're much too brittle."

"But I have hair spray on," I said, which I did, part of my new experimentation. "I have a lot of hair spray on. Without it, my hair is not so brittle."

"You don't need a perm," she said. "You need color."

Color it was. My strands stripped of their darkness and gray, saturated with something gold. My husband reacted exactly as he was supposed to, just like a husband on a perfume commercial: "Wow," he said.

I could go on. And on. I could tell you about the lid-lift I thought of getting, the tarry mascara I bought, the fancy shampoo with a lather as rich as a racehorse's. I could tell you about the pants, but I won't. The clothes are at once entirely the point and not at all relevant. What matters is this: I began to see the surface of everything, the shifting surfaces of people's faces, the grainy surface of my desktop, the surface of the sky, all slick and blue. I saw the surface of my body and ignored the bones. And this was all very good. Not only was it fun; it was somehow . . . somehow *healing,* to use a surfacy word. I bobbed to the top of life and blew a bubble or two. I began to understand that a life dedicated to appearances was not, in fact, a shallow life; it was life lived at the pitch of drama, life on a stage, life acted and inacted, almost Shakespearean. When you tend to your surface you are making an image, and images are the essence of art. When you tend to your surface, you are making a statement of faith. You are saying, *I matter.* You are saying, *The world is worth dressing for.* You are engaging in the best kind of optimism, an optimism that propels you out of bed in the morning, that directs you to the day. When you put on nice clothes, you are putting on hope; you are saying, *Here I am. This is fun. Look at me.* You are jerked out of your scrunched existence and into possibility: the pretty, the silky, the tweedy. You are celebrating the excellent malleability of human experience, that you can be this and you can be that, the fusion of image with flesh.

But at the end of the day, of course, you have to take your clothes off. Unless you want to sleep in your suit, this act of undressing cannot be avoided. The night air is cold. An airplane roars. A grandmother has just died, and as well dressed in her coffin as she was, she still looked—well, she still looked dead, the swoop of blush hideous on her sallow skin.

I wonder if there are some people who never get undressed, or who always stay well dressed, in a metaphorical sense. If there are, I salute them. To go through life clad and stylishly clothed, with all the relentless optimism this implies, is in and of itself a Herculean feat. I, in the end, do not have this stamina. I cannot run that race. I cannot bring myself, when all is said and done and stripped, to see the fabric of the universe as anything other than rumpled. Clothes are a grand vacation, an excellent adventure, but in the end, you come back to your body.

My body is aging. I have warts on my feet. My hair is brittle, with strands of gray beneath the saturating gold. I cannot stick to my surface. I sink, and in that downward decline, in the quiet moments, with the suit hung up in the closet, the flared velvet pants put away, in the quiet moments lying side by side with my infant son as he falls asleep, I think of our barbed world and so many bombed-out buildings. I think of being kidnapped. I think of how a high rise falls. And it occurs to me, in these unclad moments when the world comes at me raw, it occurs to me that my images of terror are as commodified and commercialized as my newfound interest in clothes. I mourn what the media tells me to mourn. I now dress as the media tells me to dress. Even my deepest fears have a sort of surfacy feel to them, aerosolized toxins and jihadists in Kaffiyers.

What are the real dangers here? What are the actual risks that exist beneath all our stylized surges? Perhaps it is simple. Perhaps it has something to do with a grandmother in a grave. Perhaps it has something to do with the way our faces crumple in time, our ends, however they happen. A person cannot tolerate it all; it is too much. Clothes are as fine a diversion as any. They make not remake your soul, but they give you a much-needed break. I would like a gown, pale blue, seeded with pearls at its collar and cuffs. I would like to dress my children in everything Gap. I would like us all to go forward, together, as beautifully bandaged as a human may be.

Imagining the Volcano

BRENDA MILLER

> She supposed that everyone contained a multitude, certainly a cautious and a reckless self, one who would hold back, one who would wade in . . .— JUDITH KITCHEN, *The House on Eccles Road*

I.

Watch for her: She's the young woman, still a teenager but on the verge of adulthood, nineteen years old, dressed in a soft, faded army jacket with a rose embroidered on one shoulder, a grinning skull on the other—rather like the service stripes of a sergeant at arms. The two patches award her body a pleasing balance; they equalize her as she glides through the crowd, a fiery girl whose eyes dilate to take in everything. She's wafting through the parking lot of a stadium—it could be any stadium, anywhere, Oakland or Red Rocks or Santa Cruz; it doesn't matter, for the marketplaces are all the same: vendors of tie-dyed T-shirts, bumper stickers (WHAT A LONG STRANGE TRIP IT'S BEEN), beaded earrings and crocheted necklaces, plastic vials of flowers, essences, baskets of oranges and chocolates. She's carrying a small handwritten sign that says, in a loopy childish script, I NEED A MIRACLE!

She holds this plea above her head as she steps out to the sidewalk, smiling at every passing car, every pedestrian, knowing the elusive ticket will come to her. Miracles are common here, barely noticed. She has no doubts, no worry, no fear: Those clumsy emotions will belong to her older self, a middle-aged woman who watches from her post in the future, amused but also a little annoyed, a bit peeved with that girl's care-less beauty, her naïveté, a faith that holds solid as an acolyte's.

Now a pair of bikers, bare arms cluttered with tattoos, black leather vests open at the chest, come toward the girl, drawn by her smile, her eyes, her breasts, braless beneath her tank top. They drift to her and drop a ticket into her hands, doff imaginary hats to her as they glide by. "No charge," they say. "Have a good trip." She grips the ticket between thumb and forefinger, laughs, and says, "Thanks, man. You've just bought yourself some *karma* insurance!"

They go their separate ways, melding back into the crowd, which has grown more dense in the last hour, the music from each knot a little louder, a little more discordant. She knows she's been blessed by those two men, archangels of the Dead. She knows that tonight's show will be particularly good, the third in a series of five leading to New Year's Eve. She glides back through the parking lot, and an odd sound track trails in her wake: the spacey, elongated rills of "Terrapin Station," roiling up against the twangy guitar of "Workingman's Dead," then segueing into "Fire on the Mountain," when finally she spots her friends, who see her at the same time, and she waits one beat before hoisting her ticket tri-umphantly in the air.

Tom, good old Tom, wearing an army jacket identical to hers, stands up and sweeps her into a bear hug that lifts her high off the ground. The others—Pat and Karl—watch and smile insanely; Pat reaches into his jacket and removes a plastic Baggie full of white confetti, shakes it once, and all of them hold out their hands, palms up, like children in line for candy. When she puts the tab on her tongue, it tastes only like paper—dry, faintly woody, soft as it melds into her mouth.

"Paradise," Pat says. "It's been making the rounds."

They move forward as one entity, but each with their clearly defined roles: Pat, the mellow one, benignly superior in his Dead expertise; Tom, the goofball; Karl, the slightly paranoid. And the girl—well, she's been somehow designated the spiritual one, a radiant core around which the rest of them will dance.

II.

It's the summer of 2003—years and miles away from my young, Dead-head self—and I'm staying at a yoga retreat center called Kalani, which means the convergence of heaven and earth. Everyone keeps saying we're in Paradise. All the signs proclaim it: PARADISE REALTY, PARADISE ELECTRONICS, PARADISE SHOES. Really, it's only the Hilo side of Hawaii, and while it's quite pretty—with its black sand beaches and swaying co-conut palms, the hibiscus flowers and plumeria, the blue ocean with its high, rolling breakers—I wouldn't exactly anoint it with that high moniker, Paradise. For one thing, cockroaches the size of mice lurk in the shower, and black ants run a grid pattern all across the bamboo mats. The humidity is so thick that sweat globules cling in the folds of my belly; I keep pulling my shirt away from my body and fanning it, making small exasperated noises in my throat (leave it to me to be cranky in Paradise).

It's quiet at the pool, because many of my compatriots here have gone on a lava trek this afternoon. Pele, as she's called by her goddess name, is just five miles from here, and she's one of the most active volcanoes on the planet: The lava continually erupts and forms new rock, new sand, covering what has come before, so that the island is constantly caught up in the twin process of creation, annihilation.

I used to think a volcanic "eruption" meant a spectacular blowout from the summit, a caldera boiling and overflowing in a long, undulant sheet of molten earth. But now I've come to understand that eruptions can spurt anywhere, miles from the crater; an ominous bulge might ap-pear overnight in someone's backyard, then grow to the shape of a cone, spewing cinders and fire. Kalani itself is situated in a rift zone rated a "2," one of the most volatile spots. The earth here is only about a thou-sand years old, infant earth in the scheme of things; perhaps it is the very newness of the land that gives the island that sticky, blurred, just-out-of-the-womb feeling.

I haven't signed on for the lava trek quite yet. For now, I prefer to *imagine* the volcano, because I suspect the whole event will be vaguely disappointing if I do go. Maybe nothing is ever enough for me these days, not even Paradise. Or maybe I'm scared of something more than disappointment, something I haven't quite been able to name; I think it has something to do with how heavy my body seems lately, so reluctant to do anything that challenges it. I seem to have misplaced that young nucleus, a source of energy that once kept me light enough to do anything.

I haven't gone into the waves at Kahana black sands beach, either, only watched as a naked man, dreadlocked on both his head and his beard, flung himself repeatedly into the ocean. My new friend, Ineke, also made her way through the high breakers to bob on the surface beyond. She's sixty-five years old, her silver hair shaved close to her head, her body the incarnation of the word *lithe*. I stood at the edge of the undertow, white water rushing back to the sea, and only imagined myself out there in the water, remembering how I once, eons ago, swam off the shore of the Yucatán peninsula, my naked body wholly in sync with the waves. But now I just backed away and sat on my towel while the young people around me drummed and danced and braided one another's hair.

When Ineke emerged from the waves, looking like an aged Aphrodite, we sat together and continued watching the naked dreadlocked man. Before each wave, he raised his arms high in the air, then dove forward into the force of the surge. Ineke said, "I thought he was praying, but really he's just preparing himself for the next dive." And I thought, *That's* what prayer is: the supplication of the whole body before it enters the waves.

There were supposed to be dolphins at this beach, frolicking with the swimmers who dared to dive out beyond the breakers. I scanned the water beyond the spindrift, but all I saw were waves and more waves, and occasionally the tip of someone's snorkel bobbing out there, waiting for the animals to arrive. I've been told they will come right up and nuzzle your leg, and you can pat their snouts, but only if they sense you're a good person, so to be nuzzled by a dolphin is to be somehow blessed. But for now I'll have to be content with *imagining* the dolphins and their sleek backs, those firm noses against my belly, the vigorous heads that massage a body into saying *yes*.

III.

It's 1978 and I'm sitting on my dorm bed before my first Dead show, with Pat and my boyfriend, Karl; in the few months following this moment, many things will happen: I'll get pregnant, drop out of college, have a miscarriage, and move back home to recover. I'll lie in my childhood bed and listen to Grateful Dead songs for hours on end, the lyrics soothing me, urging me to transcend my body, as all good religious texts do.

But for now we're still just kids; we don't yet know the consequences that follow on carelessness. Instead, we smoke cigarettes Pat hand-rolls from his tin of Three Castles tobacco, and the smoke forms a sweet cocoon around us as we sit in anticipation. The actual show is blur; I remember the Dead projected slides from their recent trip to Egypt as the music throbbed from the stage, a montage of camels and pyramids and desert sands, and the Deadheads swirled all around us—all smiles, all electricity, sparking off one another—and we sat on the bleachers and just watched, huddled together. Karl still remembers one particular moment from that first Dead show; it's the one he brings up whenever we reminisce: "Do you remember when you fed me the peanuts?" he asks, and I always say I do, and we sit there nodding together, smiling, because there is really nothing else to say about it except that I fed him peanuts: He sat with his head in my lap, and I cracked the shells, extracted the salty meat, placed each one on his lazily extended tongue. And such a gesture—enacted within the music, those young bodies dancing all around us in rapture—tied us more closely than sex, surpassed any other give-and-take of our bodies, or our minds.

It was easy to fall in love those days; all you had to do was look someone in the eyes and casually peel back your shell. At one of the New Year's concerts in Oakland, I locked eyes with a stranger, and we danced the second set together, never saying a word, never breaking contact, never touching, and the air between us seethed. If we stopped, we'd lose it, so we didn't stop. We danced, and the world shrunk to the circle our arms could inscribe. We danced ourselves right into Paradise. I sensed my friends watching us, their eyes bemused, and finally when the second set ended, someone came and led my dance partner away by the elbow. He looked back at me—I remember clearly those dark eyes, that beard, the blue of his tie-dyed shirt emanating like a halo. He smiled wanly and lifted his hand in what could have been either greeting or farewell. He said (out loud, or was it just a voice in my head?), "I finally found someone I can *dance* with." And then he vanished.

IV.

I hear one of the Kalani workers say to another, "You can't stay in Shangri-la forever." She says it as she juggles her juggling pins on the lanai of her lean-to; she's a slender woman with sandy blond hair and freckles, shorts that are ripped along the thigh, so they seem held together by sheer will alone. Earlier today, she came to my cottage to help me disperse the population of red ants that have decided to use my sink as a conduit to the outside world.

Most of the women here have a distinct look I'm sure I cultivated myself as a young woman: a dewy glow to the face, well-defined cheekbones, torso firm, with barely the hint of a waist, that cunning incurve just enough to hold a sarong tied at the hips. They sit at the communal tables with their lovely postures and eat heartily. They're participating in an intensive yoga workshop, a bevy of toned yoginis in orbit around a famous teacher, and you can tell who they are by the way they appear at the table in their formfitting yoga pants riding low on their hips, and tiny tank tops that bare their midriffs. They walk loose-limbed, with shoulders back, leading from their navels, and their hair either curls in ringlets around their faces or hangs in smooth ponytails down their backs. None of them seems affected by the humid heat, and any sweat they do give off seems perfumed with essence of jasmine, or of the plumeria blossoms they casually pick on the way to breakfast, tucked now behind their small ears.

I try not to look at the men, because they're all so handsome, they make me a little goofy inside. They have faces carved of bone and sinew, their smiles so wide and white, and when they turn their heads, it's like a lighthouse beam capturing everything in its path. They have bodies so thin, and yet so muscular, that I can imagine quite vividly how their weight might bestow itself over my body, how a leg would wedge between mine, how my own body would take on a man's luster as he settles himself into me. In an episode of *Sex and the City* I watched just before leaving home, Carrie finally yells to her girlfriends, to justify her ill-advised visit to her ex-boyfriend, "I don't want sex. I just need the *weight* of a man's body on me!" I don't want to look at these men, because I'm sure this desire is written all over my face, so I turn away and sip my coffee demurely, half-listening to the hubbub of yogic flirtation going on all around me, watching these bodies and the heat flickering inside them.

At dinner, the cook sits down at my table and begins talking about the volcano, Kilauea, the goddess Pele, the volcano I've yet to see. Kate's parents live just down the road, and she says, "Their house was taken by Pele in 1989." The way she says the phrase, *taken by Pele,* so effortlessly, without a hint of awe or guile, makes me understand that the volcano in these parts is an honest-to-God person, not necessarily a primal symbolic image. Just the opposite. Pele is a woman—an old, strong woman who knows what she wants and makes no bones about it. There are legends of tourists taking bits of volcanic rock home with them as souvenirs, then sending them back to the post office in Hilo. *I've had such bad luck since I took this,* the notes say, *please return this to Pele with my apologies.*

I still haven't signed up to go on the lava trek. On the waiver form, you have to check several boxes before signing: "Yes," you must avow, "I understand that large chunks of land may fall away under my feet without warning," or "Yes, I understand that hot lava may suddenly appear out of nowhere and pose a danger," or "Yes, I understand that this is not a tour, but a trip." So I just keep imagining the volcano: the incandescent earth, the crust of it collapsing, slits giving off steam, the white breath of a woman older than dirt, a woman who watches and waits for me to arrive.

V.

She's hitchhiking, that girl (don't tell her parents), putting out her thumb and heading north with a boy she barely knows, his name scribbled down from a notice on the bulletin board outside the student union: *Going to the Portland Dead shows? Anyone want to hitch together?* They are traveling about eight hundred miles, a distance that seems not insurmountable, and they get rides easily up out of northern California.

In southern Oregon, though, night is falling by the time they get a ride from a trucker carrying a load up to Canada. It's the first time the girl has been in the cab of one of these big rigs, and she exclaims, a little too heartily, about the *cute* sleeping area partitioned off from the cab with a raggedy curtain. "You can go on back there," the trucker says, "get a little shut-eye." He winks at the boy as he says this, but the boy, busy arranging their packs in the cramped confines of the cab, doesn't seem to notice.

She *is* tired, so she crawls in, shuts the curtain, and she's so excited by the prospect of another Dead show, so pleased with the whole ideas of *truckin'* to get there, everything falling into place like the *long, strange trip* the Dead exhort from onstage, that she lies there just hugging herself, doing a pretty good job of not noticing the rancid smell of the curtain, or the scratchy blanket on which she lies; but she does hear the murmur of the men's voices in the front seat, at first the obligatory "Where are you going? Where have you been," and she feels comforted by this small talk, sure in her destination and the capacity of her own body to get her there. She wears a silk scarf on her head, and tie-dyed silk pants and an army jacket that even in its very bulk and mannishness emphasizes her slim torso, her small childlike breasts.

She hears the trucker on his radio, and catches a fragment clearly: *Carrying beaver*, he says, and she thinks, *There are beavers in back?* and then knows, of course, there are no beavers, just herself, a girl, with a girl's body, lying on a man's blanket, where he has sweated and snored and jerked himself off. She sits up straight, parts the curtain a little. The trucker is now talking to the boy, asking if he's fucking the girl in back, if he thinks she would mind if he just kissed her, says that's all he wants, just a kiss, it's lonely out on the road, you know: The boy shrugs, says only, *You'd have to ask her*, and he keeps his gaze steadfast out the window.

At the next truck stop, she sees a woman going up to the cabs of the trucks lined up, all of them pointing in the same direction; this woman wears tight jeans and a halter top tied up beneath her breasts. Her own trucker has gone inside, and she nudges the boy, says, "Let's go." But he stares her down. "This ride will take us as far as we need," he says, and that's that. The trucker returns with some Coca-Cola and a small packet of pills that he scrapes off his palm with his tongue. He turns and gives her a wink, then reaches out one hand to stroke her neck.

The girl shrinks back into the sleeping cubby and passes the rest of the trip thinking about the Dead, remembering the way Bob Weir had once looked directly at her during one of his solos, the way Jerry would never let anything bad happen to anyone. At Dead shows, there's always a moment when the earth gives way, and you sense yourself dancing on air. It doesn't feel dangerous, only divine. She imagines the set they will play: maybe "Sugar Magnolia," followed by "Althea," moving into "Touch of Grey," all her favorites, the music providing its own solace. Once she starts dancing, everything will be okay; her body will become its own self again, and safe.

VI.

The yoga workshop has gone wild in the Quonset hut next to my cabin; they're having a blowout party, with loud technomusic and ecstatic dance, and I try not to sound too annoyed when I complain to the re-treat staff—"Don't quiet hours start at ten?"—and they look at me with a vague smile. "Go ahead and join them!" one woman, Althea, says. "They won't mind."

So I wander back down to my cabin and pass the dance hall. I stand outside and peer in through the screened walls, watching. Some of the yoginis are dancing in elaborate variations of asanas, standing on their heads or elongated into splits, arms waving back and forth above their heads. One couple does a routine almost gymnastic, his legs held rigid in the air, her hands clasped to his and one leg extended back above this frozen tableau for several seconds before she hops off. The rest are gy-rating in yogic version of rock and roll, hands held up to their ears as they do a sassy little French wiggle of the hips. The air *seethes* with sex.

And there I am on the outside looking in, a woman who has just re-alized she's *old,* that she has grown heavy not only around the middle but around the heart, a rope of such heft that she can't quite remember who she is anymore. Twenty years ago, I could have waded in casually, but tonight I can't breach the entry point, the breaking waves of so many bodies. I know their gazes might pass right over me, seeing nothing of interest on which to land. No one to *dance with.*

VII.

People keep returning from the lava trek with remarkable stories. "The ground, it gave way right in front of us, and the lava just started flowing out. The gal next to me started to cry. Oh no, not from fear, it was more of a spiritual experience." Or: "There's a power on that mountain. You have to feel it to understand what I'm saying."

By now, I really do yearn to feel it, to feel something more than the "Polynesian paralysis" for which Hawaii is also famous. The warm waters of the pool, the massages, the endless food on the lanai: All this can only take you so far. So I go ahead and sign up, promising to pay the eighty dollars, signing the waiver saying I won't get mad if the ground collapses and burns me beyond recognition. I won't hold Kalani responsible if the sulfur gets into my body and sears the inside of my lungs. I will remember, at all times, that this is *a trip,* not a tour.

But on the morning we're scheduled to go, I wake to torrential rains; a hurricane off the coast of New Zealand, they say, is creating monsoon weather. We huddle with Sylvie, our guide, in the lodge, and we decide to postpone the trek for a day or two. Sylvie is from Holland, her legs long and muscular, her hair black; she gives the impression she could do anything. She teaches "aquamouvance," a water therapy performed in the warm pool, and I've already felt her arms around me as she held me afloat, then flipped me over in a backward somersault underwater, so that I came up sputtering, disoriented. I started to cry then, and she rocked me back and forth in the water until I was soothed.

"It will be better," she says now, "to wait. Then we will see the lava more clearly as it flows into the sea." The others agree, so I just have to keep imagining it, the volcano. I imagine it now in the rain, the steam rising all down the slope until it billows at the edge where it meets the salty waves.

VIII.

Mount Saint Helens erupts. It's the second eruption in a month—the first one killed fifty-seven people and blew down the forests into sticks of burned lumber; this eruption is smaller, but the aftermath blows quickly toward Portland. It happens while we're in the Dead show, so we emerge into a landscape transformed by ash. We don't know what's happened: At first, we think it's snow (in June?), but the gray stuff keeps fluttering down, and it sticks in our hair, tastes sulfurous on the tongue. Finally the word passes among the crowd: *A volcano,* they say, *it erupted, just east of here,* and since everyone is on hallucinogens of some kind, this news seems occasion to rejoice rather than flee—*cool, a volcano*— and everyone imagines the hot lava oozing down the side of the cinder cone. And then, in the manner of Deadheads, the task becomes to find out exactly which song the Dead were playing when the volcano blew. We huddle together, we reconstruct the set list, and, even though it seems too coincidental, too unlikely, we all agree at the same moment which song it must have been.

Fire on the Mountain. For a moment, we're stunned into silence. Such power we had there, in the auditorium, the band belting out, *Fire! Fire on the Mountain!*, and us all dancing like crazy, arms whirling, skirts whirling, eyes whirling, feet stomping; a rain dance, but this is not rain we have mustered from the atmosphere. No, we have rent the earth, exposed its molten core. We have *moved mountains* with the dance. Everything that comes after this—hooking up with a friend to find our way to his grandmother's apartment; he has the key but fumbles in the lock of the wrong door, that ash now getting into our lungs, and a feeble voice trembling from inside, *"Who's there? Who's there?"* (the fear in it, an old woman's fear, an old woman who lives alone, and who could be at her door this late at night—with the ash outside coming down, it's like an apocalypse—*"Who's there!"*), and we giggle, *oops,* and turn to another door and the key slides right in—everything is just *a long, strange trip*: That's all it is. No need for alarm. We're safe, the volcano is miles away, and we're on fire. We can do anything.

IX.

While waiting for the weather to clear for our lava trek, I decide to check out the "Dolphin Dance" on Friday night. It's supposed to be about making authentic connections through the body, and for two hours, we're instructed to act like dolphins: nudging one another, spinning languidly in the water, wisping away, running our hands across one another's shins and thighs and backs.

I've hesitated just a tad too much, not sure if this is a sexual or a spiritual adventure (who knows I maybe the two realms are not as far apart as I think); and now I'm pushed to the perimeter of the circle, watching as several naked men arrow through the water and leap, nose-first, over one another, their torsos elegant and long, then spin under the water, wiggling between legs, rolling on the surface again, side over side. I've kept my modest tank suit on, and I end up holding a beautiful young woman afloat with my fingertips, her long black hair trailing in the water; I nudge her just a bit to watch her roll and submerge, then emerge face up, breasts up, smiling.

The next day, I say to people at the dining table, out of hearing of the teacher, "I think from now on, I'm going to do my own turtle dance instead. I'll keep my shell *on,* thank you very much," and we all laugh, but my catty remark is true: Every time I go in the pool now—surrounded by coconut palms and the trailing flowers of red hibiscus—my body seems to turn turtle-shaped in the dark. My gnarled neck stretches as I bob up for air. I tilt my head to peer askance at these unfamiliar stars.

X.

And now you're standing inside of Pele, holding hands with Sylvie, the darkness so deep, you've lost track of your own body, not to mention the others, who must be in here, too, unless they've already turned tail and run. You're in a lava tube, *inside* the volcano, and all you can do is keep squeezing Sylvie's hand, and it's muscled, it's soft, and it won't let go. *Just feel it,* she says, and so you take a deep breath and allow that darkness to settle along your eyes, your skin, that darkness like a substance, the inner walls of the volcano all around you, and it really is like an enormous body, the body of a woman pulsing with fire.

Strangely, it's cool here in the dark, but not so far away there's a heat so intense, it would incinerate your small self in an instant. Lava poured through here years ago; it's gone now, but it hollowed out this mountain, and you're *inside it;* that's all you can keep thinking, and already you're narrating it for your friends back home, *I was inside it:* this fire, this body, this woman, this heat. Sylvie's hand in your own, that tether to the world as you know it. *This is really the best part,* Sylvie murmurs in your ear. *This is where you feel Pele at her strongest.*

And she's right. You emerge and make your way down to the coast, traveling that winding road down from the summit to the sea, and you see the flowers on the trees, the symbol of Pele's tears; every so often Sylvie points out the glow from lava on the hillside, faraway splotches that shimmer erratically like stars. Cars are already parked for a mile along the road from the entry point, and Sylvie steers the van into a space, and you all trundle out, with your bottles of water and your sandwiches and your cameras. You join a flow of people, many of them in shorts and flip-flops (your own waiver form said sternly, "Wear good hiking shoes; wear long pants to protect yourself from the sharp rock"); you join this long snaking stream of people as, one after the other, you make your way up the side of Pele, toward those glowing splotches, which, as you get closer, turn into rivulets, and then waterfalls of lava, and then you realize that there is a lava tube just under your feet; you're straddling a rock where the lava gleams underneath. And it's nothing like you imagined it.

The lava does not flow; it oozes. You reach the edge of a lava field, where the lava creeps forward, the edge of it rounded; it reminds you of Silly Putty, or slime, or the burned crust of crème brûlée, and there are hundreds of people here, lots of children running alongside it; it's full dark now, so you find a seat on a flat boulder (it's warm) and you watch the lava as it makes its slow way down. It's mesmerizing, and you hear a cry from another group that's just seen the lava emerge from its tube and spill onto the ground. So you turn and watch as it, too, creeps forward, slowing and solidifying as it cools.

One of your companions has brought a small bottle of schnapps as an offering (you were all supposed to bring offerings, and at the last minute you picked some plumeria blossoms—they're in your pocket); your companion steps off the rock and tosses the whole bottle into the lava, where it bursts and explodes, the flames whooshing, and there's a park ranger who turns and yells, *"Don't throw things in lava!"* just as you make your own weak offering, the plumeria blossoms fluttering to a halt before they reach the edge of the molten earth. The strangers next to you glare in disapproval.

But there are whole families now throwing rocks in the lava to watch them melt, kids running back and forth, scouting the edges, a group of teenagers smoking a joint. The heat is intense, glaring now, the rock heating up under your butt, and after awhile you all get up to make the trek back over the black rock, rock sharp as glass; the slightest touch opens a gash on the ankle. You keep turning to look back at the lava, which grows small, inconsequential; tonight it will not reach the sea.

The next day, you'll have a pain deep in your sinuses, and your massage therapist, Nancy, will say it's a volcano headache. She'll massage you with an oil called *Sacred Mountain,* the smell of cedar and pine and ylang-ylang clearing your body of Pele's breath. Afterward, you'll slip naked into the pool, even though sanctioned nudity doesn't start for another hour, at sundown. But the yoginis sunning in their bikinis poolside won't notice your body there in the water, unpeeled, and the way it gives off a sure fragrance, like smoke.

Middle Age All Over Again

ANTONYA NELSON

I think I have always been middle-aged—if "middle-aged" is defined as being burdened with that paradoxical combination of a hyperactive imagination for catastrophe coupled with a physically exhausted affect. This is the posture of the worrier, the person not *doing* but *thinking,* telltale crease in the center of the forehead. As a young child, I would lie in my bed wide-awake for hours after the rest of my family had gone to sleep. It was a big house, and we were a big family, so the diminishment of noise would provide a kind of helpful backdrop to what I called "worry." "Why can't you fall asleep?" my depleted mother would ask, she who was summoned to my side night after night once the clatter had died, after even the pets had settled, when I couldn't stand being alone any longer with my anxiety. "I'm worried," I would say. About what? I didn't know; I still don't know. Intruders, illness, car crashes, clowns, nuclear war. I have a busy fantasy life. I bite my nails; I am a hypochondriac. I write stories and novels in which awful things happen to people not so very different from myself. Sometimes I think this practice is a way of warding off these same events, as if dramatizing the imagined disaster might preclude its actualization. And sometimes, since I'm a worrier, I believe the exact opposite: Writing about an event brings it crashing down upon me. Character is fate, said Heraclitus; what sentence does a worrier have to serve?

Other children lose their startle reflex when they grow teeth and verticality and gather their wits to fight back. Me? My first job, when I was sixteen, was at Dairy Queen, where I had to stand before a sliding window and exchange frozen deserts for cash. No matter that this was the sum total of my job description—greet the stranger on the other side of the glass, satisfy his need for ice cream—every time someone stepped up, I gasped, throwing my hand to my uniformed heart.

I had some siblings to look after, both older and younger. We're spread apart, the five of us, so while my eldest brother was getting arrested—stealing cars, selling drugs, skipping school—my sister was still in diapers. That's a lot of territory to cover, for a worrier. Sometimes I was joined in my fretting by my brother David, who is only two years younger than I, and also situated in the middle of the sibling spectrum. What a pathetic pair we were at Joyland, our city's amusement park. For our straight A's (middle-aged youth always make straight A's), we'd been awarded free tickets to ride the rides. Because we were also frugal (another of our middle-aged traits), we could not reject the tickets. Yet we hated those rides; what was the point? "It's like being a cat in a clothes dryer," David complained, terror-stricken, as we swung around on the nauseating Ferris wheel. We envied our legitimately middle-aged father, who sat below us, reading a book on a bench like a sane person. After we'd dutifully spent all of our free tickets, we sighed with relief and piled back into the car, locked the doors, buckled our seat belts, and returned home.

Older, on our way to Mexico for a six-week college course in Spanish, David and I freaked out at a hotel on the border, flushing away a great deal of expensive illicit pharmacopoeia before crossing over. The thing is, we were going *into* Mexico, not out. It was only after we'd stepped onto the train and settled with our suitcases that we realized no one had paid any attention to our entry whatsoever. We'd flushed our fun for no good reason. This was a classic middle-aged moment, overthinking the danger, preparanoid.

Most of the time, however, I suffered alone in my worldly wizened self. Put in charge when the grown-ups were gone, I circled the house, locking doors and turning on lights, jamming broom handles under beds, shrieking into the closets. At twelve, I ratted out my father when he took up smoking cigarettes after a twenty-year hiatus, organizing a campaign of guilt-inducing notes and pictures to be placed strategically in his pants pockets and underneath his razor, on the mirror where he faced himself every morning. His photo, with *X*'s over his eyes to signal his certain demise. At fourteen, I was the one who quit speaking to my brother when he foolishly divorced his first wife, whose hair I envied and whose name was Leslie Starr. What was he *thinking*? My parents and I shook our heads around the kitchen table. I referred to the other children in the family as "the little kids," promoting myself out of their class. Whenever our cats got run over on the busy street outside our house, I took responsibility. I should have brought them in the night before, no matter the weather, no matter the hour; I'd known, hadn't I, that something awful would happen if I let down my vigilance? Wasn't that the cost of not listening to my gut instinct? Ignore it once, and you can be doomed, poor Peter Rabbit, poor Ink, poor Panther.

At school, I was a competitive nightmare. I don't think I am particularly gifted IQ-wise, but I'm driven, so that helps. I'd cheat—look over shoulders, plagiarize, you name it—to be awarded the *A* that would lead, inevitably, to those Joyland tickets I didn't actually want. I started early on the boring capitalist treadmill most adults find themselves slaves to, where work begins equaling the objects in your house, where your labor translates directly into the completely useless knickknacks you yearn for. By the time I was seventeen, I had graduated from high school, started college, and was holding down four jobs simultaneously: waitress at a pizza parlor, lifeguard (of course; where else would a worrier sit?) at both the YMCA and YWCA, and substitute instructional paraprofessional for the Wichita Board of Ed.

This last was my best job. Every morning, some genderless soul named Percy (from Personnel) would call to ask if I wanted to work. I always took the tough assignments, the special ed stints at Starkey, our local school for the mentally handicapped. I appreciated the extremity of those kids' situations. They seemed, perhaps, like embodiments of a menacing force in the universe—the girl born without eyes; the boy who, at age five, was the size of an infant and who spent his days in a beanbag chair, having his limbs manipulated, blinking milkily up at the light; the thirteen-year-old who liked to drop trou and jerk off every twenty minutes (his penis was extremely large). Why, I wonder, did their grim and often hopeless seeming situations not paralyze me with despair? I can't say; I just know that I was well suited to the job and highly requested.

With all that money I earned (I was still living at home), I bought antiques. Antiques! Glass candy dishes and velvet chaise lounges. Like the future grandma I was, I liked willowware, and had a full set waiting like a dowry in my bedroom. In the evenings, after work, I would go home and drink hot tea, read *The New Yorker*, listen to public radio. Just like my parents, the real middle-aged people in the house.

Some evenings, I went to bars instead, and, as usual, I took advantage of seeming older than I was. And some mornings, I was hungover when I went to work, also just like a grown-up, alternating milky coffee and aspirin. I would open the Y a little early just to breathe the eucalyptus fumes in the sauna, sweat out last the previous night's beer. My friends and I liked to frequent the Fraternal Order of Police bar; those men seemed supremely uninterested in our underage status. I don't recall ever being carded at the FOP. My date for senior prom (although I'd graduated, I went back for the party) was in his late twenties, prematurely bald, wearing a hideous green leisure suit and carrying a can of Bud when he came to pick me up. It was as if we were already a married sitcom couple, spatting, me annoyed by his manners, him bored by having to indulge these foolish social engagements.

Since I'd gotten partying out of my system by the time I reached college, I did not know what to do with myself on Friday nights. I'd moved three hours north of Wichita by then, so I couldn't just keep traveling back to my parents' house when the weekends rolled around. I didn't have a job, my roommate was a born-again Christian, and the rest of the women on my dorm hall were busy going to fraternity parties and getting "wasted." They were so excited to lose control of themselves, stumble around and puke in the halls. They were such amateurs. It's not that I felt motherly toward this group of pretty girls I now lived among; it was that I felt like their jaded, vaguely scornful aunt. I would hold the hair of the one ralphing at three o'clock in the morning in a trash can in the hall; I would write the Dear John letter to the boy abandoned in Winnetka; I would counsel the one caught stealing dorm mail about the root causes of compulsive kleptomania.

I shopped at a used-book store that catered to the town spinsters. I preferred British mysteries, full of decorum and dry wit. I was a virgin until I was nearly twenty, as if saving myself, as if taking the wise, dull advice of other middle-aged do-gooders.

Was it maturity? Was it fear? Lack of confidence? Surplus of hubris? When my baby sister came to visit me in college, I thought it my duty to get her drunk—at age fourteen, her first time, me her spirit guide. And then I led her wandering the safe streets near my dorm, feeding her starchy potato chips and fresh hot doughnuts to soak up the alcohol, showering her to remove the foul odor of bars, putting into her hand glass after glass of water so that she wouldn't suffer a hangover.

In the middle of whatever intoxicated state I have ever found myself, whether flying on acid, floating on Valium, or sloppy on alcohol, there sits a sober nugget like a cherry seed, like the metal BB in the spray-paint can. There, inside, I am sane, rational, capable of making decisions, capable of discerning up from down, right from wrong, smart from dumb, dumb, dumb. Don't drive, this dutiful take-no-prisoners conscience says. Don't kiss that boy. Move your fingers away from the fire. This judging capacity seems both a gift and a curse. It has both saved and doomed me. My friend Karen calls it my "Wise Soul." I think it would be better named Middle Age, some curmudgeonly voice of consequence and reason. I've been carrying it around since I was very, very young. It appears to be getting larger, like other unfortunate transformations wrought by middle age.

Even physically, I developed too rapidly: I lost my first tooth when I was only three years old, swimming at that same Y where I would later work and cure myself of hangovers. One day, when biting at my inner tube, a tooth flew out of my mouth. I had no idea they came out; it was like losing an eyeball or a little toe. I nearly drowned, in my panic. After it had been explained to me—the fairy, the profit margin—I made my older brother dive for a long time in search of that valuable body part.

I got breasts early, too. This occasioned a long walk in the snow, during which I wept, despairing of my lost innocence and certain oncoming unhappiness. I already missed my youth; I'd been missing my youth since I was capable of thinking the feeling. Maturity never particularly pleased me. It gave me fodder for ennui. It made me the confidante of a lot of unlikely types. It got me into bars and through difficult written texts. It's provided me with way too much information about my own imminent decline. But it's never really been a pleasure.

Knowing stuff? Highly overrated. And not the brainiac stuff, like historic world events or political leaders or intriguing math formulae. It's not like I could quote pithy literature or sexy song lyrics. I knew middle-age stuff, like what to do if somebody chokes on a grape, or how to talk to a person who's considering suicide. I could tell you why it was crucial to protect your credit rating, the statistics on being single after the age of thirty-five, and how to get out ink stains (hair spray). Defuse a two-year-old boy's tantrum? Yes indeed. And a fifty-year-old's, as well. Create a meal from what otherwise looks like the makings of compost? I'm your girl.

Maybe I'm confusing the character traits of motherhood with that of middle age. Surely it was a maternal impulse that brought me my first pets as an adult? Those two kitties I hauled out of Kansas, onto the road to Arizona, for graduate school? But surely it was maternal extremis, Munchausen's perhaps, that led me to my intimacy with the emergency veterinarian near my rented home. (And, as a sidebar, let me describe my graduate school digs: a four-bedroom ranch house, complete with family furnishings, fruit trees, and swimming pool; my peers were living in garages or guest houses within walking distance of campus. They were also dating one another, while I was carrying on with a man my father's age, which is to say middle-aged. Why had I found this middle-aged man? Why was I living out in the desert in a house whose owners were going through midlife crises?) Out into the desert my kitties would go; back they would come, full, like pincushions, of cacti needles. They were neurotic cats, those sisters; one of them used to climb the hollow-core doors inside the house and leave excrement on the top, from which it would fall whenever I moved the door. The other took to eating tarantulas; I think she understood how creeped out finding the bodies made me. But perhaps it was my constant, completely over-the-top concern for them that drove them to their rebellions. Every evening, I would confine them in the house, where we would listen to the coyotes out in the hills or the sand snicking at the windows. In the morning, they would escape between my legs into the desert, digging up all their lethal playthings. And if I thought they were feverish, off to the vet we would go. It was always after hours; it always cost at least a hundred bucks. I spent a fortune on those cats.

It wasn't just the animals I've owned who've been victim of my warp-speed ability to arrive at the worst-case scenario. Hypochondria comes with this particular territory. Going back to, say, fourth grade, I have suffered the following potential afflictions, in roughly this order: brain tumor, breast cancer, pleurisy, anemia, herpes (complex and simplex), pregnancy, pregnancy, heart murmur, pregnancy, pregnancy, pregnancy, chin cancer, melanoma, TB, rickets, OCD, Lyme disease, the hantavirus, rotting flesh, and Mad Cow.

The only things I have actually suffered (so far, knock wood) are back spasm and bulimia—the latter of which might be, when you think about it, a perfect kind of middle-aged disorder: having your cake and heaving it, too—and pregnancy on purpose. I am the kind of person who should not have had a medical encyclopedia in my house, let alone an illustrated guide to dermatological disorders; the Internet has exponentially increased the amount of time I can waste, on a daily basis, substantiating some far-flung notion about my own, my husband's, or my children's corporeal condition.

And here I am, forty-something, officially arrived at middle age, still lying awake at night worrying. But, unlike my eight-year-old self, I now have worries I can name. They concern my adolescent son and daughter. When they were babies, I checked on them a few times every night to make sure their hearts and lungs were still soldiering on, beating steadily, lifting the chest, expelling the breath. And then I could sleep. Until I woke again, panicked and needing reassurance. That monitor on the nightstand? Useless: How do you know that the rhythmic snoring isn't the sound of the sleeping dog, or the wily intruder who's come to do the unimaginable (unfortunately, for me, it is imaginable) to your baby? When my children spend the night away from me, I find myself in that nocturnal hell that is completely of my own making.

When the twin towers fell on September 11 and America suddenly grew frightened, I found myself for one brief period not alone in my thinking. Suddenly, everyone was afraid of flying; we were all convinced that an apocalyptic force was afoot, ready to hijack our planes, blow up our icons, slip a questionable white powder into our children's lunch or our congressman's mailbox. We hunkered down; we counted our blessings. For just a little while, I had the strange sensation of having been joined in my condition of apprehension. Perverse as it sounds, I sort of liked those late months in 2001, when I could sense so many of us, out there from coast to coast, wide-eyed with anxiety in the dark, imagining the worst.

It's probably not surprising that I'd give birth to a middle-aged child, that old soul in a baby suit. His sister is a wild thing, reckless and fun-loving, gregarious and adventurous, but my son is a homebody, a door locker, a worrier. Endowed with one myself, I can fully appreciate his fretful nature. When he grabs my hand as the plane bumps down the runway, I say, "Would I let you ride in this thing if I really thought it would crash?" When his dogs cry pitifully in the night, alone in their kennels, I say, "Would I ever let anything bad happen to Roscoe or Oscar?" When he lays his head on the pillow at night and creases his brow, his concerns vague but there nonetheless, I say to him, "You go to sleep. I'll worry for you."

Happy Birthday to Me

LYNN FREED

Within a culture that is reaching the breaking point in its search for a real cause for celebration, women have come up with something quite novel: themselves. Celebrating—cousin to those other horrors of modern parlance, honoring, affirming and challenging—attaches itself like a weed to every damp spot along the female path, birth to death. And now, several reaches beyond the halfway mark, is the fiftieth birthday.

For a whole generation of baby boomers recently turned fifty, this birthday is being called upon to celebrate the coming out of womanhood. Perhaps this is because for so long it signaled precisely the loss of same. Menopause, once a tiresome, even a dreaded inevitability of middle age, has been dragged out of the closet, dusted off, tarted up, and invited to the party. Now, women, high on age, discuss their PMZ (postmenopausal zest), their newly degenerating bodies, and the men who still desire them. Goddesses are invoked. Rights are invoked. We have the right to let the inner child out, the right to cry. We are, after all, celebrating Life and the fact that we're still in it after half a century on Our Planet. Our Bodies, Our Power, the Joy of Life's Passages—for all this we feel Grateful.

Has anxiety ever run to a higher pitch in the name of celebration?

Has the hysteria for public confession taken root even here, at the fiftieth-birthday party? So that to utter what either goes without saying or was heretofore unutterable in the company of strangers is to be miraculously unburdened? Simply listen to the birthday speeches, the catalogs of reverses overcome—ex-husbands and other illnesses, hostile tenure committees, rebellious children. And then to the inevitable embrace of ordinary happiness that follows—the sun that shines one day at a time, the treasure of friendship, of grandchildren, of second or third husbands. Nearer my God to thee, and pass the nuts, please.

Every decade brings with it its own anxiety—at twenty the madness to experience life, at thirty to establish a life, at forty to change it. But for the aging woman, beset by concerns about lasting the distance, there is now the added requirement that she look forward rather than back, that she do so with hope, and that she do it in public.

America is not the first society to go in for mass public confessions. The Chinese were fond of them in the third century A.D., and they have popped up regularly since then. Nor is the count-your-blessings mode of celebration new, either. It is simply that when one of life's true milestones is colonized by any group and turned into a mass coming-out, then the milestone itself is trivialized in the process. And privacy, already radically undermined in our culture, shrinks further toward the horizon.

Perhaps my antipathy toward such trumped-up celebration stems, in part, from the fact that I grew up in the buck-up, grin-and-bear-it, pull-up-your-socks culture of a once-British colony. Both at school and at home, the mawkish and the sentimental would bring on gales of derision. Let anyone be foolish enough to lapse into self-pity and she would be pounced on with caricature and exaggerated sympathy. Even at home, where my mother, an actress, threw herself regularly into tragic poses, we simply rolled our eyes, or just ignored her completely. If it didn't bring her out of it—if her fits and sulks kept the whole family on edge—at least we had the satisfaction of letting her know that we were not taken in.

Not even she, however, would have dreamed of dramatizing anything as normal as menopause. In a house composed largely of women, the only nod made in the direction of female biology was an incinerator my father had installed in the servants' yard to dispose of the plethora of soiled sanitary napkins. For the rest—cramps, quick tempers, tears—these were to be ignored, or, if not ignored, considered in the same category as bad weather. To hold a ceremony celebrating a girl's first menstrual period would have been as unthinkable as sacrificing a virgin to the moon.

By the same token, menopause was considered a family inconvenience—windows to be opened, fans fetched, and so forth. The decades came and went. Sometimes, when one turned into the next, there would be a particularly large party, usually for my father. Because my mother was a few years older than he, she kept her decades to herself until, when she turned eighty, she had no choice: We threw the party for her. Forty or fifty members of our large family came, as well as a number of friends going back to my mother's youth and even to her childhood.

Perhaps, if extended families were still intact, the milestone birthdays themselves would be back where they once belonged—within the family and among those of close acquaintance. There the journey makes sense, with the past and the future all around us in the persons of those who went before, those who accompanied us, and those who will follow. Now, however, it is often friends who take the place of family, who flatten out the whole idea of generation itself, who conspire, somehow, to banish all thought of the certainty of death. Friends give us the parties, or they enjoin us to give them for ourselves. Fifty, sixty, seventy and loving life to bits.

Some years ago, at my first experience of such a party, I had no idea that there was a birthday involved at all, certainly not a fiftieth birthday. I was a new acquaintance of the hostess, who was herself new in town. And I would never have imagined that this woman—sophisticated, successful, intelligent—would have agreed to such an event. But there she was in the corner of her living room, opening gift after gift, blushing like a bride-to-be. She slipped the cards into the boxes and then handed them to the friend sitting at her feet.

Men looked in, putting on a show of interest. But men have been turning the decades in triumph for centuries. For them, women jump out of cakes, and wives grow fearful. Here, on the other hand, was a woman of substance, giggling about a gift plonked into her lap by the giver, the friend at her feet, who was around fifty herself. There was whispered debate as to whether the gift should be opened at all in public. Yes. No. Yes.

Sexy underwear, I thought, oh dear God. All around the room hung photographs of the hostess as a young woman, a very beautiful young woman. Clearly, although it is an important creed of the new cult of celebration to find the fifty-year-old even more beautiful than, say, the twenty-year-old—evidence of life *lived,* the spirit settled, et cetera—the message wasn't quite selling.

Off came the bow, then the wrapping. The company fell silent as she lifted the gift out of the box. It was a book after all, only a book. But then she clutched it to her bosom. She laughed, embarrassed at last. So did the friend at her feet and a few women around them. Even the men looked interested now. And then the hostess turned the book around to face the audience. It was *Listening to Prozac.*

SOON AFTER I turned fifty, a routine mammogram showed evidence of breast cancer. Sitting on the examining table, waiting for my initial examination by the surgeon, I was startled when a woman walked into the room. She was not the surgeon, not even a nurse. She was about my age, bleached and teased and sprayed, and smiling with frightening determination. "*Hi!*" she said. "Mind if I sit down?"

I did mind. It was all I could do to keep from losing control myself, and I didn't want a stranger there to see me if I did.

She handed me a flyer. "*Hi!*" she said again, unsure, perhaps, as to whether I spoke English.

I nodded, taking the flyer.

"*Well,*" the woman said, "*isn't* it a lovely day?"

At this point, her false cheer began to do its work. A lovely day for cancer, I thought, cheering up a bit. Had a friend been with me, we might even have managed a laugh.

"*Well,*" the woman said again, "I've come to tell you that you are not alone. Did you realize how many support groups we have out there?" She gestured out into world, still smiling intrepidly.

I stared at her. I was as alone in my life as I had ever been. My father had just died, my mother had sunk into senile dementia, my lover had decamped, and the college at which I taught would not allow me the six weeks I needed for radiation. I was reliant completely on my daughter and my two closest friends. And even so, it was as if a glass wall separated me from everyone, everyone in the world who did not have cancer. Still joining a group, any group, especially one composed of strangers who had nothing more in common than breast cancer, was inconceivable to me.

I am no good at Group, any group, even one promising hope. Nor can I stand a parade, militant causes, causes of any stripe. Pink brooches, yellow bangles, armbands, T-shirts—any badge of right-mindedness sends me right back to the cultural shudder with which I grew up.

I handed back the flyer with thanks.

As it happened, I had turned fifty with great relief. A bad marriage was behind me, my daughter was finally out of her teens and becoming bearable, I had a man who made me laugh, my books were being published, and I was free to run my own life.

And then, soon behind, came the shock: breast cancer. Until that point, I had often pondered the torque between the allure and the terror of death. Having grown up in the wake of the Holocaust, in a family that felt itself saved from it by a mere trick of history, I had stood on the edge of that mysterious, horrifying terrain, staring in, wondering how and whether I would have survived myself.

And now here, at last, was the knock at the door: statistics, percentages, informed guesses, groups of fellow sufferers. Quite soon, I came to understand that any allure death might have held for me until now was a sentimental indulgence. I didn't want to die. After surgery and radiation, when I was given my life back, I was filled with uncomplicated relief.

But I conducted no celebrations; I am far too superstitious for that. What I longed for as much as I had ever longed for anything was the peace of a simple life. I kept returning to an image of two rooms overlooking the sea. All the excesses of life—things, people—would be jettisoned. I would savor my time as I had squandered it before. I would consider the present as once I had considered the future.

But what I failed to consider in this fantasy was myself—that, mutatis mutandis, the person I was at fifty was the same as the one who had gone before. And that the life of peace I had imagined I wanted would quite possibly have felt like death itself. Perhaps it was simply that I did not have the strength of character for such denial, that the wisdom of peace and simplicity was not my portion. Whatever the case, I feel sure that I would soon have begun acquiring back the things and the circle of acquaintances that I had jettisoned, filling my rooms and my life with them again, even as I continued to long for peace and simplicity—to look toward them, as I still do, for hope of relief from the noise and rattle of what passes for normal life.

AND STILL I am disinclined to celebrate what I do not consider to be an achievement. Which is not to say that I am not glad to have been spared. I am, I am. One needs only to visit an old cemetery to see the tombstones of women who died in childbirth before reaching the age of twenty-five to understand that fifty is a lucky thing to be. And even if twenty-five itself is not what it once was—how many parents have their twenty-five-year-olds back in the house with a college degree and no job?—nor, indeed, is fifty. A fifty-year-old woman is no longer an old woman, even in our youth-mad culture. There is still life in her. Certainly there is spending power.

And so, if she can handle the jump in her health-insurance premiums, join the AARP with insouciance, shed her girlish little voice, and resist the pull of merchandisers of every stripe, including those of the medical profession, to move her backward in time and dignity—if she can sidestep the determination of her fellow celebratees to make a virtue of an inevitability, and can emerge herself into middle age with the wisdom and dignity that *should* go with the territory—if she can do all this, then indeed this aging woman might have something to celebrate.

My Red Dress Voice

JOY PASSANANTE

I am a woman who laughs. I laugh often, often inappropriately. And I don't just laugh; I bend at the waist, wrap my arms around my middle, shake my shoulders as if I'm the lead singer in a rock band, hyped up on ego and drugs. And I roll under tables, slide from chairs. I make, well, noise.

People are continually commenting on my laugh and the voice that produces it. Even people I've just met and whose names I haven't caught have informed me—with varying degrees of goodwill—that my laugh is "contagious," "infectious," and just plain "loud." I can call my insurance agent, whom I don't speak with more than once a year, or the mother of a friend I haven't seen in decades, and they will say, "Hello, Joy" as soon as they hear me ask for whomever it is I want to speak with. The sounds I make are, apparently, familiar, distinct.

And as I stride (still-muscular short legs pumping, pewter hair flying around my neck) toward what statistics indicate will be my third and final trinity of decades, I have a ripple of a suspicion that my most significant, monumental, and perhaps important escapist pleasure is this laugh. No matter how stressed I am, no matter how many problems I have spent the day enumerating or feeling helpless against, when I laugh with all the stops pulled out, I feel released. I think of a volcano, a geyser, Sisyphus on a holiday. For those seconds, I am the freest woman I can imagine.

Or at least I used to be this woman.

Flashback to the sixties. After I had dated my husband-to-be a few months, my parents invited him to dinner. Our relationship was in its fledgling stage, and before him, I had had the same boyfriend for years—a good-times, no-holds-barred type, who had done odd, if intriguing, things to my sense of propriety. This new love-of-my-life, Gary Williams, with his WASP name, Sunday school inhibitions, and pew-rigid work ethic, was (among other things particularly pleasing to my parents) a book lover, on the path toward a Ph.D. in literature. He was a churchgoing Methodist from Montana, who hadn't had anything like the Jewish-Italian Passanantes in his experience.

That night, at dinner in our suburban St. Louis dining room with my parents and two younger sisters, I was a little tense. Just as my mother was about to clear away her homemade cannelloni to present her Bavarian cream with brandied chocolate sauce, my sister Judy, still in high school, began reminiscing about a long-forgotten member of her second- or third-grade class, who had, in protest at having to return from recess, hurled a volleyball against the teacher's head. The main thrust of the penance for the class was to write a song, while the teacher was at home recuperating, the refrain of which was "We're sorry we hit you on the head with a volleyball." Face twitches, volcanic rumbling of giggles. My sister Jeannie then chimed in, "And then there was the time the ninth-grade geometry teacher took his small ruler out of his desk drawer and announced to the class, "When in doubt, I always whip out my trusty six inches." Seismic tremors. I felt my lips stretch out, my mouth open, my eyes squinch, my head fling back, and my laughter erupt, and before we knew it, all three of us siblings had slid down my mother's white patent-leather dining room chairs to the carpet under the mahogany table, while my father, calmly spooning canelloni into his bow-shaped Sicilian lips, looked at the bewildered young man to his right and said dryly, "They're always peeing all over themselves. Want some more pasta?"

When the Passanante women were together, we laughed as if the sun were, any nanosecond, about to hurl itself into the woods on the outskirts of our suburb; we laughed as if the impact of our noise could heal the have-nots and wretched of the planet, could transform dirt to diamonds. Our laughs were sudden thunderclaps, libations to the gods of pleasure and liberty. Apocalyptic. Apoplectic.

I learned early that my voice was my ticket to victory in the battle against ignorance, hormones, laziness, and family conflict—as a teacher. While I waited for Gary to complete his degree (though I had sworn for years that I wanted to be a writer and had no intention of teaching), I said yes to teaching grades nine through twelve at Homer High School in upstate New York. While I was struggling to master the content of the ten different courses I was assigned that first year, I became increasingly aware of a profoundly more important responsibility: how to awaken the dormant intellects of my reluctant charges, who I just knew were waiting for that magic kiss of inspiration. And how could I—a not-quite five-footer, who had only a few years on my students—deliver this to them? Well, through my voice.

And it worked. For the next three years, I developed and honed the habits that would give me the inside track on inspiration, not to mention popularity. I became one of those up-front, pacing-around-the-room, in-your-face teachers who ratchet up their already-loud voices and thunder up and down the spectrum of pitch to reach and engage even those who try to shrink into the back wall of the classrooms. I projected to punctuate and drive home particular points, but mostly to keep all of my one hundred and thirty students each day turned toward me and tuned in. I can still hear myself bellowing out " 'Et tu, Brutè?— Then fall Caesar' " in such an explosive voice that it made the class— and their young teacher—laugh. I greedily soaked up every manifestation of positive reinforcement (the clamoring to get into my classes, the thank-you notes signed "love," but mostly the attentive and astounded looks on my charges' faces).

GARY AND I were still in our mid-twenties, when, just weeks after he brought his dissertation back from the bindery, we moved across the continent—to launch his first job, to embark on our journey through parenthood—to a college town cradled in the undulating wheat fields of northern Idaho. I found myself suddenly stripped of identity. As I navigated the uncertain waters of my new roles as the faculty wife of the novice assistant professor and the first-time mother of a baby who had arrived in a strange land a continent away from where she was conceived, as the conversations I got sucked into at social gatherings drifted increasingly toward exchanging trivial information about our children's height charts and baby-sitters, I longed to feel still aligned to that spontaneous free woman I used to be. I longed to laugh with those other free women, my mother and sisters, who now lived more than two thousand miles distant.

Idaho was a foreign place to a young mother with a premature baby and a husband with his teeth set on tenure. And then, in that small and isolated community, there was nothing but us to do. So laughter took new forms. We went to party after party. Unfettered by a bra (it was the seventies, and I wanted people to notice me, but I also just wanted, literally, to *feel* free), I often wore an ankle-length, plunge-necked red dress, my cleavage luring the eye down to my convex belly, and I could feel the tingle of the gazes every inch along whatever flesh the red silk concealed. I remember my body, my dress, my laugh, and my voice.

In some ways, I spent the rest of my young adulthood in that dress. I believe I was among the luckiest of women because, except for the few pitch-dark months when my marriage plunged me into depression, I felt damned good about myself: Even in a sweatshirt and jeans, I could conjure up the way I felt in that dress—spinning out from myself, experimenting with words and phrases, collecting, if not always alluring looks, then at least admirers for being so uninhibited, so cocksure. It was the transitional era between Woodstock and disco, and on scuffed platforms in bars and in the living rooms of friends, who slid back the furniture and clicked on the boom box, I danced in that dress wildly—arms above my head, neck stretched, sometimes shimmying in a back bend until my hair grazed the floor.

And slowly, incrementally, year by year, I found another version of the laugh, of the red dress—another kind of voice. When my children were napping, or visiting their grandparents, and more often, later, when they were riding the middle-class merry-go-round of dance lessons and cheerleading practice and slumber parties, I began to write again. To my surprise, this wasn't the same voice I had left behind in graduate school: This voice was erotic, a typed-out and in-print version of the red dress. I wrote on the electric typewriter my parents had given Gary to use for his dissertation, I wrote on hikes, using a yellow pad; I wrote while the kids slept; I wrote while I was supposed to be cleaning the house or doing laundry. I wrote when I knew my husband would be angry about the counters being dirty, the living room scattered with toys. And as I heard the red dress voice boom from page after page, self-confidence oozed from me. I was hot. And free. A pinnacle of still-youthful energy. I had my voice.

I also started teaching again, as a lecturer in the university's English department, and in some ways my fiction-writing voice—and the red dress?—influenced my classroom voice. I explained, I cajoled, I elucidated, I mollified, and I exemplified in the same way I had in those earlier days—that is, I boomed until I croaked—but I also suspect that radiating from this repertoire of voices was more than a suggestion of seduction. As a sideline to my university teaching, I began to give presentations on business writing to banks and organizations. I had to muster enormous amounts of vocal energy. In my youth, after some assiduous preparation, I could present for an eight-hour day. Someone would have had to hook a cane around my neck to extract me from the podium. I once kept up my combination of informative banter and laughter for a regional telephone company for six straight hours, forgetting to give the participants a break. The lesson was focused on what standard business form-letter phrases not to use. I can still hear my voice scream out my favorite example: "May I take the liberty," I said, mocking the phrase in my highest-volume, perilously low-pitched voice. "MAY I TAKE THE LIBERTY?" I repeated, my voice ricocheting off the hotel's conference room walls. "The answer is NO. N-O!" And one evening, after I had lectured to a bank group for two and a half days, I realized my chest and throat and some other spot I couldn't quite place inside me between my chin and stomach actually hurt. I sounded like a man pretending to be Lauren Bacall. But I ignored my pain—yes, pain, I'll admit now. I've been humbled by the powerful and pesky god of irony, the one who had apparently been watching the woman who flashed at the world in red.

ONE APRIL MORNING, after a few days sniffing my way through a sinus infection, I wake up immediately knowing something is wrong. Gary, now my husband of over thirty years, has brought me my coffee in bed—our morning ritual—and I open my mouth, flex my throat muscles, move my tongue . . . but nothing comes out. I squeak, but squeaking hurts. Suddenly, I flash back on a party three decades before. The party lasted until 4:00 A.M. and I, who had had a bout with laryngitis following the flu (prophetic, I now see), spoke over the alcohol-infested din alternately in my husky it's-too-smoky-in-here voice and in the high-pitched staccato of Minnie Mouse. At the time, it made us laugh. Now, on what should have been an ordinary spring day, I struggle to activate, or capture, or energize, or even just plain find the muscles farther down in my chest. Nothing. I grab a pen and the back of a receipt. "I can't talk," I write in a shorthand I will get to know all too well. "Call office? Sick leave today?"

"Today" stretched into three, then five. I try to be practical, assess my lifestyle. I'm a teacher (I imagine a musician without her instrument, a policeman without his gun). And Gary and I are social folks. We have a wine-tasting group, a commitment to grad students to attend their monthly symposia, an obligation to hear readings from visiting writers and poets, an expectation that we will host receptions, a propensity for candlelit dinner parties around our large dining table. And besides, I have things to say.

I call the local doc, get a prescription for an antibiotic. Take it. Still no sound. Now panic creeps into my sleep, and I am jolted awake. I travel the ninety miles to Spokane to see an otolaryngologist, who gives me steroids, a prescription for voice therapy, and a diagnosis: dysphonia. This, he explains, is a voice disorder, and my particular kind involves a swelling and inflammation in the vocal cords.

Over the next several weeks, I, who have bragged in every class for years about how I have been absent for only four days in my career—and that for major surgery—stay home from school. I walk the dog but cannot give her the expected commands or praise her; I cannot call Gary to ask him to pick something up at the store for dinner; when the postal carrier brings me a package, I cannot thank him; I cannot talk to my children or sisters or mother on the phone. When a friend has a small birthday celebration for me, I have to mouth the words I want to say, watch the others talking to one another, and I am the first one to leave. I feel ineffectual, hollow. And I cannot laugh.

I begin to see my voice as a visitor. I have no ownership rights over it; maybe it is just a scarlet-feathered bird nesting in my body. It is my fortune, and I am aware that it might disappear forever.

After the steroids kick in and I somehow finish the semester, I go to voice therapy. I am dutiful; I attend twice a week. This process might take as much as an entire semester, my therapist projects. The first semester, I practice with her tapes, speak at a higher pitch, speak at a lower volume, try not to speak at all. I do my homework sporadically, not confident that there is a cure for me. I practice techniques to help me relax.

My friends ask, "Did they ever find out what it was?" "Dysphonia," I try to explain, sounding like a Web site labeled Voice Problems 101. "Stress makes acid in my stomach rise into my voice box. And then there was that sinus infection or virus or whatever it was, and"—and here's the one that saddens me and in some sense embarrasses me—"nearly a lifetime of abuse of my voice."

These friends are solicitous. I have sent them E-mails saying that I need to rest my voice, but they call anyway. I tell them I can't talk long because I am not allowed to. Sometimes the notion of this restriction elicits a chuckle.

Or: "I'm so sorry about your laryngitis," they say.

"It's *not* laryngitis. It has nothing to do with *laryngitis*." I tell them I can't talk long because my voice hurts.

"You sound fine," they retort, no doubt trying to be supportive. But I am by this time well trained—I can envision my bloated vocal folds, hear them smacking together, grating, jockeying for room in my throat on their way up the larynx. And I can sympathize with them, my sad, swollen folds, as if they are unattached to me, just distant relatives, as they strain to find room to vibrate unencumbered and produce sound.

"Well, it isn't really fine," I say, wondering why I feel defensive, why I have to be defensive.

"Whatever," they'll add perhaps. But the next time, Whoever It Was will ask me the same question. *Whatever,* I keep trying to think, but it suddenly matters that people know what is really happening to me. I have turned inward, like a tunnel of air in me, my voice trapped and flapping inside it like that bird. The voice trying to fly from within my neck. Fly out into someone else. I think, *Can you hear me?*

One day, my therapist says something mildly amusing, and I laugh. The disembodied sounds I make crack in the air. She draws back, says, "Ouch." My heart steps up. "You've got to muffle your laugh," she says. "Can you hear what you're doing to your vocal cords?" After that, I find myself smiling and nodding more when I want to burst. Still, even nodding hurts that elusive place in my throat.

My out-of-therapy life is a jumble of strained discussions, during which I croak or squeak or develop the breaking staccato syllables of an eighth-grade boy being dragged into puberty by forces beyond his understanding. My voice is choked with gravel.

A colleague offers, "We're hoping you can come to the gathering we're having on Saturday night. You're always the life of the party." Immediately, my heart kicks into gear; I clench my fists. I know this is a script that is yellowing in the trash can. I replay a fleeting image of myself holding forth, deploying wisecracks, stories, jokes at my own expense, my friends' pleasure and mine swelling with the volume, with the laughter.

THE ONE SEMESTER of therapy stretches into two (during which I'm advised to take sick leave from work), then a summer. My therapist, though she admits that I have made some improvements, declares she doesn't understand why I'm not substantially better. She brings in a singing coach to assess my way of lecturing in class and show me how to stand, how to align my throat with my vocal cords, how to breathe from my diaphragm. In other words, how to change my entire teaching style. My therapist's student assistant also makes a stab at my case, and when her efforts fail, too, she pop-psyches me: "Do you think you're not making progress because you don't want to be a quiet person?"

Since I want to please my therapists, as if that were a measure of success, my head nods as if I am considering, perhaps even agreeing with this analysis, but my heart scoffs: Silly. Ridiculous. Absurd. And yet, now that my consciousness as well as my vocal cords are many months older, I wonder. My identity seems suddenly, almost impossibly, tenuous and elusive.

I memorize my two-page "Rules for Vocal Hygiene," which I keep crumpled in my backpack, and set about the process of learning: that my vocal cords are too large, the sounds I have spent my youth and much of my middle age throwing out to the world too intense. That I have to relax. *"Relax,"* my therapist keeps repeating, trying hard to inculcate a mantra to chant me through the silence into the world of sound.

Phrases like "hard glottal attack," laryngeal tension reduction," "easy onset," "lower intensity," which form the lexicon for my semiweekly therapy sessions, seem like the least poetic and appealing words I've ever heard. And it begins to strike me slowly, like a chiming bell at a Buddhist funeral, that I am becoming the least poetic and appealing rendition of *me* that I've ever known.

I have to learn new tricks: how to loosen my jaw muscles; how to align backbone, hip, shoulder, ear; how to wait for others to stop talking before I utter a sound; how to respond to someone without voicing "uh-huh"; how to lower the volume and raise the pitch; how to steer clear of the bottomless pitfalls of smoke and dust and furnaces and restaurants and dances and traffic and running water and background music, which all now say one thing: DANGER. The trade-off is clear: I have to change everything, it seems—the way I hold my body, the way I open my mouth, the way I cough and clear my throat, even the way I breathe. And, of course, the way I laugh. The alternative? A lifetime of silence. But this threat for me has an even more alarming consequence: that I will be confined to a lifetime of being someone else.

When I finally return to work—and to parties—I feel like a child in an aging adult body. I am muted. I speak through cotton, or perhaps (on days when I feel better about myself) layers of silk. But not red silk. That red dress seemed destined to remain in the closet, under some dusty cover.

Even so, I *could* say that in my fifties I now have wisdom to bestow and that I dreadfully miss a reliable voice to do this. Oh, what I could tell my ingenuous students, my newly adult children, and, with my precise and amply informed choice of words, how I could use my voice to open windows and doorways onto the world. But a chilling honesty has taken root in me, and the truth is that as I age, I want to reflect more, want to give less. Perhaps my fragile and mercurial voice has presented a way of easing me into the life I am being invisibly escorted into on the twin arms of biology and fate.

NOW, I KNOW, it's just a matter of time. I go to a party and try to pretend I am not there. I wander around the room, examining the photographs on the wall. I am not, needless to say, wearing a red dress. I hear myself laugh, and I sound like my laugh is creeping up to the surface through blankets, through straw, through dirt. It's buried. I'm my own ventriloquist, my own dummy. I am going through the motions—for social purposes, I might say, but I'd be lying. I'm going through them so that I can be part of the group. I dance, but when my partner talks to me during the dance, I can't respond in words. He thinks I am not having fun, or that he has garlic breath, or . . . well, who knows. It's what I think that counts. I think I feel self-conscious.

The deepest panic here arises not from the being quiet (I can do that), but from the fear that I have little to say. Saying little, or—why not admit it?—saying *nothing,* like my multiple ways of abusing my voice, is threatening to become a habit.

An odd transformation has been taking place against my will, but it seems not lodged so much in my vocal folds as in my cranium. What *do* I have to say? What if no voice equates with no words? The words swing through my brain and clatter inside my chest. Feelings no longer leave my body in the form of recognizable syllables that impart meaning. They're there, but since they can't link themselves to words, they float away. And my laugh, too, seems detached from my voice. Maybe it's that life is less funny? Maybe it's that my sisters are too far away? But now I feel everything is filtered through a flannel lining.

Sometimes, when my problems tug at me and threaten to pull me under, I look around for something to laugh at, just to test myself, perhaps to make sure I am I still here. But I think I am past that moment—or month or year—of panic. The red dress may be gone—so be it—but I feel, now, I need a different voice, a sotto voce voice, to sustain who I am.

One day near the end of my year of therapy, I have coffee with a young man who asks me to serve on his thesis committee. Yes, I say. Certainly. But what I want to say are the things that I wanted to say years ago, before my years flew away. I want to spew off words at a hearty volume, without so much as a forethought; I want some of them to be unpredictable and spontaneous, to teeter on the edgy and outrageous. I want to laugh in a thunderclap. And I am about to be forlorn, when I abruptly think I can feel a new voice swimming up into some sort of shape, though I don't think the shape is English or even recognizable syllables. That voice under my voice is silken, delicate as a cream-colored orchid, and it bubbles up under the tongue, delivering gorgeous words like *mellifluent* or *millennium, lugubrious* or *languid* to the clarified air. And then the cadences of sentences. The love affair between tongue and throat.

My voice is still dancing. But now, instead of shimmying untamed, it's doing a tango, handsome and admirable in its control—a snug embrace, a shadow kick here and there, a rock to the fan position, reverse promenade, swivel to tango close—a cream-colored orchid bobbing with every sweep and sway. Can you see this?

Oh, my future listeners, can you hear me?

PART II

THE PERSON
TO CALL

Love is much nicer to be in than a tight girdle, a higher tax
bracket or a holding pattern over Philadelphia.

— JUDITH VIORST

•

Age does not protect you from love. But love, to some extent,
protects you from age.

— ANAÏS NIN

•

"Love is the answer, but while you're waiting for the answer,
sex raises some pretty interesting questions."

— WOODY ALLEN

•

Middle age is when a guy keeps turning off lights for economical
rather than romantic reasons.

— LILLIAN CARTER

·

She is a friend of mind. She gather me, man. The pieces I am,
she gather them and give them back to me in all the right order.
It's good, you know, when you got a woman who is a friend
of your mind.

— TONI MORRISON

·

One of the signs of passing youth is the birth of a sense of
fellowship with other human beings as we take
our place among them.

— VIRGINIA WOOLF

The Person to Call . . .

JOYCE MAYNARD

The old dream, of course, is to find a lover. A life partner. A person with whom you could share not just your bed but your bathroom. Someone whose name you could write down in the "Person to call in the case of emergency" line when you go in for a root canal. In my case, there have been an embarrassing number of crossouts here. I still hope I can write a man's name down on that line someday, in ink, and keep it there. But in the meantime, the name I put down belongs to my best friend, T.

I met T six years ago, when we served on the planning committee of the annual scholarship auction at the progressive private high school our kids—my two, her one—attended. We were assigned the job of auctioneer assistants, which turned out to mean we were supposed to wear gowns like Vanna White and display items to fellow parents at the annual Auction Gala as they came up for bid—things like a football signed by Joe Montana, donated by some sports merchandiser dad, or a bottle of merlot that represented one of a case, donated by the owner of a Napa winery, whose twin daughters—I'll call them Betty and Veronica—were classmates of my son. (Betty was the same girl who, some years later, when she turned sixteen, was offered a Toyota Land Cruiser as a birthday present from her parents on condition that she remove the little metal stud she'd had inserted in her tongue a few months earlier. At which point, sister Veronica, who didn't have a stud in her tongue, went out and got one, which meant that their father had to make a similar offer to her, naturally. Betty's Landcruiser was white. Veronica's was forest green and featured a superior sound system, since when she'd gotten the tongue piercing, she'd thrown in eyebrow and nose rings, which she later agreed to remove, but for a price. Namely, the price of the superior sound system.)

So there we were, in our evening gowns—me in a vintage number I'd picked up at a thrift shop a couple days before, T in one of the designer creations left over from her married days—standing up in front of all the more affluent fathers and mothers of our children's classmates as they waved their paddles, bidding away. One minute, we were holding up pictures of a château in France, owned by the parents of somebody from my son's class (a week for two, airfare not included, bought by the parents of someone else in the class for eight thousand dollars). I modeled a fur wrap donated by a mother who had recently (on the stern recommendation of her daughter) become an animal-rights activist. T sashayed around the room, carrying an exercise ball, to indicate one particularly hot item—a year's sessions, three per week, with somebody's personal trainer, who was also in attendance that night, in spandex, to further inspire the bidding, which he definitely did.

After the gala was over, T and I found ourselves sitting around, eating leftovers and drinking a half-finished bottle of champagne, and we realized something: Out of all the school parents in attendance that night, we were the only divorced women. Several divorced fathers had come, with their significantly younger dates. One of them had bought a week's use of some other parent's forty-foot sailing yacht in the British Virgin Islands—a trip that, from the look on the girlfriend's face as he raised his paddle and from the French kissing they engaged in when he came out the top bidder, she was planning to be part of.

We weren't the only mothers of students at our children's school who were no longer married to our children's fathers, of course. What we figured out was that most of the others couldn't afford the hundred-dollar admission price for the banquet. Neither could I, but because I was doing Vanna White duty, my fee was waived.

Then there was the other part of it. When you're a divorced woman, with a child the age of ours, you may not find it in the best interests of your mental health to spend a Saturday night in the company of a mostly married crowd, all with enough disposable cash to do things like purchasing a spa vacation in Palm Springs, or a week at a château in Provence, on a whim.

It wasn't that I felt some burning need to fly to Provence that accounted for the particular wave of sadness that hit me when that item went up for bid. What got to me was the vision of having a partner to fly off to a château with. Or to take me on a fishing trip to Idaho, and never mind the fishing part. I would have been happy—thrilled—if there had been someone out there bidding for the chance to give me the darned calligraphy set (donation from a single mother, not in attendance that night, who manages an art-supply store; estimated value, forty-five bucks).

"All I really want is someone who would treasure me," I told T later that night, after everyone but the organizing committee had gone home. We were picking over cold chicken Florentine with carrots in mint sauce, "Just one time, I'd like to ride home from one of these school events in the passenger seat."

We don't always feel as sorry for ourselves as we did that night, I want to point out. But there was something about being around all those married people that did it to us.

"I bet at least half of them are miserable," T said.

"That's one good thing, anyway," I told her. "At least our horrible divorces are over with, and they haven't even started in on theirs." I said a similar thing after my mother died, fifteen years ago, some years after I lost my dad: "At least I don't ever have to lose any more parents." Which was about as close to looking on the bright side as I was ever going to get on that one.

Even in the depths of our self-pity that night, T and I understood something else: As much as we longed to be adored, that wasn't the whole story. In fact, we had both experienced adoration from boyfriends in recent years—ex-boyfriends now, men whom we chose to leave, not because they didn't love us well enough, but because we couldn't love them well enough back.

Or maybe we did love them, in our way. Only there was this absence of common ground. Our children, our friends, our life rhythms simply weren't compatible. When you're twenty-three, those things are still in transition or haven't even been formed yet. By the time we reach our forties, few of us are likely to change in any fundamental way. And it's a foolish woman of any age who embarks on a relationship with a man while supposing that she'll change him.

So there we were, my new friend and I, with enough common ground between us to host a football game or a rock concert on top of it. We shared a similar outlook and sense of humor, not to mention age, gender, marital status, shoe size, and feeling for art, music, gardens, cooking, and our children. Except for the little matter that we were both women (and neither of us gay), we were a perfect match.

With close to two decades of divorced living between us, T and I had been on our own long enough that we knew how to do it, and a little knowledge (never mind a lot) can be a dangerous thing. We had learned how to start the barbecue even if (like mine) it wasn't gas-fired, and get the garbage disposal working with that special tool only men and a few divorced women know about. We had functioned long enough outside of the protective shell of marriage that we could take care of ourselves. Our vocabulary did not, unlike that of married women, contain that word *we* used interchangeably for *I* when talking. One more thing: We had been alone long enough to know the preciousness of a good female friend.

"Admit it," T said to me that night as we polished off our chocolate mousse. "Was there a single one of those husbands you wished you'd been going home with tonight?"

No.

We had spotted each other, however—she in her white gown, me in my red one, both of us with our wealth of a kind of experience we recognized in each other's eyes—and that was the beginning of our friendship. Three and a half years later, it's as much a part of how I start my day to dial her number as it is to brush my teeth.

I don't want to imply that all my friend T and I do is talk about men. We go to see art. We talk about books, and what's happening in the world, and our professional lives. We make meals. We work in her garden and confer on each other's kids. But there is no question that one of the things that has bonded us together has been the shared experience of single life and our quest, in what we must reluctantly acknowledge to be middle age, for love of that other sort: the love of a man who might become our life partner.

There's some irony here in the fact that it has been the absence of one kind of relationship in our lives that has brought us this closeness with each other. We have reflected that if either one of us had had a great partner the night we did Vanna White duty, T and I would not have connected as we did. It is a rare thing for either of us to have as good a time on a date—to laugh as much, to speak with as much candor and trust, to know that the person we're with possesses the kind of perception and compassion we know we will get with each other—as we do together.

The truth is, I have never known, with any man, the kind of regular, honest, intimate conversations that I share with my good female friends, T in particular. Because I live in Marin County and she lives thirty miles north in Napa, we don't even see each other as often as you'd think, but we talk on the phone every day, and often several times a day. Last time I went to Guatemala to hole up and work on a book for a month, she said she wasn't sure how she'd get through the weeks I was gone. One time, she got laryngitis, and I thought I was going crazy, it got so lonely. I could still talk, of course, and she could listen, but there would come a point in the conversation where I'd miss what I'd grown accustomed to—her Alabama voice saying, "And then what?"

We are both in the market for someone we could love forever, someone who'd love us back. We are looking for that person whose face we'd like to see looking down at us when we're on our deathbed. (There's a sign of age for you; back in my twenties and thirties, I never used to include that one on the list of desirable attributes for a mate, but lately it's an image that's been popping up with increasing regularity. That one, or its corollary: I'm looking for a face I could look down on lovingly if he were the one to go first. Not for some time, one hopes. But the kind of person who, when he dies, would inspire large amounts of sorrow and not—as might occur with some of my past boyfriends—a certain sigh of relief.)

And as much as we share a common goal for the future, we share, too, the frustrations of more than a decade of being out in the world as single women, interested in a partner.

We share an understanding of the frustrations of the quest: the dance we do as we spin around the ballroom, bumping into partners, giving it a try, falling into step for a while, but ultimately stumbling and moving on. Sometimes a wallflower, sometimes in possession of a filled-up dance card. But always—up to this point anyway—driving home alone. Like T, I knew the state of marriage for twelve years, but I have known the state of divorce, the state of singleness, for longer.

BACK IN THE old days, when I was newly divorced, living in a small New Hampshire town where just about everyone but me appeared to be married and raising three young children, my main method for locating a potential partner was the personals.

Thinking back on that period now, the image that comes to mind is of sitting in some coffee shop, waiting to meet some SWM or other. Times when I greeted the wrong person ("Are you Bob?" "Are you Bob?" "You must be Bob?"), and times when I saw who it was and wished there was a back door to the restaurant. A few times, I actually went out with the man for a while. And many times, the man would be a good one, too, and lovable, and someone who genuinely loved me. The reasons for the ultimate breakup varied with the men, of course. But the last line was always the same. It didn't work. And I was on my own again.

Once, during a period of particular frustration, a dozen years back, when the whole business of going on blind dates and sorting through the stories of my potential partners' divorces, custody arrangements, property settlements, and visitation schedules had gotten too depressing (add to the list their medical histories, the ex-girlfriends they never quite got over, the fatal flaws with the Red Sox pitching staff, the delicate digestion and psychology of their cats), I signed up for the services of a professional matchmaker in Boston, a two-hour drive from my New Hampshire town.

The idea of signing up with the matchmaker had been to turn the whole sorry mess over to someone else (a kindly, motherly person, if there is such a thing as a mother who would accept a hefty check for mucking around with your life, when the more likely story is that you couldn't pay your mother *not* to do that). The kind who would sort through the chaff for me and call when she'd located the wheat. And come to think of it, the death, a few months before this, of my own mother—the real one, whom I adored—no doubt accounted for at least a part of Hedda's appeal.

My $2,500 got me Hedda's handpicked choice for my life partner: George, an attorney with a prominent Boston law firm, who wooed me for close to a year, during which time I tried hard to fall in love with him but never did. When I called Hedda to ask for another candidate, she politely explained that my contract had run out.

Over the years of my life as an unattached woman, some major changes have taken place in the dating world, of course, and one has been the advent of on-line dating. One agreeable aspect for me was the price of membership on a dating Web site—$29.95 a month for Match.com, which was $2,400 and change less than the services of the matchmaker. You could get a better deal if you went for the six-month package, and after fifteen years of what is known as "midlife dating," you might have thought I'd recognize that as a sensible option, but I seem to be an incurable optimist. Even at that late date, I still chose to believe that I wouldn't need a full six months of browsing on Match.com to locate my soul mate.

The first thing I did after deciding to become an on-line dater was to make sure Jane signed up, too, and right away, so she and I could cross-reference each other's prospective suitors and analyze their remarks.

I might have been worried that we'd find ourselves attracted to the same men and in some kind of competition, except that she and I are very different types. T is southern, for one thing, and even here in California, you can spot me for a New Englander. She likes a smooth, well-dressed sort of person—likes nice restaurants, hates beards, gets pedicures—whereas I have this fatal weakness for men with tool belts, men who drive trucks, and players of stringed instruments. She's a very petite person, which means she could date a five-foot-seven-inch man and still wear heels. I prefer the six-foot types, and if they are a little rough around the edges, that is just as well, because so am I.

It's a generalization, but not so far off the mark, that the higher the income a man reports, the more likely he is to set his sights on younger women. He may have had kids thirty years ago, but now he's ready for a new set he could actually spend a littletime getting to know, and though he may not live to dance at their weddings, by the cruel joke of biology, he can still (particularly with the assistance of few handy blue Viagra pills) procreate with the best of them. All of this, of course, I discussed at some length with T.

We agreed that it's easy enough to spot these men on an Internet dating site: Even when one specifies his desired age range as twenty-nine to forty-nine, you know which group it is he's really looking for. The higher-end age bracket is just thrown in for a little camouflage, not unlike the unnecessary toiletries I used to pile in my shopping basket at age thirteen the first few times I had to buy tampons and felt embarrassed by the prospect of the cashier knowing what I was up to. I didn't pedal my bike three miles to the drugstore for bobby pins and cotton balls, that was for sure.

T and I have meditated on this age-preference question at length, naturally. "Any man who thinks he might want a twenty-nine-year-old is not a man for us," she tells me firmly. We concluded long ago what these men's real problem is: They're insecure. They cannot deal with our strength, our sense of ourselves, our sexual power. They think it's only flat stomachs and perfect skin they're after—perky breasts, a tight rear end, enthusiasm for activities like snowboarding and going to clubs—but we know better. These men just can't handle us.

So we reserve particular respect for the rare few who mention an appreciation for older women, though less so if they haul out that old line about "aged like fine wine," as all too many do. These are the discerning ones. Either that, or they just know (here, a quick check of the income bracket can be helpful) they don't have a prayer of nabbing one of our younger counterparts.

Then there is the old geography question: How far would I go to find my perfect match? The choices are: Five miles beyond my zip code. Ten. Twenty-five. Fifty. Or more. Truthfully, where *wouldn't* I go? Only how would I ever get to find out he was our perfect partner if he lived in Minnesota? E-mail and the telephone can only extend so far. I chose the twenty-five-mile-radius option, hoping I didn't seem like not enough of a romantic, when the truth is, I am nothing but. No doubt this has been one—just one—of my problems.

When I was finished with my free introductory questionnaire, a bunch of tiny hearts appeared on my computer screen and whirled around for about thirty seconds like a swarm of blackflies in May, until the screen changed to reveal a lineup of faces: My potential matches within the twenty-five-mile radius of my zip code, as specified.

The first few were easily dismissable, and, more than that, they might have been downright depressing:

LoveMeDo, age 49, never married. Fun-loving guy, likes watching Jeopardy, *playing video games, karaoke. Five foot ten, husky build* [translate: carrying an extra fifty pounds]. *Occupation: sales.* You'd think, even if a person's real favorite activity was playing video games, he'd know enough not to admit it.

HaveAHeart, age 52, divorced. Looking for a woman to put on a pedestal. Favorite activities: Making you happy. Willing to relocate—any-where—for my partner. No kids, but would love yours. No baggage, besides saltwater aquarium. (Never mind the aquarium. He could give it to his paperboy.)

CorvetteGuy, age 42, divorced. Looking for dating, fun. Woman who looks good in a bikini or out of one.

SoccerDad, age 47. Shares custody of three great kids—ages 7, 9 and 11. [Elaborate description of kids' lovable traits follows here.] *BUT there is room in the station wagon for one more passenger. Favorite activities: Water parks, paint ball, my kids' ball games.*

FarmerJohn, OperBuff, ZenWhat, Thirdtime'sACharm. All hopeless.

Then I spotted Robert46. *Attorney. Mountain biker. Owns a golden retriever. Has season tickets to ballet. Recently took a class in Italian cooking, ready to cook you fresh pasta. Or we could just fly to Tuscany. . . .*

He had all his hair. Clicking on his photograph to enlarge it revealed a trim physique, a sort of Kevin Spacey look around the eyes. . . . I hit the phone, punched in T's number.

Together, we analyzed his profile, wishing he'd chosen something other than Gwyneth Paltrow's first kiss in *Shakespeare in Love* for his favorite on-screen sex scene, but all in all, he was promising. He didn't have any kids and was inconclusive about wanting them, but we figured, the dog (plus our own offspring, naturally) might be enough for him.

As we soon learned, once we'd ponied up our charge-card numbers, which allowed us not simply to peruse the candidates for our affections but to write to them, Robert46 had not actually logged on to this particular dating site since spring of 2002. Robert46 being—as Jane and I would learn—precisely the kind of man who sticks around a place like this for about ten minutes before someone snaps him up. You could call his appearance on the dating site a perfect example of the old bait-and-switch style of salesmanship: advertise Robert46, give them LoveMeDo.

But by then, I was hooked. This was better than other kinds of shopping. This store never closed. You could log on at any hour of the day or night, and, as I would learn soon enough, many did: LoveMeDo could be found on-line at 3:43 A.M., though, then again, who was I to talk? I wouldn't have known if I hadn't been on-line at that hour myself. You never knew when the next Robert46 might wander in, and, as Jane put it, you'd better be there ready to pounce when he did.

So we posted our profiles, filling in the answers to questions like "Describe your perfect first date" and "Celebrity I most resemble." In preparation for posting her profile, Jane sent me an E-mail with a bunch of digital pictures of herself from her recent vacation in Costa Rica with her son, Jake—one with (untypical for her) no makeup, wearing hiking gear, standing in front of a waterfall, and a more glamorous shot, from an interior designers' dinner she'd attended awhile back. I voted for the Costa Rica picture, with the fancy dress photo as her secondary image.

For myself, because I didn't own a digital camera, there was only a single option: a shot taken by an old boyfriend's son of the two of us six months earlier. With the help of Photoshop, Jane managed to cut the boyfriend out of the picture, though one telltale hand rested, ambiguously, on the shoulder of my red dress. I figured this wasn't so bad, when you thought about it. Were these men really going to believe I'd spent the last half century of life sitting around waiting for them to send me an E-mail?

The fifty-one years part was a major discussion point, actually. Jane, being a southerner, felt reluctant to put her real age in her profile, and "never mind" was not an option, since the age you give for yourself determines whether or not you show up in a particular bachelor's search. As for me, I felt no choice but to put it out there in black and white. "What kind of a relationship would it be if I started the whole thing out with a lie about something as basic as the year I was born?" I asked her.

"You could pass for forty-two," she pointed out. "Particularly in a dark room."

T is a kind person and a loving friend, but this actually may be true. There's another part to it, however, that took me a while to recognize, which is the part about a person's age that has nothing to do with how she looks. It's about what she's lived through, what she knows. In that way, I am every minute of my fifty-one years. So I typed in the numbers. Birth date, 1953. Let them do the math.

We decided on our monikers. I chose two words that popped into my head for no particular reason except that they seemed to fit. Red Shoes. Maybe someone out there, reading that, would get the sense of me as a woman who wished she went dancing more often, someone with what my mom would have called a "zest for life."

It was a Friday afternoon when we signed up. I remember that, because I was thinking, as I typed in my Visa card number and expiration date, that I could be out dancing by Saturday night.

I pushed enter. From where she sat in her messy office thirty miles north, T did the same. Ten minutes later, there were our two mug shots up on the screen, smiling out hopefully, like a couple of women who still, after all these years, believed in such a thing as love, which truthfully we did—do.

"If I like you enough to walk down the street with you at all," I had written in my profile, "I'll probably want to hold your hand." I might as well have stood up at my daughter's school auction with a big red X on my left breast and a sign saying UP FOR BID.

An hour later, the first message popped up on my screen. I had mail.

THAT WAS A year ago. Since then, we've had a few dozen cups of coffee and dates with our male counterparts in the world of so-called midlife dating. We have met men whose photographs, posted with their profiles, probably dated back to the Reagan administration. We have, of course, received duplicate E-mails from men who have informed each of us how utterly and uniquely charmed they were by our eyes, our smile, our je ne sais quoi. We have fielded proposals to fly to Paris for the weekend, or to be someone's date for his company Christmas party (we passed). We have heard from young men who expressed deep appreciation for older women ("like fine wine . . .") and older men who promised to take care of us forever. Now and then, a man writes to us who has posted only a photograph of his abs, or no photo at all. Those, we now understand, are the married ones.

Now and then, someone comes along in T's life, or mine, who seems like a candidate for a real relationship, and sometimes we have found such a person, though never yet one who's stood the test of time. You will not hear me say there are no good men out there. I believe there are many, and I have found a few. But a life partner, after all these years? There is a tougher challenge.

We reflect that life has taken its toll on the men who constitute a significant portion of the dating pool of women at our stage of life, the men who are left, still available, at this point in the game. (Of course, life has taken its toll on us, as well.) Now and then, a widower may show up who had a happy marriage and a great life until his wife dropped dead—and if he does show up, he may represent our best shot at locating a bona fide normal man, but only if the experience of his wife's death (not to mention the trauma to his kids) didn't do him in, which very likely it did.

I dated a high-priced litigator one time, marveling to Jane how someone who could be so tough in the courtroom that he charged $425 an hour could be so sweet to me—a mystery whose solution was finally revealed when I ended the relationship six months later, not because anything about him was terrible, but because it just wasn't great enough. Four days later, I received by registered mail a letter tougher than anything my ex-husband's lawyer ever drafted during the whole of our divorce, accompanied by a bill for every long-distance phone call I'd made from his telephone over the duration of our relationship, as well as my portion of the rental-car bill for the vacation we'd taken together, and a formal letter on his office letterhead indicating that in the event I failed to pay up within thirty days, he'd be taking me to court.

The insomniac. The fitness fanatic. The one who wanted me to be his mother, and the one who hated his mother with such a passion that when I inadvertently served rice pudding for dessert one time (her specialty, it turned out), he ran out the door, jumped in his car, and never darkened my door again.

I could teach a whole class on "The Effect of the Vietnam Experience on Men Born Between 1945 and 1953." I could edit a collection of astonishing, brilliant, and deeply moving letters from men in prison. Then there is the alcohol factor, the marijuana-dependence factor, the too-little-sex factor, the too-much-sex factor, and (increasingly, of late) the touchy-prostate factor. For all the times I had to call a love affair off for insufficiency of love, there was at least one that taught me love is not always enough. It can also be too much.

The funny thing is, I still like men. I don't mean simply that I want one of them to dance with me, or kiss me, or drive me home. I mean that for all their failings, I like them. When women sit around and tell stories about men, as divorced and single women the age of T and myself tend to do—if they haven't given up entirely—they often say some pretty nasty things. Sometimes these women are so bitter and hate-filled, you wonder why they'd even want to be with a man at all.

At times like those, I tend to remain silent, or offer up excuses for the trying behavior of the men. The attitude I take about these men being almost motherly, or sisterly. They're probably doing the best they can, I say. The best they can simply falls short, often. Same as it does with many women, I would concede.

SO HERE I am, at fifty-one. *Red Shoes1105*, a number that refers to my birthday. A woman who—depending on what day of the week it is, and what hour—might alternately describe her life as rich and full and exciting, or lonely, frustrating, and tough. A woman who will sometimes climb into bed at the end of the day and say—out loud, though no one is there to hear it—"Thank God I'm alone." Same woman who will sometimes announce into the phone, to her best friend, "Never mind the passion part. Just give me a nice warm body to put his arms around me and carry out the trash."

For a while, I kept a piece of paper in my top drawer, under the bras, with the heading "The List." If I were a man, a list like this would refer to sexual conquests, but it wasn't that. It was the names of all the men who had come in and out of my life over the twelve years since my marriage ended, to whom I had given pieces (maybe only pieces, but sometimes substantial ones) of my heart. Men who continue to occupy space in my memory. Names that conjure happy times and hopeful ones, as well as times of grief.

Partly, I stopped maintaining this list out of the fear that if I were hit by a car and my kids found it, they'd misinterpret it. But it wasn't so much the fear of my children finding the list that persuaded me to abandon it. For one thing, T and I made a pact, early on in our friendship, that if one of us were to die a sudden tragic death, the other would pick herself up from despair long enough to hightail it to the other one's house and remove a few crucial items: the Hitachi vibrator, one or two skimpy outfits designed for the kind of romantic assignation we always pictured ourselves having with someone but seldom did. First thing we'd retrieve for each other, however, would be my list and the equivalent notebook in her own top drawer.

The real reason I gave up on keeping the list was because it just made me too sad, reading over the names and conjuring the memories attached to them. I didn't want to say good-bye to any more men I used to love or care about. I didn't want to have to cross out any more names in my address book, or forget any more numbers that, for a time, had been programmed into the speed-dial function on my phone.

I wanted to get to the last line on the list, the line that didn't exist, the one where I'd have written "The End." I think that may have been what allowed me to stay as long as I did with one boyfriend I had awhile back, with whom I got all the way past the two-year point—a truly good man, even if he wasn't, in the end, a truly good man for me.

I can remember, when he and I were having dinner in a restaurant, seeing a woman I recognized immediately as a divorcée (almost certainly a single mom) out on a blind date. Seeing her, I practically shivered, though it was summer when this happened. It was as if I were catching a glimpse of myself—walking over my own grave, you might even say—and I was just so glad not to be that woman anymore.

But it did end with that boyfriend, and then I was that unattached woman again after all. As T and I concluded regretfully awhile back, neither of us is very good at making the best of a so-so situation. If we were, we'd have been paired off by now.

It has also begun to occur to us, at this point in the game, that maybe an amazing relationship is something you painstakingly build, not something that hits you like a lightning bolt. We've stopped looking for a particular person, a particular set of qualities and interests, a match, a destination, instead viewing the process of the search more like a road trip to parts unknown. Not so much "Here's what I want" as "Let's see what I discover."

Looking back, I doubt I could have made a go of it with any of my past sweethearts—from the personals, the matchmaker, or any of the other odd ways I have found myself bumping into a partner over the years. But to say the fault was in the men is not the real story, either. The woman I was when I chose those men, and the woman who conducted those relationships—much as she would have said she longed for a partner—was still engaged in the many-years-long process of grieving the marriage that had ended, raising the children it miraculously produced, and discovering who she might be. In my case, the journey of discovery has taken around half a century.

I have always said that I am looking for continuity. Someone to treasure me. But lately it occurs to me that I have those things. There is a fixed point in my universe—a whole constellation, in fact. But it's not a man. It's my children, of course, and it is the women friends with whom I share the experience of life without a man. "My sisters of choice," I call them, T in particular.

And it came to me the other day that perhaps one reason I have so uncompromisingly held on to a certain high standard for the level of communication and connection I look for with a man comes from having experienced such a high quality of those things with my women friends. The bar is high. As T says, "Before I go out with someone, I ask myself, Who would I rather have dinner with—him or you?"

So for now, I have my coffee—over the phone—with T. When all else fails, it is the treasured woman friend on the other end of the telephone line who may be counted on to know and love and treasure us.

OW/YM Q&A

KAREN KARBO

When people discover that my boyfriend, J., is sixteen years younger than I am, they are intensely curious. Friends, acquaintances, old college chums, the mothers of my daughter's friends, New York magazine editors, and my favorite Russian pedicurist all want to know how I do it, as if I'm the mother of quintuplets, or am supporting my family solely on bottle-return refunds. It's outlandish, loving the thirty-year-old J.

When I first began dating J. almost five years ago, people who hadn't met him would ask what he was like. I would enthuse about his sense of humor, his generosity of spirit and urge to shake people up occasionally, and the fact that he looks the love child of Johnny Depp and Leonardo DiCaprio. This was all disingenuous of me; I was hedging. I knew the moment I mentioned that J. was twenty-five (I was forty-one), I would provoke one of two responses.

The first would be alarm. "Oh my God!" an editor at a women's magazine said to me upon learning J.'s age. "How can you do it? I could never be with a younger guy." This woman was twenty-seven and had just enjoyed an awkward three-week-long courtship with a twenty-four-year-old. I did not have the heart to tell her he barely qualified for merely younger, forget much younger.

I wish I could report her dismay stemmed from the fear of something substantive, like how I, a baby boomer, could possibly share a life with someone who wasn't even alive when Kennedy was shot, but it's never about that. It's always about looks and aging, and the fear that loving a younger man means a life where you're eternally reminded that you're not as young as he, that every time you look into his eyes, which will have no bags under them, you'll be brought face-to-face with your own self-loathing and mortality.

The second response is the ridiculous "You go girl!" The message here is that I've done something zany and reckless, like quit my job and moved to Tahiti. "You go girl!" is rarely uttered when the age difference is less than ten years.

Then come the questions, some ruder than others.

Next month, J. and I have will have been together for nearly five years. In celebration of half a decade of taboo breaking, I thought I'd take the opportunity to clear up certain matters once and for all.

Q: *How on earth did you meet? Could you tell, by following his line of sight, whether he checked out your crow's-feet first, or your sagging bosom? How did he see past your obvious decrepitude to the lovely soul that lies within?*

A: J. and I met on the Internet. There I was, lurking in my favorite chat room, CraddleRobbers. Ha! Just kidding. In point of fact, when I met J., I was on the job, researching a story about the popular on-line role-playing game EverQuest. The world of EverQuest is Dungeons & Dragons by way of the Renaissance Faire. I'd created an elven magician in an emerald green robe who, one night while adventuring in a place called the Estate of Unrest, met a wood-elf bard in blue plate mail who looked unnervingly like David Cassidy from his Partridge Family days. I typed out this joke when I met "Mozi," and he LOLed.

This is the unsung advantage of dating a much younger guy as opposed to the merely younger guy; the much younger was weaned on Nick at Nite, and can easily sing along when the urge arises to belt out the theme from *Green Acres*. He can appreciate a good David Cassidy joke. The merely younger guy was probably already in college when Nick at Nite debuted, and he won't share your cultural references.

Thus J. and I began an on-line courtship that was positively Victorian in nature. I, being middle-aged, thought it was pretty fucking weird to pursue a relationship with someone I knew best as a shaggy-haired cartoon character with whom I spent hours every evening killing cartoon monsters. So, I was timid. What if Mozi was a big freak? Or a girl? Day by day, I got to know him. What impressed me most was that he knew *a lot* is two words. You wouldn't have *that* information about someone you'd met in a bar.

Between slaughtering frogloks and orcs, there was a lot of downtime. I learned he owned his own condo in Southern California, did consulting as a computer-network engineer, had sailed to Hawaii on a fifty-three-foot Passport when he was seventeen, once owned a Peruvian Paso named Maria, who tried to buck off the first person to ride her on any given day, despised country music, was a fan of Jamie Lee Curtis, and preferred his fries with ranch dressing rather than Catsup.

He learned that I had an ex-husband, a daughter, a chocolate Lab with a walleye and a chronic case of colitis, and that I was forty-one.

After two months, I revealed my first name. After two and a half months, I passed along my E-mail. Until the day we traded pictures, it was a meeting of the minds, as if we'd been old-fashioned pen pals. We didn't expect much. We met on a video game and either or both of us could have been repellent to the other. Instead, he looked like my first boyfriend, and I was the brand of tall redhead after which he secretly lusted. It was, quite literally, a virtual miracle.

Q: Do you do nothing but have mind-blowing sex all day long?
A: Pretty much. We've both given up our jobs, friends, family, and gym memberships to stay in bed 24/7, in the spirit of John and Yoko (also an OW/YM couple).

I've taken to giving the above answer, since no one believes a relationship between an older (experienced!) woman and a younger (horny!) man could be based on anything other than rampaging lust, despite how we met (see above).

For it's common knowledge that by virtue of being the OW, I've been miraculously transformed into the modern-day equivalent of the sexually ravenous French courtesan who knows all the moves and when to expertly apply them, and J., by virtue of being the YM, is as well endowed as a porn star, eager to learn, and indefatigable. (It's one of the intriguing stereotypes: The OW/YM hookup is always presumed to be about sex, and the OM/YW hookup is always presumed to be about money.)

Where and when we OWs developed this legendary sexual expertise is a mystery, since before meeting our YM, a lot of us have been otherwise consumed by marriage and divorce, kids who were conceived, carried, toilet-trained, and now dole out the back talk while needing to be chauffeured around to endless sleepovers and riding lessons, careers that took off with varying degrees of trajectory, and a lot of other grown-up stuff.

One thing OWs have learned, however, is that guys are simple contraptions. They like sex, and they like it when their women like it, and that's about it. Younger women tend to make things more complicated. They worry far too much about cellulite. Basically, if you're naked and smiling, men are pretty happy. And if you feel generous and want to toss a blow job in there on occasion, he's yours for life.

Q: *How is it possible to have a meaningful relationship with someone pre-dated by Watergate?*

A: It's not easy, especially since all my previous relationships relied heavily on an ongoing speculation about whether Deep Throat was G. Gordon Liddy (he wasn't). Sometimes, when J. and I are in a restaurant, involved in a discussion about the fate of Social Security, or whether the president should be held accountable for the fact that Iraq wound up WMDless, I glance over at a couple who look as if they may have graduated from high school within a few years of each other and think, I bet they're talking about Watergate! I wish J. and I could be talking about Watergate!

Q: *Do you have to listen to a lot of Bon Jovi?*

A: Rather more than I would otherwise. The upside is, no Neil Young. There is no truth to the assumption that the rock music of your own coming-of-age decade is in any way more bearable than that of any other decade.

Q: Do you have sex with the lights on?

A: You mean, am I afraid that if the lights are on he's going to get one look at my yes-I've-given-birth belly and realize I'm not twenty? (As if he can't *feel* the difference, no matter the lighting scheme, but whatever.) But to answer the question: Mostly, there is some form of light in the room, but rarely the overhead. We like candles. We like a full moon. We like a gray, rainy morning.

Then again, we almost never turn on the overhead for any reason. It's got a hundred-watt bulb in it, and we always forget to change it to something a little less reminiscent of movie-set lighting. However, it would be disingenuous for me to fail to report that (a) I'm fortunate in having had parents who were lanky and, for their era, athletic, and (b) I am no stranger to the Butt Blaster at my local gym, where I work out about five days a week.

Q: Aren't you afraid he's going to leave you for a younger woman?

A: I would HOPE he would leave me for a younger woman. If he dumped me for another forty-five-year-old, I'd have his head on a plate.

It's one of the liberating things about being the OW: However terrific you may look, you are not now, nor will you ever again be, a nineteen-year-old-in-a-bikini-walking-on-the-beach. You may own a bikini. You may own a beach house with its own private beach. You may have abs of steel, but you'll never be a nineteen-year-old-in-a-bikini-walking-on-the-beach. If J. decides one day that that's what he wants (doubtful: when he was seventeen, he was already pining for a thirty-year-old), I hope he goes for it.

Part of my sanguine attitude has to do with the fact that God, in his infinite mercy, has seen fit to allow me to remember quite clearly what it was like to be nineteen. I grew up in Southern California. The summer I was nineteen, I spent plenty of hours trudging up and down the wide, flat shore of Newport Beach, where I was renting a beach house with three sorority sisters. I was five nine and weighed 130, give or take. I had a yellow velour bikini held together on the sides with gold rings. I had a smooth golden tan. And, of course, I was consumed with self-loathing. Why was I so tall? Why was I stuck with this mop of wavy brown hair that turned red in the sun, never blond? Why did I have to have all these freckles? Why didn't I have blue eyes? Why did I have such big hips? Why weren't my boobs bigger? Why were my knees so weird-looking?

None of these questions obtain anymore. I'm not sure why. I've already outlived my own mother; maybe I'm simply glad to be alive and healthy. In any case, I'm happy with the body I've got, and, as J. likes to point out, there's nothing more appealing in a woman than self-esteem.

Q: *Do you feel a kinship with Demi Moore?*
A: I love this question, which presumes that all of us OWs belong to some secret society, like Freemasons. However much I admire Demi for the one-armed push-ups she performed in *G.I. Jane,* she should be ashamed of herself for making the rest of us OWs feel that unless we can afford—and have geologic expanses of time to endure—four hundred thousand dollars' worth of surgery we daren't hook up with the cutie-pie likes of Ashton Kutcher. Demi clearly does not believe she simply needs to be naked and smiling. She is also operating under the misguided notion that with her sucked-out belly and bright pale blue teeth, she can be a nineteen-year-old-in-a-bikini-walking-on-the beach. (Impossible; see above.)

Q: *What does J.'s mother think?*
A: There is possibly no better time in human history to get yourself a much younger man, since there's a good chance he sprang from the loins of forward-thinking hippies. J.'s mom has straight blond hair and still knows all the lyrics from "Me and Bobby McGee" and is impressively tolerant, as mandated by the I'm Okay, You're Okay counterculture values she embraced as a teenager.

She sees that her eldest son is happy. She sees that he eats well, has color in his cheeks and a bounce in his step. Once, I asked her point-blank whether our age gap bothered her, or whether it bugged her she was a scant eight years older than I. She said there was no guarantee that if J. hooked up with someone closer in age that the relationship would be any happier. It also helps, I suppose, that she has three other children poised to give her grandchildren, and so she can be philosophical about the fact that unless we adopt, J. and I won't be having any of our own. Which leads to the next question . . .

Q: *What about* children?

A: My usual flip answer: I already have a twelve-year-old daughter from my first marriage, so I'm set.

I do understand what everyone's getting at. When two thirty-year-olds hook up, the question of children is unresolved. There's a Christmas Eve feeling about the possibilities: Will we have one? Two? Four? Twins? Girls? Boys? The assumption is that if you want 'em, you can find a way to get 'em. The option remains tantalizingly open, and we Americans love keeping our options open.

In an OW/YM situation, the future is known: Unless you adopt, or do some wacky Joan Lundenish surrogate mom thing, you know going into it that children won't be part of the equation. For some reason, this bothers people. Perhaps there's some mammalian impulse that makes adult humans overly concerned with whether another pair of their species is helping propagate the race. If there is such an inborn impulse, it must be ancient, because the world is groaning with humans. Have you noticed how all of us middle-class American types have conveniently forgotten this? We still act as if having a passel of kids is our birthright.

But the world does not need one more human being; it especially can do without another First World consumer of global resources. I once read a statistic that I will now misquote, but you'll get the idea: By the time the average American child is sixteen, he will already have consumed more than two hundred times the amount of natural resources as has a sixteen-year-old Afghan.

The friend who worries most about the kid question is one of those lovely blond environmentally conscious moms who shops at Whole Foods and is raising her children not to litter and to walk softly upon the earth. She advises me on occasion not to get too invested in J.— too late, too late—because one day he'll wake up and feel the urge to populate the world with little Depp/DiCaprio hybrids, and I'll be unable to accommodate him, and off he'll trot in search of good breeding stock. Maybe he will and maybe he won't. In the meantime, I told my friend she should thank J. and me for remaining childless, since our lack of kids balances her overabundance of offspring.

Q: *Have you ever been tempted to break it off because of the age difference?*

A: On the morning I heard George Harrison had died, J. was still asleep. I stood at the end of the bed and announced, "George Harrison died." I thought, If he says "Who?" or "The owner of the Yankees?" I will immediately vote him off the island. Instead, from beneath the comforter came a muffled, sleepy voice: "Uh-oh, we're running out of Beatles." This ability to crack wise straight from a dead sleep is one of the things I love about him.

Q: *So what's your secret, then? How do you keep J. interested?*

A: This is a direct quote; I found it in my journal. I'm overlooking the subtle insult because it's a question worth answering. I would like to think that J. stays interested the way anyone does in anyone: because he finds me interesting, and what we've got going is interesting, but the point is well taken. In an OW/YM relationship like ours, society doesn't provide any natural glue for the union. We don't have parents invested in the merger of our respective families. We won't have children for whom we might one day decide to stay together. I don't depend on him financially, nor he on me. We're a nontraditional couple, and as with every nontraditional couple, the continued success of the relationship is based on our efforts to make it work, because there's no real reason for the love affair to exist, other than our own determination and desire. We can let it slide, as many more obviously well-matched couples sometimes tend to do, but that will surely spell the end, and so we attend. We pay attention to what's going on between us. I certainly pay more attention than I did in my marriage to my grad school sweetheart, which appeared on paper to be a perfect match.

Q: *Don't you worry about what the age difference means in terms of health and longevity?*

A: Well, to quote Joan Collins, who married Percy Gibson, thirty-two years her junior, "Well, if he dies, he dies."

The strange thing about all these questions is their inherent sexism, which is—surprise, surprise—more insulting to men than to women. Yes, there's the obvious subtext—that women, as they age, lose their evident beauty—but what these questions imply about the character of men is more damning. No one quite believes that a man would choose a partner with wisdom, a sense of humor, ease of being, sexual confidence, financial independence, and, say, the ability to listen, instead of someone with washboard abs. Ever. No one asks an older man how he expects to relate to his much younger woman, because it's assumed that her having a nice ass makes up for the fact that they have nothing to say to each other. We believe that at the end of the day, men are shallow, and that youthful female beauty, however superficial, callow, unimaginative, high-maintenance, or downright boring, will trump any other female attribute.

I asked J. the other day whether he thought this was true. He said there was one mitigating factor that made me, and not some sweet young twenty-something type, deeply appealing. He said, "You love me for who I am. Women in their twenties still are under the impression they can change a guy. They snag you and then they think, Okay, here's what I have to work with. You don't do that." And it's true. At my advanced age, I have no other agenda. I enjoy J. He makes me laugh. I don't need him or want him to be anyone else, and that, in his mind, is huge.

Oh, and there's also the mind-blowing sex.

Tearing Up the Sheets

A Meditation on Middle-Age Sex

ELLEN SUSSMAN

I love sex. I love middle-age sex. I love married sex. I'm almost fifty and I've never felt sexier. But damn, it took a long time to get here.

Middle-Age Sex

My husband and I prefer to make love in the afternoon. In the evening, we're, well, tired. And we like energetic, tear-up-the-sheets kind of sex. So we steal away from our work and spend some time imitating porn stars. Then we take a long middle-age nap.

Married Sex

I met my second husband when we were on the early side of our forties. We're now on the late side of our forties. Sex was great right from the start. And now it's better. We have a running joke: After I come, I lift one finger high into the air. It's shorthand for "That was the number-one orgasm of my life." He thinks I might be suffering from early senility—that I just can't remember yesterday's orgasm or last week's. I remember them well. This one was longer, wilder, deeper. Tomorrow's will be even better.

I've learned to trust my body, to trust my lover. The older I get, the further I let myself go. And the further I go, the more I come.

It wasn't always easy for me to love my body or to love my partners. I was raped when I was eighteen. It has taken me many years to deal with the repercussions of that horrible experience. And so I celebrate middle-age sex—because I got here, because I deserve it, and because it keeps getting better.

My Body, After Rape

Hours after being raped at age eighteen, after being taken to the hospital, to the police station, and back to the house where I had been staying in a foreign country, I stood in the shower. I let hot water beat on my body. I couldn't touch myself. At the hospital, they had cleaned my wounds, but my body was filthy, from the field where I was attacked, from the men who had raped me.

I stood under the water for a long time. I never touched my body. My arms hung at my sides and I turned under the hard spray of water.

Middle-Age Sex

I'm still fit and thin at forty-nine. But my breasts aren't perky and my buns aren't made of steel. Mid-sexfest, I might glance down and cringe at the sight of an extra roll of flesh on my hips or too many dimples on the backs of my thighs. But hey, my guy's got a bald head and a chestful of gray hair.

The frolic builds to a fury of breast wagging, bun shaking, flesh shivering, thigh thumping. Who cares about these tiny flaws when you're experiencing a miracle of bodies at work?

Ten, twenty years from now, the picture won't be any prettier. We'll be sure to keep cameras out of the bedroom. But I'm hoping we'll still be in there, tearing up the sheets.

Sex and My Wardrobe

Over the years, my clothing reflected the way I felt about my sexuality.

After I was raped, I began to drape my body in layers of clothing. I have a small frame and large breasts. It takes some work to hide my breasts. I got good at it—I wore flannel shirts and baggy sweatshirts. I never tucked anything in. I wore overalls.

And then at some point, in my twenties, when enough time had passed since the rape and I no longer feared every man and every dark street, I claimed my body back. For about ten years, I wore clothes that fit, clothes that made me look good.

Ten years into my first marriage, my husband started paying more attention to the curves of the stock market than those on my body. I starting wearing clothes that were too tight, too young, too tucked in. I bought a red leather jacket. Luckily, that period didn't last long.

Now I wear clothes that fit again. If they're sexy, it's because I'm feeling good and don't mind showing it. If they're not sexy, it's because I like that tunic and those wide-legged pants and I don't mind hiding my curves. Sometimes sexy isn't defined by Lycra or lace—just the other morning, at breakfast, my husband found my oversized cotton pajamas alluring enough to take me back to bed.

It's taken years to make peace with my wardrobe.

Sex and a Stranger's Glance

I lived in Paris for five years and now I often go back to visit. There's something shocking that happens to middle-age women in Paris: They're ogled by handsome men—Young men, middle-age men, older men. These men, who have plenty of lovely leggy twenty-year-olds to admire, choose to look at middle-age women—with desire. Their eyes stroll over our bodies; their mouths turn up into small, shy smiles. They wouldn't mind if we ogled back. And if we did, they might even invite us for an espresso or a *bierre*. But if we don't, if we just walk on by, they're fine with that. They're just appreciating the view.

Naked Dreams

I have a reoccurring nightmare. I don't remember the nightmare, but I wake up, suddenly terrified. I find that I'm naked. (My husband and I always sleep in the buff.) I know that someone is in bed with me and I shouldn't be naked. My heart hammers against my ribs. I tear from the bed, run to hide in the bathroom. Usually, midway across the room, I come to my senses. I dare to look back at the bed—there's enough moonlight filtering through the blinds that I can see my husband's head on the pillow. That's his familiar close-trimmed beard, the curve of his shoulder. My breathing slows. My body relaxes. I don't need to cover my bare skin. Nothing terrible will happen to me. The rapist isn't lurking in the bed or behind the closet door.

How much time has to pass?

I climb back into bed and wrap myself around my husband. I feel the rise and fall of his back against my chest. Soon I match the rhythm of his breathing with my own, and I can almost believe that it is that easy to calm the terrors of the night.

Middle-Age Sex

Boys come quickly. Men do not.

Hallelujah.

Sex without Love

After I was raped, I broke up with my boyfriend because I couldn't imagine making love with him again. Wasn't what he and I did in my college dorm room just weeks before my rape the same thing that my rapists did to me in the middle of a field? Or was it something else entirely?

After a few months of celibacy, I decided that sex had nothing to do with making love. It was just sex. And damn it, I was determined to prove that I could have sex, again and again. My rapists weren't going to ruin a good thing.

And so I found lovers. I was scared of all of it—being touched, being entered, being vulnerable. I had sex with one boy, then moved on to the next. I liked fast sex, hard sex, more sex. I never let any of the boys stay around for long.

It took years before I ventured back to making love. It took a long, long time before I really opened my legs and let someone in.

Sex without Love

My husband spent much of his adolescence and his twenties looking for love. He kept finding sex. He's handsome and very physical and he listens to a woman. Women kept taking him to bed. He didn't complain.

But in the middle of the night, these women would slip away.

Once, a female friend fixed him up with her girlfriend. He spent a wild night in bed with the woman, but he decided in the morning that she wasn't someone he could love. He never called her. His friend gave him a message from this woman: "Stop avoiding me. I don't want a relationship. I just want to have sex with you again."

When I met him, he made it absolutely clear: "I want love with my sex."

I was forty-two. For the first time in my life, I was ready.

Sex and Death

When I was fourteen, I went to visit my grandmother in Miami Beach for Christmas vacation. On my first morning there, I stopped by the corner market for a Coke. The boy who worked there asked me if he could take me to the Blood, Sweat & Tears concert that night. He was movie-star handsome, twenty-one, ponytailed. Nothing like this had ever happened to me before. The world tilted on its axis, and I spent a week lying to my beloved grandmother so that I could meet Brett to make out in his VW van. He had a mattress back there and curtains around the windows. Before Brett, I had kissed a few boys and had let a couple of them fondle my prepubescent breasts. My week in Miami took me into foreign territory—beyond anything my girlfriends and I had practiced during our sleepover parties. Brett took off my clothes, covered my body with kisses. He made me come with his fingers, with his mouth. His was the first penis I played with—he taught me how to hold it, how to move my fingers around it.

We didn't have intercourse—I remember telling him I wasn't ready for that yet. Now it seems amazing to me that I was ready for so much at age fourteen! I sneaked out to meet Brett every night and sometimes during his lunch break. At the end of the week, he borrowed a friend's taxi to pick me up, pretending to my grandmother that he didn't know me. He kissed me at the airport and told me I was his girl forever.

On the airplane, I got my period for the first time. I was terrified—I thought perhaps Brett had damaged me somehow, causing me to bleed. I stuffed my underpants with toilet paper and tried to convince myself that it was not some fatal sexual wound.

My mother met me at the Philly airport. I remember thinking she looked different—but then, the world looked different after my wild week. She took me in her arms and held me for a very long time.

"What's wrong?" I asked, scared that she knew, the way mothers always know.

"Your father's in the hospital," she told me, not letting go.

My father died of cancer a year later. And somehow, in my mind, I lost him that week that I was in Miami, discovering sex.

Middle-Age Sex

When I was younger, I thought that when men and women have sex, men come and women sometimes come.

Now I think: When men and women have sex, men and women come.

I grew up in the feminist seventies. I joined a consciousness-raising group; I formed a campus women's center; I grew hair on my legs. But somehow, one key message never took hold: Women have the same rights to the same kind of fun in bed that men have.

The men I slept with hadn't learned that, either.

I've always been a bold person, willing to fight for my rights. But back then, in bed, I was silent. And often, after the boy came and fell asleep in a heap on top of me, I stayed awake, my body humming, my mind churning.

Why is it so hard to say "My turn"? Why don't most guys think, Your turn. (Or even better: My turn to enjoy making you come.)

Today's high school kids have made blow jobs the fad of the moment. But wait: Why are only boys getting oral sex? Why aren't girls?

It took me years to learn to ask for pleasure. I found a man who loves to give pleasure as much as he loves to receive it.

Now I'll collapse in a heap on top of my husband, or he on top of me—we're both out for the count.

Sex and My Mother

A few weeks after I was raped, my mother came into my bedroom. I spent most of my time in there, sleeping, watching TV. I rarely came out, except to eat a meal with her, quietly. We didn't have much to talk about.

Once, she asked me if I was going to go back to college in September. I told her I didn't think so.

She stepped in and closed the door to my bedroom behind her, as if there were anyone else in the apartment. There wasn't—it was just my mother and me for that long, awful summer. She walked to my bed, where I was tucked under piles of blankets. The temperature hovered in the nineties, but I can only remember how cold I was.

She sat at the edge of the bed, careful not to touch me. I felt the weight of her, though, as the bed dipped and sank. I pulled my eyes away from the TV—a game show, probably. Bob Barker perhaps. The summer I spent with Bob Barker.

"I want to ask you something," she said. She wasn't looking at me. She looked toward the window, where the shades were pulled low. There was a blinding line of light that curled under those dark shades, like the promise of some other world.

"Go ahead." I said it like a dare. Try me.

"Were you a virgin? You know. Before."

I thought about Jeff, my college boyfriend in Boston. I pushed the thought away. He had called, but I hadn't spoken to him. My mother always talked to him for a while—I couldn't imagine what she said.

"No," I told her.

"Good," she said. And then she touched my cheek, her fingers as light as a kiss.

Good. I couldn't imagine then what was good about it. But now, as a mother, I can imagine. She wanted me to have known something else.

Born-Again Sex

One of my closest friends spent too many years married to a man who hated oral sex. Performing it, that is. He certainly loved getting it. He convinced my friend that there was something wrong with her because she didn't enjoy sex. She and I would go for long walks and talk about her despair. "I'm just not a sexual person," she would insist.

And then the marriage broke up. My friend met a new guy. "I'm a sex fiend," she told me. She's now fifty, a good age to be a sex fiend. "I can't get enough," she says. "We made love five times last night."

Her sexual revolution began when she took her body back from a man who didn't love it and made it her own playground.

Naked Dreams

Once, a man woke me in the middle of the night and said, "You're clawing at yourself. In your sleep."

I had my hand buried in my crotch. I was scratching, pulling at myself.

I did not tell this man that a few years before I had been raped, that I had been left to die in a field, that bugs had covered my body while I lay there trying to die.

I climbed out of the man's bed, got dressed, and left.

For a long time, I would not spend the night after having sex with a man.

Sex and Monogamy

A year after I got married the first time, in my mid-twenties, I went to a writers' conference and met a guy who made me think about sex all the time we were talking about literature. I couldn't sleep at night. I worried: What the hell is going on? I'm a newlywed! I love my husband! Get me out of here! I'm in heaven—I mean hell!

I spent years in that marriage, lusting after other men and going home to my husband. Lusting and flirting. Lusting and keeping secrets. It was exhausting.

My new husband and I talk about lust. He understands that when I watch the Lakers with him, I'm really following Rick Fox down the court—and into to the locker room. He's going to want to watch any Angelina Jolie movie, no matter how bad it is. And then we take each other to bed, leaving Rick and Angelina alone in the TV room.

Middle-Age Sex

When I met my husband, seven years ago, we tried to stay out of bed. We were both newly separated, too raw for a new relationship. We talked for hours, our bodies trembling. We spent a week like that, like teenagers who hadn't yet made it past first base. Somehow, without talking about it, we knew the stakes: If we do this, we're going to do it right.

And when we finally took each other to bed, we made love in a way I had never experienced before. It didn't have to do with unusual positions or sex toys or acrobatic feats. It had to do with the way he looked at me, and kept looking at me. The way he wanted me. The way he made me want him.

In the morning, we passed his neighbor. "Did you hear the coyotes last night?" she asked.

Sex and Death

When I was eighteen, two men took turns raping me. One stood over me with a baseball bat while the other fucked me. When I screamed or struggled, the bat crashed down on my head, my shoulder, my chest. I remember the surprise of a boot in my ear when I whimpered.

One month before my rape, I had lost my virginity. I was a freshman in college—my boyfriend, Jeff, was a first-year medical student. I had spent my high school years practicing what my Miami Beach boyfriend had taught me. I loved boys and petting and the surprise of what bodies could do when they rubbed up against each other. But I still hadn't let a boy slip his penis inside of me.

Jeff and I made love. And then I went away for the summer.

I knew the men would kill me. They had already dragged me far into a field, where no one would hear my screams. While they raped me, I thought, Kill me. First. Now.

I can die, I thought. Before they kill me. I screamed and the bat thundered against my skull. I felt my legs kick spasmodically; I heard the breath go out of me. My eyes closed. My body went slack.

I could still feel the man pounding my body with his cock, but it felt as if I were far away from the pain of it. I couldn't hear them anymore. I couldn't feel the pain in my head, on my shoulder, in my legs. I couldn't feel my chest move with my breath.

All movement stopped. Then my feet lifted while one of the men tried to drag me. He couldn't. He dropped my feet and my legs thudded to the ground.

Nothing happened. I didn't know if they were still there, waiting to kill me. I didn't feel anything. I didn't dare try to move. Maybe they think I'm dead, I thought.

Maybe I am dead, I thought.

I don't have to return to consciousness, I thought. I can stay here. I won't have to feel anything again.

After a very long time, I opened my eyes. I saw the sky, ice blue. Clouds pulled past the sun. I lifted my head and looked down at my body. I was covered with bugs, with blood, with dirt. My shorts were bunched at my ankles. My bandanna was stuffed between my legs.

I lay there a moment as feeling gradually returned to my body. Pain, cold, thirst, fear. It didn't flood back; it seeped through the cracks, filling me slowly.

I finally stood up, pulled my torn clothes over my broken body, and stumbled out through the field. In the distance, I saw a tractor. I waved my arms in the air and finally found my voice. I screamed.

Sex

My husband and I have been reading by the fire. We've finished dinner; our daughters have gone to a movie. The dogs are asleep by our feet. We're sharing a glass of cognac; he only poured one because I told him I didn't want any—until I saw it sitting on the table between us and began taking sips. We reach our hands for the glass at the same time and our fingers touch.

"Shall I get you your own?" he asks.

"No," I tell him. "I only want yours."

He takes my hand, brings it to his mouth, presses his lips against my palm.

He runs one finger along the inside of my arm. I make a noise, something between a sigh and whisper.

I put my book down and move to his couch, tuck myself into the space in front of him.

"Very hard to read this way," he murmurs.

"Who's reading?" I ask.

His mouth moves to my neck and again his lips press into my skin like a blessing.

"You have too many clothes on," he finally says.

I sit up and begin to unbutton my shirt. He doesn't help me; he watches. For a brief moment, I think of what he should see—young breasts, firm skin, taut stomach—but then his hands lift my breasts to his mouth, his fingers swirl over my skin, and his kisses run from nipple to navel.

I fumble with my jeans, pushing them down and off; I scramble to pull his T-shirt over his head—wait, it's caught in his glasses—and the shirt and glasses fall to the floor. We swipe away books and a cat and pillows, trying to fit ourselves in the space of the couch. He grunts when he turns toward me—an old hip injury—and I cringe when I lean into the cushion—my damn back. And then we've got it right—the fit of body to body—our legs intertwined, my arms around his back, his mouth on mine. When we have kissed and petted and turned too many times on the too-small couch, we do what any reasonable middle-age folks would do: We climb the stairs to our king-size bed, our clothes bundled in our arms, one sock left by the fire for the puppy to chew.

In bed, we pause a moment, facing each other, smiling like mischievous teenagers. I run my fingers along the lines etched in his handsome face.

My husband touches the small of my back, and the sensation, like heat, spreads to my feet, my groin, the back of my throat. He touches my breast and my blood courses through my body. He touches the inside of my thigh and my body opens to him. Every inch of my skin is awake, tingling, full of the sense of him.

For a moment I think, I am so lucky.

And then I stop thinking. I'm much too busy for thinking.

When he enters me, he fills me. I pull him close, wanting all of him. I give him all of me.

Coffee Dates with a Beefcake

PAM HOUSTON

Whose job was it, I wonder, to decide when the respective sex drives of men and women peak? Whose idea was it, specifically, to give the average woman forty years, say, to figure out that she has a sex drive, that she has sexual power, that her longings are valid, that her curves are sexy, that her breasts are the right shape, that there are at least three different kinds of orgasm and she can have all of them? Now that she's finally learned to give a blow job without dry heaving. Now that she can use birth control consistently and effectively without embarrassment. Now that she's ready to call up all those men she turned down out of shame or fear or loyalty to someone else long gone. Now that she has learned to truly feel her feelings and a whole bunch of them are about wanting to get laid. Who decided to let her figure out all of this and so much more, just when she starts to become utterly invisible to most of the men on the planet, just when her husband has realized he prefers twenty-two-year-olds, or SportsCenter, or chocolate ice cream, or men. Where have all the eager beavers gone (long time passing . . .)? In a universe of dirty tricks that have been played on women (menstruation, menopause, and those big, big babies coming through that tiny little hole), this particular failure of timing might be the cruelest of all.

NOT SUCH A long time ago, I met a man, a man who has devoted his life to many things, among them twenty-one years of quality hands-on single fatherhood and, more recently, sustainable organic Scottish Highland cattle ranching. The man is also an ex–high school state champion quarterback. He throws pots, he plays guitar, and he has built custom homes. He sits in the coffeehouse late at night reading *The Unbearable Lightness of Being.* He is about as easy on the eyes as men come. When my husband, Martin, and I met him at the farmers market a couple of years ago, Martin dubbed the rancher "the Scottish Highland Beefcake," which my friend Tami shortened to "the Beefcake," which my friend Fenton translated to "Monsieur Gâteau du Boeuf."

Monsieur Gâteau du Boeuf and I had enlivening conversations each. Saturday morning at the farmers market, where I would pay in the neighborhood of twenty dollars a pound for what was truly the best meat I had ever tasted, counting Neiman Ranch, counting Kobe, counting the organic Black Angus ranch I worked on, north of Billings, Montana, many years ago. But people bought the Beefcake's meat, not because it was the very best beef—though it was indeed the very best beef—but because of the Beefcake's great beauty, his unending charisma, and his rugged, seemingly unself-conscious charm.

I have always been a sucker for men who devote themselves entirely to something, who pursue whatever goal they pursue with every fiber of their being. I recognize myself in these men, I suppose, my own passions, my own single-mindedness, the way I throw myself into a book project, or a teaching assignment, or a conversation, and then, upon the completion of that book, or that class, or that conversation, I throw myself entirely into the next thing. It makes me difficult to live with, I am told over and over, the on/off switch inside me that has no dimmer. I hurt people repeatedly, I am told, because I am either right in their faces or a million miles away. So, I am guessing, it is with the Beefcake, and for a very brief time—less than a month, as it happened—the Beefcake turned his full attention and all of his great beauty toward me.

IT IS AT this point where I should probably mention that my husband, Martin, and I have always given each other a great deal of room to flirt. I should probably also point out that Martin doesn't prefer twenty-two-year-olds or chocolate ice cream or men, though we are both pretty dedicated to SportsCenter. We are also dedicated to the notion that no one person can provide all things for any other—we nearly didn't get married because of how strongly we felt about this—and so we give each other a lot of space to have meaningful relationships with other people of both sexes and various sexual orientations. You probably think I am speaking euphemistically here, but I'm trying my best not to. To the best of my knowledge, when push comes to shove, Martin and I have been faithful to each other. He is a stage actor; I am a writer. We often live in different states and we give each other a lot of slack.

What the Beefcake wanted, I can only guess now, was to see if he could win me. The writer in town, the minor celebrity, the one who wrote the books that all the younger and prettier girls who chased him around town all day read and recommended. And although I believed with every fiber of my being that I had learned my lesson about beautiful men all too well and all too often—in fact, I would have said, if you had asked me, that I no longer even saw all those dirty-fingernailed, wolfish-cheekboned men walking around out there—the Beefcake found me far too winnable, far too quickly, and lost interest so fast, it made my head spin.

One hates to be a clicheé of oneself. One hates to have to wonder if that thirty thousand dollars' worth of therapy was all a lot of killing time. One hates to have revealed exactly how quickly all those self-caring tendencies and all that commitment to living in the present moment, and all that dedication to getting beyond the superficial when assessing one's self-worth, go flying out the window in the presence of one Gâteau du Boeuf.

The Beefcake made me stammer and shake. It has been a long time since I have either stammered or shook, and all but a tiny part of me would have liked to have thought I was over that, too. I would liked to have thought that once we leave forty in the dust, there are many more important things to do with our time than to stammer and shake over a man. Never mind that he is a perfect specimen. Never mind that he really knows how to wear a pair of dress pants. Never mind that in forty-seven years he's learned to do that thing that some men never learn how to do, where he listens with his whole body when a woman talks, and that he does that bumping up against us thing, chest-to-chest, right before he leaves us standing on the sidewalk, which must take us back somehow to the apes or the protozoa or whatever we were before the spoken word came along and screwed everything up. Never mind my happy and calm and reasonable marriage to a man who does not build custom homes or raise Scottish Highland beef cattle, throw pots, or play guitar, but who does many, many things well and above all puts up with me in rather grand fashion. Never mind my utter dedication to my new novel and my wonderful graduate students and the writers' conference I've been given a whole bunch of money to get up and running. Never mind the 453 other reasons that I don't have time or leftover energy to stammer and shake. Never mind that, on one of our first going-out-for-coffee dates, the Beefcake wanted to talk—unironically—about how much he loved the song "Desperado." Never mind that I wrote a whole book fifteen years ago about why it is better not to stammer and shake around a guy who loves the song "Desperado," and that book has given me my livelihood, my profession, nearly every single thing I have in my life.

MY FRIEND LYNN wrote, "Darling! Oh! Oh! A sexy cattle rancher! How absolutely delicious! Were I there, I could talk about the risks, if any, of the cattle rancher. As it is and from this distance, I want to say, seize any chance of delight (I hesitate to say 'love') in any guise for every reason. And if heartbreak follows, well, you've been there before, my darling."

My friend Fenton wrote, "I recall your saying, and wisely, about my Kentucky reverend, that good-looking men were/are at some level all alike. I knew that what you said was true, and I proceeded anyway (though I am glad to say with some reservation, as I knew what was coming). It was, in fact, only a matter of time before he took me out to a restaurant called—no kidding—the Last Supper, to confess that he'd met someone else."

My wonderful non-guitar-playing husband wrote, "He was reading *The Unbearable Lightness of Being* in the coffee house at age forty-seven? Aren't you supposed to read that when you are, like, nineteen?"

———

THE BEEFCAKE CAME over at all hours of the night, and we would sit on the couch talking and talking. He seemed to see around all my little cities of defense, and so few people, so few men, especially, are ever willing to challenge those. He gave me the gaze, the one my best dog always gave me, the one my mother never did, and I was blinded by the beauty of that gaze and believed it was sincere, and, worse than that, I briefly believed I needed that gaze to keep breathing. Then he asked me how he was supposed to know if *I* was sincere, and when I opened my mouth to answer, he said, "Never mind. If you are that good, then just go ahead and play me."

He invited me to a black-tie dinner in the city, a fund-raiser for an organic-food cooperative he belongs to. I said I would be happy to go and he said, "There's just one thing. The tickets are a hundred and fifty dollars a piece, and I just can't see paying that kind of money for dinner."

"And so . . ." I said.

"Well," he said, "I thought if you would pay for your own ticket, I could pay you back in meat."

(I know you don't believe this, but it is true.)

I narrowed my eyes and said, "I'm pretty sure I got over you fifteen years ago."

He said, "You've never met anyone like me before in your life."

MY FRIEND LUCY wrote, "I know why you are going to the dinner. It is because you have to see what happens next."

My friend Mandy wrote, "Coffee dates can be deadly, all right."

My friend Lynn wrote, "I hope to hell you aren't paying. If heartbreak is to follow, at least it should do so at no expense to your pocket. If only they knew how much they could have for forking over $150—the cachet, the appreciation. You'd be his without looking back. Stupid man, beautiful or not. Still, carpe diem, darling."

ONE NIGHT, THE Beefcake called at 11:30 and I was in bed. I had an early flight; he had an early market. I heard myself say, "Sure, come on over," and I splashed water on my face and pulled a sweater over my flannel nightgown and we sat on the couch, talking until I had to leave for the airport at 4:30 A.M. We talked about violent fathers—you might have guessed we had those in common. We talked about travel, places in the world that had changed us. We talked about raising children. He told me how empty my life would ultimately feel because I had made the decision not to, and I agreed completely, as if I'd suddenly lost faith in all of the years of soul-searching that had led me to that complicated decision. We talked about teaching and mentoring as an alternative to parenthood, and he said there was no such thing as a good teacher, only a good learner, and what startles me more than anything is that I agreed with that, too.

It was like I had lost my mind. It was like relationship Groundhog Day. It was like I had gone back to the time when I knew absolutely nothing about anything, and I felt so at home there, I decided to stay.

MY MOTHER HATED getting old more than anything. She had face-lift after face-lift, until by the end of her life she couldn't quite close her eyes. She dyed her hair and tweezed her eyebrows and never weighed more than 125 pounds, and she successfully willed herself dead, I believe, because she couldn't face seventy. I will not, I tell myself daily, follow her footsteps into this maelstrom of despair that she created for herself by throwing all 125 pounds of herself continually up against the inevitable. I barely wear makeup, I hardly use sunscreen, and I feel affection toward my laugh lines as they deepen, my freckles as they turn into liver spots. I wouldn't get my face lifted for all the money in the world.

My friend Lucy wrote, "If every single thing always goes back to our mothers, then what are all the people who come after our mothers for?"

MY SECRET FEARS are often the ones that get me in trouble. With the feminists, with my therapist, with my writing, with myself. Do I subconsciously quake at the thought that men don't find me attractive anymore? How much was my crush on the Beefcake evidence of my clandestine—even unconscious—fears about aging, and how much was his quick dismissal of me evidence that all I secretly fear will come true? Do I harbor some big secret motherlike fear of becoming old and ugly? Not too much, I hope, because what I consciously feel is that to even consider such a thing makes me feel like taking a shower.

Maybe my attraction to the Beefcake was some last-ditch effort on the part of my genetic encoding to mate with a beautiful specimen before I run out of eggs. Go ahead, my ovaries might have been saying. Just agree with everything he says. We've got something to get accomplished here.

And what, in the end, does simple sex have to do with it, that animal urge that hasn't had the time or the patience to keep up with all the reading in the feminist literature, but sits up and bites us just when we are sure it has finally gone to sleep?

The good news, in retrospect, is that the Beefcake and I never had so much as a kiss. On the way home from the black-tie dinner under the glass rooftops of a beautifully restored building in the city (yes, I coughed up the $150 and he never paid me back in meat), he spent forty full miles of interstate letting me down easy. He talked about friendship camps and romantic camps—a conversation I have had a few too many times before and would happily never have again—and said it might be horribly presumptuous of him to speak so soon, but he didn't see how he could help it if he didn't feel the necessary physical attraction. He said he was just so terribly, terribly tired of hurting everyone. He said he didn't want to take the color out of my cheeks. He talked at length about the irony of attraction, and during that part of the monologue, he made gestures with his hands, like airplanes approaching each other and just missing, flying off into uncharted space.

I said that I didn't believe in camps, and that I didn't think he was capable of taking the color out of my cheeks, but that I would be happy to be his friend and I would be a good one. He said that he would hold me to that—by this time, he was standing mostly behind my front door, with only his head left in my living room (while I sat quietly on the couch), as if at any moment I was going to try to get him into a headlock.

He said, "You don't like to have limits."

I said, "Who does?"

He said, "Tough girl, you don't scare me a bit."

"Look at yourself right now," I said, "Look at your body language." And then just a quickly as the Beefcake entered my life, he was gone.

MY FRIEND TAMI wrote, "I think you should have *IT'S NOT TRUE* tattooed on the inside of your forearm."

My friend Lynn wrote, "The bizarre thing is that now, men are to strong women as women used to be to strong men. I mean, if you wrote that scene with the woman standing at the door, it would nicely fit into early- and mid-twentieth-century fiction. But now he's revealing himself so nicely before the heart is even lassoed that you can consider yourself spared. What a fool. You are being smiled upon with this one, darling."

My wonderful non-guitar-playing husband wrote, "He got your complete attention and then decided he didn't want it? Well, that proves he's a total idiot."

I KNOW WHAT you are thinking. That I don't deserve the wonderful non-guitar-playing husband, and in some respects you are right, I don't. But that is the subject of another essay. Or maybe you are thinking about the Beefcake. Maybe you are thinking he was just a female midlife crisis that didn't bear fruit. I've never been sure what the words mean, *midlife* and *crisis,* but the day before the fancy dinner in San Francisco, I did buy my first pair of high heels in ten years—Donald Pliner: made in the mountains of Italy pumps—black patent-leather toes and four-inch heels, mid shoe covered with closely cropped holstein fur and a little patent-leather strap at the ankle. They are perfect and ridiculous. Just like the Beefcake. Just like me.

Twilight Zone

A Midlife Episode

LISA NORRIS

F ive o'clock on a Saturday in Boise, Idaho. High-desert summer but not hot enough for hallucinations: That guy outside the Bittercreek Alehouse in his baseball cap, T-shirt, jeans, and shell necklace really could be twenty-nine-year-old movie star Ben Affleck. I can see the characteristic long-jawed face, modest nose, and well-drawn brows. Puckish mouth. He's too young for me, of course—I'm forty-three. Besides, I'm married. Sort of. My second husband and I are embarking on lives in separate states, pursuing our separate academic careers. For everyone else, we're calling it a commuter marriage, but we've agreed it's a trial separation. Marital limbo.

I'm also in limbo geographically. Idaho is a state where neither my husband nor I live. I'm here waiting for my twelve-year-old son to complete his custodial time with his father, my first husband. While I wait, I am alone. If my second husband and I divorce, I could be alone for a long time. What an idea for someone who's spent half her life married. It's not a change-of-life story for which I'm prepared.

While Ben Affleck (if that's who he is) talks to a blond woman outside the pub, Eighth Street restaurateurs are outside checking their wrought-iron tables, raising umbrellas for shade, instructing their wait staff and hostesses. Though shadows are lengthening, the sun doesn't give up this time of year until nine o'clock or so. Before long, locals will gather to eat and drink at those tables, tanned and fit from their activities in the nearby rivers and mountains. Three-quarters of Idaho is national forest. To the north, mountains provide a panoramic backdrop to the state capitol's rotunda. A ski resort there, Bogus Basin, opens during the summers for mountain biking. More trails lace the closer-in sagebrush hills where my longtime friend Jane and I lost control of our bikes, pitching into sharp rocks in separate crashes, just a few days ago. Jane was with me until this morning, when she left for her home in Ohio. I'm here now, watching this Ben Affleck double in downtown Boise, because Jane and I spotted him at the Bitter Creek Alehouse last night. He was pretending—or so we thought—to be a bartender. I've returned to find out if it's true.

There are other arenas in which I'd like to know the truth of things, too. Stories to resolve the future of my marriage have been muddying my mind for several years. If we could just figure out who was to blame for what—my thinking goes—then maybe my husband and I would agree on how to fix what's broken. That's one story. However, my husband tends to think salvage is impossible because it would require us to change who we are. Which is it really? Which will it be? Not knowing the future because I can't interpret the past is making me a little crazy. But this Ben Affleck thing—*that* I can get my mind around. He's either Ben Affleck or he's not. Simple. All I have to do is figure out how to get the information without embarrassing myself.

Last night, it was easier because I was with Jane. We met fourteen years ago in a writer's workshop at the University of Idaho, and our group still gathers annually near there. Driving together to Boise from the writers' retreat six hours north, we arrived in town the night before at 10:00 P.M., hungry and thirsty. One of the only places still serving was the bar. A blond hostess led us through a maze of crowded tables. Fan blades turned near the high ceiling in the dim light. A mirror reflected the faces of customers seated at the long, curved bar. TVs were placed up high in the corners, but the sound wasn't audible above the buzz of the patrons' voices. Neon beer signs and colorful framed pictures of cigar ads and cowboys gave the place a festive air, while the cheesy smell of warm nachos sharpened my hunger.

I walked behind Jane, who—like me—was dressed casually in sandals, shorts, and a tank top that showed her arms, still scabbed from the bike wreck. Men followed Jane's movements with their eyes, admiring her well-defined calf muscles. Tight rear end. V-shaped torso with muscular shoulders and arms. Brown hair cut in wisps around her heart-shaped face. She has big, round, vividly blue eyes. Symmetrically balanced feminine features that add up to *very pretty*.

I'm taller, more willowy, with baby-line darkening blond hair cut to my chin. Broad shoulders, broad hips. Not much in the way of breasts or muscle. Unlike Jane, who walked with the confidence of an athlete, I could feel my desire to hide.

Before we'd finished our first margaritas, I nodded toward a blond man at a neighboring table and said idly, "That's one of the best-looking men I've ever seen."

Jane glanced at the table, then stared. After a long pause, she said, "Well, he should be. That's Brad Pitt, and I think the guy sitting next to him is Matt Damon."

We took turns pretending to go to the ladies' room so we could pass by, getting a closer look. After a long spell of jittery consideration, Jane finally decided to approach them directly. For a few minutes after she crossed the room to their table, I watched from my seat. Matt Damon, knees open, turned toward her in a friendly way, while Brad Pitt leaned across the table to hear what she and Matt were saying.

I remember how—when the night was over—we went giddily out on the sidewalk into the cool night air, hooting and congratulating ourselves. After Damon and Pitt had left, we'd identified the Affleck look-alike at the bar, and Jane had spoken to him as well, though she hadn't asked for his identity. Now we had theories about what was going on. Maybe the whole restaurant had been involved in the making of a movie. Perhaps Damon and Pitt were really who we thought but Affleck was just a bartender look-alike. Then again, maybe they were all doubles. It was a *convention* of doubles, we howled, and the other patrons were all extras.

My face felt numb from the rush of tequila. My spirits soared, as if sighting the rich and famous signaled a fabulous turn of luck and I, too, would wake up tomorrow with a million dollars in my pocket. The wreckage that was my marriage momentarily forgotten, I wondered if I could forge a whole new identity for myself, become a professional celebrity hunter, barfly extraordinaire.

SATURDAY EVENING. I approach the podium at the front door of the alehouse, where Ben Affleck studies a seating chart. I smile and greet him, thinking, Yes, he looks just like his picture on the Internet. Yes, that has to be him. Then I walk past into the dim light, letting my eyes adjust. At five 'o clock, all the tables are empty. Only a few people are seated at the long bar. One of the bartenders, a man with Hollywood good looks and Arnold Schwarzenaegger muscles—with whom Jane chatted from a bar stool the night before—gives me an enthusiastic greeting. "Where's your friend?"

I'm flattered, even if it's Jane he's remembering. I slide onto a bar stool between a young couple to one side and a lone older man smoking a cigarette on the other. I repeat: I've seated myself on a bar stool *by myself* and ordered a beer. This is a first. At the age of forty-three, I've rarely been to bars at all—certainly never alone. I'm not much of a drinker.

I keep my hands on either side of the frosty mug, wondering where to look—not into the mirror opposite me. Not at the bartender. Not at the couple to one side, lest I appear to be eavesdropping. Certainly not at the lone man, who might get the idea I'm inviting him over. I gaze, therefore, into the froth in my glass. When there's movement behind the bar, I look up and am surprised to see not one but two muscular bartenders who look exactly alike. I ask the obvious question. "Are you twins?"

They nod.

"Identical?"

Nod again.

It's too weird: Ben Affleck, Matt Damon, and Brad Pitt look-alikes. Bartenders who are identical twins, built like weight lifters and good-looking enough to be Hollywood stars. Maybe it's a convention of doubles after all. And who is that woman who looks just like me in the mirror behind the bar? Could she be some evil twin, sitting in a place I'd never go alone, acting like a hanger-on, a groupie?

Ben Affleck leaves his post at the podium by the door and sits down next to the man at the other end of the bar. They seem to be having a friendly conversation. I find it endearing that someone as famous as Ben Affleck takes time for an aging drinker. Of course, I'm no spring chicken myself. Looking in the mirror, I can see the telltale neck wrinkles. Beneath my sundress, chosen for the way it hides some of my less-than-flattering curves, my pouchy belly folds in on itself. My thighs spread, no longer tight, onto the seat of the bar stool. Maybe my tanned shoulders and sun-streaked hair compensate for the rest. Maybe I'm in better shape than most, able to (sort of) keep up with Jane, who's eight years younger, on the mountain bike. Nevertheless, I've hit midlife. And I look like it. Nothing I can do about that.

Will I become like the man to my left, a solo drinker at a near-empty bar, hoping a stranger will slide over and talk to me? To quell the panic this thought encourages, I take a deep drag of my cigarette, feel the burn of nicotine at the back of my throat. My husband was addicted. He gave it up years before I met him. To keep him from temptation and be certain my son wouldn't see, I have smoked rarely and always undercover. It feels deliciously subversive to have my cigarettes in full view.

The couple to my right heads out the door. The lone man and Ben, pretending to be the bar-manager, continue to talk. I've got a full beer. There's really nothing for the twins to do, so they head back toward the kitchen. Jane would have known how to get them into a conversation, but once I've exhausted my questions about their genetic makeup, I'm at a loss. I sip at my Corona. Feel the seat cushion under my haunch. Rest my sandaled feet beneath the bar stool. What must the bar staff think of me? Do I look pathetic, like I'm hoping for a pickup?

I want to say to them, *No, I'm not like that. I'm here doing research. This is about getting an answer to last night. Not about getting laid.*

Or is it?

Last night when Jane approached the Brad Pitt/Matt Damon table, her opening line was this: "I just want you to know I'm a happily married woman. I'm not trying to pick you up. I just want to know if you are who I think you are."

Matt Damon eventually showed her an ID card from his wallet to prove he was, in fact, the celebrity. I couldn't hear what they were saying from where I sat at our table, but I could see Jane's lips move as she spoke directly to Damon, who smiled. After that, Jane started shaking people's hands—Matt's and Brad's and the hands of the women who accompanied them, dressed in tight tops and frayed jeans. One of them seemed to be hanging on Damon, but it didn't stop him from stroking Jane's scabbed arm, as if to say he was sorry for her pain.

Brad Pitt looked over at me with interest and—according to Jane—asked, "Is your friend married, too?"

What if Brad Pitt reemerges to keep me company on the next stool. I'm no longer a happily married woman. What will I do?

I haven't forgotten the motel room scene from *Thelma and Louise*, in which Brad kicks off his cowboy boots and wriggles free of his pants to make mad, passionate love with Geena Davis. Nor have I forgotten that, after the sex, he stole her money and left her to continue the road trip, until she and her girlfriend drove off a cliff.

Really, what is it I'm after? A beer, a cigarette, some attention from a man—famous or not—to prove to myself that I can still attract a lover, even if only for a night? If I could just accept the uncertainty of last night's experience, I'd be out of this adventure altogether, safely back at the place I'm house-sitting, waiting for my son's time with his father to be up. I'd fix myself a stir-fry dinner, take a walk in the sagebrush hills at the edge of town with my dog, and return to the kitchen table to surf the Internet on my computer. The anxiety of waiting—for my son, for the outcome of my marital situation, for the resolution to this story of Hollywood sightings—is what I'm avoiding. I don't want to be in the company of the storyteller I become when it's dark, one who tends to send me into a well of fear and self-pity.

Ben finishes his conversation and rises, heading toward me on his way to the kitchen. Though my mouth feels dry and my tongue thickens, I manage to turn casually, smile, and say, "Remember me from last night?"

He grins charmingly from beneath his baseball cap, pulls up a stool. "Sure. You were with the mountain biker."

Jane had played a game with the muscular bartender last night—What's My Line? He'd looked at her athletic body, tank top, shorts, and scabbed-up arms, and said, "I think you're a mountain biker." Though

Jane was, in fact, an English teacher, she'd grinned and nodded. "How'd you know?"

Now I say to the bartender, "Jane had to go home to Ohio."

"Too bad," he says.

"Hey, would you mind if I asked you a question?"

He leans back on the stool, blue-jeaned legs open, hands on his thighs, wary. "Okay."

"Look." I edge forward, feel the knocking of my heart against my ribs. "I'm not a reporter. I just want to know what was going on here last night. What were Matt Damon and Brad Pitt doing here?"

"They were here?"

I nod.

He swivels around toward the empty tables scattered from the bar to the back wall, where Jane and I started out last night. "Where? Which table?"

I point to one at the center of the room, explain how Matt Damon showed my friend Jane his ID.

"Boy." Ben shakes his head, looking toward his feet. "I wish I'd known they were here." Very convincing. But then, he *is* an actor.

"It's okay," I tell him. "I know who you are."

He cocks his head, looks at me suspiciously. "Who am I?"

"You're Ben Affleck, right?"

He laughs. "What?"

"Well, you look just like him."

He shakes his head.

I pause, pondering how to get at the truth. "Okay, if you're not Ben Affleck, then would you mind if I see your driver's license? Just to be sure."

Obligingly, he takes out his wallet. He has an Idaho driver's license with a name I don't recognize. A fake?

"But hasn't anyone ever mistaken you for Ben Affleck before?"

He shakes his head, then admits, "Well, once someone asked me to be his stunt double. I was stupid enough to say no."

I raise my eyebrows, wondering why he acted surprised when I asked about his identity if he's been mistaken for Ben Affleck before. "Come on. You can tell me. You're all making a movie here, aren't you? I mean, half the restaurant was on cell phones last night. Something was going on."

"This is getting too weird," Ben says. "I have to go." He escapes to the kitchen, and I hear him saying to the twins, "She thinks we're all in some kind of conspiracy."

I shake out another cigarette. If he isn't Ben Affleck, then I'm a smoker. I light one up and try to look like Joan Crawford or Lauren Bacall, slitting my eyes and forming my lips into a pouty *o* as I exhale. All right, maybe with my height and my head of bone-straight hair, I bear more of a resemblance to Darryl Hannah—sans breasts and with more nose. I rest one elbow on the bar, hold the cigarette between my fingers expertly. Before long, the man with bottle black hair slides over to ask if he might have a cigarette. I oblige.

"He used to be a bartender at a place across town, too," says the man, nodding toward Ben Affleck.

"Oh really," I say.

"You know." He pauses, takes a drag from his cigarette as if for effect. "People used to tell me I looked like Mark Spitz."

I take another gulp of my beer. He *does* look like the Olympic medal–winning swimmer Mark Spitz—if Mark Spitz were sixtyish, down-and-out, and dying his hair shoe-polish black. How old would Mark Spitz be by now? I do the math—it doesn't add up. Either this guy is the best actor in the bunch or he's the real thing: a genuine alcoholic. I sip my beer, listen to the Mark Spitz look-alike tell me the sad story of his failed marriage, his difficulty spending time with his son, who lives in a different state. Since his divorce, he's been in and out of jobs and relationships. Nothing has really worked. Really, I don't want to hear it.

By now, Ben has disappeared into the kitchen. Last night's waitress walks right by me, avoiding my friendly wave as if she's afraid I might accuse her of being Jennifer Aniston.

Meanwhile, Mark Spitz and I sit companionably, smoking our cigarettes, sipping at our drinks. He wears the garb of a workingman—plaid shirt and jeans. There's a heaviness about him: thickened neck, fleshy cheeks. He's seated, so he doesn't seem big, and nothing about him frightens me—maybe because he doesn't look directly at me when he talks. He glances at his cigarette, or into his drink, or across the bar at the mirror. He seems like the most authentic person here. He *belongs*.

I've never been told I looked like anyone beautiful or famous, but right now I can't say that I look like myself, either—unless, and this is a terrifying thought, unless that woman in the mirror behind the bar, either being tricked or thought insane by the people here, represents who I've become. But no. That isn't how I'd write this story. My developing protagonist might be confused right now. She might have a headful of illusions about what might be workable in her marriage. She might enjoy a little fantasy about Brad Pitt. But she still has choices.

The Mark Spitz look-alike has grown silent. The identical twins polish the bar, flexing their muscles. Ben Affleck's double glances toward the bar from the door of the kitchen, keeping plenty of distance between himself and me. I take the last gulp of beer from my mug, grind my cigarette into the ashtray, push the pack of smokes toward my new friend, wish him good night, and make my way to the door. As I stand in the threshold, I glance at my watch. Only thirty minutes have passed.

I'm not drunk after only two beers, though I'm certainly feeling like everything is slippery. I make my unsteady way down the sidewalk. No amount of distraction, alcohol or celebrity-related, can keep the truth of my life from me now: The only certainty is uncertainty—that, and the twilight deepening over the mountains of Idaho.

Sources of Pleasure

JOAN SILBER

rovence seemed like a good idea. Groves of olive trees, ocher cliffs, fields of lavender. Colette, whom I read avidly in my twenties, wrote that the sky in Provence was so "exceptional" in its blueness that "around the scarlet zinnias and the red geraniums there vibrates an indefinable violet halo." A place, I now decided, I'd always meant to go.

I was forty-nine and some crucial areas in my life had taken a distinct turn for the worse. A twelve-year relationship with a man I still speak well of had ended a few years before, without bitterness, and I'd assumed I would meet someone else right away, but I definitely had not. My writing career was suffering a switchback—an early novel had won a prize and I'd had a story in *The New Yorker,* but no one was buying my current work and the famous agent who'd taken me on decided we'd better part ways. But I was not at a loss for ways to enjoy myself. Had I lived this long not to know how to have a good time? I had not. That June, to celebrate what an English friend called my golden jubilee year, I set out with her for ten days in Provence.

I should say there was nothing wrong with Provence. The house we rented (which belonged to my friend's friends in London) was simple and pleasant, wedged in a tiny village, and we drove past landscapes of blooming flowers and waving grasses, visiting small towns, eating goat cheese and *pain au levain* and white peaches. The weather was mild and sunny. I had spent time in Europe before (this was my eighth trip, and I once lived for a year in Rome) and my French was passable enough to be useful. One of my better memories is of translating the words for chestnut leaves when we asked what a cheese was wrapped in. It was not the fault of either Provence or my friend (though we quarreled quite a bit) that I could not stand to see another marketplace or charming square after the first few days. How had I ever liked just wandering around idly, sifting through bins of antique underwear, buying jars of lavender honey—who could anchor a day on something as airy as that? I was too old for this crap. I could only think (though not clearly), These are empty pleasures. On my birthday, I felt that I had been sorely mistaken about something important, and was now, after all these years, in a false situation. How had this happened?

I arrived home in Manhattan with the feeling that I had come to the end of something. The ideas I'd relied on—pretty usual ones about what makes for a satisfying existence (good company, good work, and a well-cultivated life of the senses)—weren't going to be enough to get me through the rest of my life. I began reading about religion, particularly Buddhism, and I began thinking about finding volunteer work; both these realms had a certain lyrical quality to me, I have to admit; they sounded like something I could do in a seemly way.

Finally, I signed up to be a Buddy for Gay Men's Health Crisis. It seemed less institutional than other volunteer work; being a Buddy (I liked this coinage) meant you showed up once a week to help a person with AIDS with errands or housework or whatever. Now that it was clear I was not going to have children—a subject I had very complicated feelings about—I envied my friends who were parents their ease in taking care of other beings, the skills they'd grown in the natural course of being the adults to rely on. I felt young and lightweight and underdeveloped compared to them, more frivolous than I wanted to be. Being a Buddy seemed like a route toward at least a little practice in being the responsible party.

I was very eager to begin; though I was teaching in three writing programs, being single gave me time. But I had to wait months for an available spot in the Buddy program, as if I'd requested space in an exclusive resort, and I was given two weekends of "training" with social workers who invented role-playing games that seemed totally dumb and childish to me. The medical lectures were complicated and depressing. Protease inhibitors were new on the market and barely mentioned. A friend who was closer to the epidemic than I was said, "You'll be with someone for *maybe* a year."

I was assigned a guy close to my own age, and for my first visit, I wore a favorite sundress, as if I were getting myself up for a date. And a good thing, too; he was a handsome and picky man, a former decorator, and one of the first things his boyfriend said when I walked in was, "You're not fat!" They had assumed any woman who wanted to do this must be ungainly and grossly unfortunate, which at least I was not. John (I was sworn to anonymity and still cannot bring myself to use his real name) was jokey and charming, with beautiful manners. He had a hoarse, endearing voice and a gorgeous slow smile. His way of referring to his ailments had an offhand irony, with some awkwardness under it. He talked of having been in the hospital with a "smorgasbord" of problems: "Take your pick—a little KS, a little CMV in one eye, a little pneumonia." He was very thin but broad-chested, and though a report had described him as "emaciated," he seemed livelier than that, with his bright blue eyes and his head tilted in attention.

When he called later that week to say he was "looking forward to it"—our Buddyship—I was as thrilled as if I'd won something. I had been afraid I wasn't actually going to want to do this, afraid of a secret coldness on my side, but the opposite happened. I could not have been more intensely interested, more ready to be obsessed. I came to feel I had taken an absolute vow.

Mostly my duties consisted of having lunch with him every week. We went to an old dark Village bar that had great hamburgers, a stylishly goofy British tearoom for egg salad with watercress, a place on his block for Cuban pressed sandwiches. (One of my strengths as a person is that I will eat almost anything.) He narrated the story of his life in installments: He'd had some fame as a "baroque minimalist" decorator and had part-owned a shop that sold hiply designed objets, where (thank God) I had actually bought things. By a classic New York coincidence, it turned out we had friends in common: two guys I'd met the year I lived in Rome. John always paid for our lunches, which was against the rules, but I didn't want to fight his gallantry. One of his favorite stories was about how he'd celebrated his last release from the hospital by treating all his friends, and his doctor, to a great gala dinner in a restaurant.

Right away, I felt better about being single. In John's world, plenty of people—as old as I was and older—were without spouses or offspring. In the world of gay men, my life looked okay. I'd listen to John's tales of old romances, and he'd remind me to absolutely tell my old boyfriend he finally *had* to move his cartons of stored stuff out of my loft.

For some years, I'd been struck by the way gay culture had modified itself in response to AIDS—the way its fabulousness, its sublime reliance on style, had deepened and darkened. As someone who'd lost both parents before I was out of my twenties, this was compelling for me to see. John seemed midway in this process, sometimes brittle, sometimes frank. He'd brag foolishly about old glories (did I know he'd been to a lord's house party in England?), he'd mouth platitudes about his illness (attitude was everything), and then he'd be bravely direct (when I looked at a photo of his toddler niece, he said, "She's my heir"). The shifting appearance of these components in him was sometimes very moving to me.

It confused him that a straight woman had wanted to be a Buddy. We both knew he had imagined a gorgeous young man at his beck and call, and he'd gotten me instead. I had no clear reason I could give him, except that I had felt a need, and, since I had no children (and, as it happened, no aging parents), there were parts of me that weren't being used. Once, when we were driving back from his boyfriend's house in Queens, he seemed to think I might give up this Buddy thing if I stopped liking it. "No," I said. "I'm in it for the long haul." For a second, I was afraid this was too blunt a reference to the road that would end with his dying, but it was not. This was a crucial moment between us, one he mentioned later, more than once.

It gratified me very much that we took to each other so well. I talked about him quite a lot—by way of pride and showing off and also with some sense of spreading the word. I liked being part of a large and good idea. When people said, "Oh, I could never do that," I took this not as the compliment it was meant to be but as a sign of an old way of being that I wanted to leave.

Though my labors at this point were no more than shopping for very specifically commanded items, they were a useful exercise in going outside myself; one thing about being a Buddy, it was not about me. I read as much as I could about the virus; I was now a part of its community. If I'd never had much of a capacity for devotion, I seemed to now. Whatever I was doing, and for whatever oblique reasons, it gave me a better opinion of myself. Which is worth a good deal. I began to think that volunteer work should be recommended to all depressed people.

After the first few months, each time I asked John how he was feeling, he'd say, almost brightly, "Oh, I've been better." A lot started to go wrong very fast—he had trouble keeping food down, was losing weight, suffering ear and sinus infections. He was less focused in conversation, seemed sealed in his own landscape, and was often peevish or dazed. After he came back from a trip to see his family in Canada, a friend of his called to tell me John was in the hospital. My first response was relief that someone was taking care of him.

He was snappish and gloomy on my first visits, mellower as the days went on. I got to know his two closest friends: Carolyn, a motherly woman in her sixties who had known him twenty years, and Ron, a painter with a sterling character. People he had not seen for years showed up; a French restaurateur brought him meals, designer friends brought him astonishing flowers. I was at the hospital so often, everything in the neighborhood—the bagel shop, the newsstand—turned familiar. He did not seem to be getting better. His family came from Canada. Weeks passed. We came to think he would never leave the hospital, and we began to take shifts, keeping vigil in the room so that he was never alone.

In the middle of the night, while Ron and I kept watch, John's breathing grew so labored that we summoned his family. What was I doing in the midst of this sacred emergency, witnessing these ultimate moments with people I hardly knew? As his parents struggled to say their good-byes, I started to edge out of the room, not sure I should be there, but they called me back. He made it through that night. Before I left, he asked me, like a demented good host, if I wanted some oxygen. At home, I canceled plans to go away and I waited for the dreaded phone call; I scared my dog by bursting into tears at intervals. A day later, in the hallway of the hospital, his boyfriend told me cheerily that John was lucid now, really fine, much better. All John's friends hated this boyfriend, who was flaky, unintelligent, and unfaithful, so I thought he was fooling himself. But when I walked into the room, John said slowly, "Hi, honey. What's happening?"

He was back. As the others arrived, he became his fussy, bossy self. He wanted a certain crocheted throw brought from the apartment to brighten the place; he wanted a favorite pudding brought from the British tearoom; he wanted Ron to hang one of his paintings up in the room, right over there. Last year when he was here, he'd had vials of flowers taped to the needle-disposal unit. You could do something with these rooms if you knew how.

It was a moment of great beauty. Who knew there was going to be this reversal? You can have good luck as well as bad, I thought.

Within a month, he was settled back in his own apartment, and his return was an especially jubilant occasion. He was grateful to all of us, and when I came back from an extra trip to buy his favorite Jell-O, he looked over at me, as I was finally about to go home, and said he loved me. This was as thrilling and hard-won to me as if he had been a lover, and yet (I have to explain this) it did not feel like a substitute for having a lover, or a poignant echo of something once known. It felt as if I was in a different landscape altogether, with its own heights.

He was fragile and very skinny that winter. Just before I'd met him, he had been put on a cocktail of new drugs—he liked to brag that his doctor gave him Crixivan, "the Rolls-Royce" of protease inhibitors—but no one really thought they could help someone as advanced in infection as he was. That spring, he called me with the sudden miraculous news that his viral load was down. A viral load of over 50,000 classifies a person as having AIDS; John's had once been as high as 600,000 and was now down to a mere 15,000. At the very least, it meant that he had more time. I was so wildly happy and manic when I got off the phone that I ran out to buy a Little Richard album so I could keep dancing to the stereo. That night, for his birthday dinner, a group of us took him to a favorite corny Spanish restaurant, where he polished off a three-pound lobster (was this the man I'd had to scold into downing his Ensure only months before?). Hs friends got blitzed on sangria, and Ron, usually the most reserved of us, recited dirty limericks, Carolyn cracked her usual bad puns, and we were all very jolly.

THAT SUMMER, WHEN an adult student asked me what I did for fun, what my hobbies were, I almost said, Being a Buddy. Then I realized this would sound leaden and sanctimonious, or just plain weird. But it did provide me with exactly what is meant by diversion, in that my attentions were directed away from small everyday aggravations. Minor troubles tended to seem minor (and I was a really poor audience for other people's social gripes). I had kept a trace of that perspective that comes after a great emergency.

All during these months, I was also testing out an interest in Buddhism, taking courses and reading. I visited as many different kinds of meditation centers as I could, and New York, a city rich in variations, has a lot of them: Zen, Chan, Shin, Tibetan, Vipassana. Meditation itself often made me impatient. And at one point, I came to think that being a Buddy might be my own version of a practice, as Buddhists use that word, that it might serve me in that way.

I couldn't know what I would need. At the end of that summer, my older brother, whom I had not seen in seven years, lay in a coma after a heart attack. He had lived alone and had no intimates; I was his only kin, and all decisions lay with me. Since childhood, he had been solitary and withdrawn, uncompromising and absolute in his opinions, and not like other people. He died within a few months, the last of my immediate family. When I flew out to California for the funeral, John left a message on my phone machine, with his own jaunty sympathy ("Chin up") and offers to help ("Whatever you want, you got it"). I was so harrowed by my brother's death, I remember thinking I had been "only playing" when I'd been in anguish in John's hospital room. In my worst moments, no ideas of any kind, no "larger views," consoled me; I was solaced only by marks of tenderness (like John's message), and not always by that.

For a good part of the next year, my friendship with John was especially bright and companionable. He gave me advice on wardrobe (that beat-up, tacky leather coat had to go) and on redoing my loft (I didn't). We'd share our lunches, shop at street sales ("Never buy just one towel—you need two to match"), and he'd hear my out on the complications of my revived dating life, muttering due warnings ("Grain of salt, Joanie"). Once, when I was potting plants for him, he had me change into a pair of his old shorts so I didn't get dirty, a small domestic intimacy.

He had various passing ailments, but he kept out of the hospital. In the spring, he was upset because he'd tested positive for hepatitis C, an illness I knew little about and was sure was treatable. What was one more infection? A week or two later, when he was home seeing his family in Canada, his mother called to tell me he "was not doing well" and would be with them "indefinitely." His liver was very enlarged; she thought this was "it." How could that be? I cried and then I called Ron, and we decided that his family always got much too alarmed. They were overprepared for bad news. We all talked to John on the phone and he seemed cogent and very much himself.

But he was saying he knew he didn't have a lot of time. I was too cheerful and upbeat when I spoke to him (we had never been falsely blithe) before I understood that matters truly were grave. He invited friends to visit him—there was a nice little B&B down the road from his parents, he said—and I bought my plane ticket. Ron and another friend arrived in Canada first. When they got there, Ron told me later, John was sitting on his parents' lawn, lighting up one of his Camel lights. "I've decided," he said, "not to give up smoking."

He died the next day, before I could get there. Hadn't I known it would come to this? I had and I hadn't. I spent that night and the next drinking with his friends. I was the only one who hadn't known him before he was sick, which amazed them to think of. I belonged to him and I didn't. We were all tickled to hear that he'd asked that one of Ruth Draper's elegantly comic monologues from the 1950s be played at his funeral. Had you seen us across the room, you would have thought we were a group highly amused by one another, yukking it up.

My house is still full of items that were his: the paint-by-numbers *Last Supper* that hangs in the bathroom, an old silver perfume atomizer from Paris, handsome ikebana shears from Japan, bowls and pots he wanted left to me because "Joan likes to cook." There is an irony somewhere in the way all the artfully orchestrated sense pleasures I was fed up with when I first sought to be a Buddy figured so prominently in my ties to John. One of the better dinners I made for him and his friends involved a tomato and orange salad from a Provençal cookbook left from that unsatisfying trip.

A close friend of mine, who had listened intently to my long, highly detailed accounts of everything about John, was shocked when she heard I was planning to sign up to be a Buddy to someone else. I would do this again? From my monthly meetings, I knew plenty of people who did. Why would I stop? How would I do without it? I was bound up with this altered version of myself.

So who had I been before? Not a mean person, certainly. But someone more strained by the work of looking out for her own interests, more petulant and more confused about what the hell she was supposed to do for herself. More worried, it later seemed, about very little. I was more relaxed now, more at my ease; of all things to come from being around suffering. I knew what was what—what counted—a little more clearly.

I am still a Buddy. Sometimes I can hardly remember the days before I knew John. My life as an author, once so full of bad news that I thought of giving writing up altogether (I knew this was like saying I was going to go eat worms), made a step-by-step upward turn, and three books have been published in the years since.

Not that everything's been so exceedingly perfect, but my luck is better. For now. I can't know what I'll need or what's around the next curve. Being around sick people is a big reminder of impermanence, a favorite word of Buddhists. From all the time spent hanging around hospitals, everything I've seen thus far indicates that in time of extremity: you need human love and you need something that is independent of love.

Every year on my birthday, I get a card from Carolyn. She always picks ones with a message like "Go do something illegal, immoral, and fattening on your birthday" or "Forget about aging like fine wine, just drink the wine." The cards stay on my refrigerator for months, spotted with butter and soy sauce. I like these suggestions that I am irrepress-

ible and light of heart, not to mention roguish. In truth, I am more buoy-
ant, less fearful and less touchy than I used to be, less at the mercy of
circumstance. I wouldn't have done it on purpose (I only took the high
road because the low road was closed to me). I wouldn't have guessed
any of it might qualify as a cheering activity, but I would have been quite
wrong.

A Measure of Grace

CLAIRE DAVIS

On the first approach, Scout balks, a sputtering stop at the cross rail, his knees touching the wooden X. I make him stand, facing the fence. It is the pony club grounds in Deary, Idaho, a landscape of rolling fields and solemn hills crowned in conifers. The day is hot, mid-nineties, with a dry heat that founders the grass in dust and leavens saplings. I'm at the end of a three-day riding clinic and half-surprised to find myself still upright in the saddle. It's the last set of jumps for the day: an oxer, one stride, and then a triple. My horse, Scout, is a Connemara-Arab cross—just barely fifteen hands, and, at four years old, still considered a baby. He's a stylish little animal, a deep dappled gray with personality, which is to say a good horse but with a dollop of attitude. I hold him at the rail, pop him with the small riding crop, once, twice. His head swings up, and I feel him tensing beneath the saddle. I turn him away, and we circle the field, cantering down the brittle fescue and packed clay. There's the musk of pine duff and pitch in the air, and from beneath the saddle brews the sweet-sour smell of sweat. I wonder how much of his lather is from the day's heat and how much is nerves? He's as new to this business of jumping as I am—a short four months—but one thing I've learned in this time is that he always jumps higher when nervous. Overjumps. The helmet feels like a clamp on my brow, and as I look over my shoulder at the course, the doubt comes on, as it has so often. I am fifty years old. And jumping horses. I can almost hear my mother: Pretty damn old to be starting this nonsense, don't you think?

I push aside what I cannot afford to examine at the moment. We swing around and canter to the jump. As we near the fence, I feel my stomach shriveling like an insect in its casement. Be brave. I focus on the horizon, that point of light over the fence, beyond the rim of the arena. Don't look down. But I can feel Scout sucking back, his gait slowing. I turn my heels into his side, give a quick punch in the ribs with my boot heel.

It's shocking how stridently he responds. His hindquarters bunch and release, and then the ground is leaping from beneath us. What the others talk of afterward is how the compact form of him rises up and up, and I hear the gasps of bystanders, the lone voice—"Oh my God"— somewhere off to the right as Scout executes an utterly square jump. I am catapulted, riding the slipstream of air at his side. Strangely enough, I have the presence of mind to look at him. I'm an arm's length from his head. I see his eye. No. It's more than that—I can see how I hold his interest throughout the long drop, his eye following, that orb black and wide, pondering me even as I ponder it.

I discover the fall from grace is not quick. There's time enough to think, Son of a bitch, to think, I can't believe . . . and, Where's the rail? Don't hit the rail. But when I do hit, it's dirt. I land on my right hip, my left knee driving into the clay so that the leg ratchets back on its socket. I feel my arm being tugged on, and I see the reins still gripped in my hand, along with a sizable hank of silver mane. Scout's tethered by my grip, swinging wide around me, his eye rimmed white with fear; he snorts and pulls harder, the bit sawing like a hasp in his tender mouth. I remember to let go, and he trots to a cautious distance.

Friends on horseback and spectators on foot converge from the wood line. "Are you okay? they ask. Can you move?"

There's a patina of dust settling on my breeches, my arms. I can taste the dirt, bitter and clotting on my tongue. I lie still, wondering if I can breathe—and then I do. In the distance, a woodpecker drills a drumroll. The tops of the pines sway. I feel my body, the flesh and bone and gristle resonant with pain. I cannot quite own up to this, though. Instead, I assure everyone, myself foremost, that I'm just fine. I'm always fine. I've taken tumbles before. More than pained, I'm embarrassed to be so plain-facedly clumsy. Most of those riding with me are in their teens or early twenties. They want to comfort, but, still head-shy around age and pain, they hang back. Some nearer my age—in their late thirties, early forties—take matters in hand and brush off my backside with a brusque familiarity. So I'm putting off their hands, their concerns even as I roll onto my right hip, because somehow I know, in a way outside of reason, that my left hip will not tolerate a whole lot more. I pitch up onto my right knee.

"See?" I say, and, as hands help me up, "I can stand."

I attempt to walk off the pain, to circumvent the curious mistrust I have suddenly developed in my own good bones, but find I cannot step forward, nor backward, nor to the left. I crab-step right.

"See? I can walk," I say. After which, I insist on getting mounted again. Friends lead Scout up to the same grassy bank we'd jumped earlier in the day and hold him as I crab-step over. I ease onto his back. The pain's no worse for sitting astride. I walk him in a wide circle.

"Want to try a jump?" someone calls out.

I nod. "Why not?" I say, and set him into a cautious trot. I lift into half-seat and it actually feels better. I perk up. I circle the small area at a slow, steady trot, past spectators returning to lawn chairs, and past the ranks of horses and riders waiting their turns, thumbs up and faces smiling. I hear a few relieved laughs. It's going to be all right after all, I think as I aim him at the gymnastics—a series of three jumps, one stride apart.

It's when he lifts over the first cross rail that I feel it—the cattle prod—that long rod of charged steel boring up the length of my spine, and then, when his feet hit the ground, how that rod fuses my eyes shut in a burst of white light, my left side spasming in the galvanic air. We are between jumps, and to stop now would invite catastrophe—the distance too close to pull up at this speed, my legs unable to bear me to a stop. In the moment between strides, I imagine Scout unbalanced by my teetering body—his collapse into the next jump, the rails splitting, standards buckling inward—but his next stride drives the pain up my spine once again, and I yell, settle deep into my right leg, grab mane, and just manage to hang on as the small horse safely carries me over the next two.

IN THE HOSPITAL, in the luxury of hindsight, I become wise. That is, after the long drive home, having shrugged off all offers of help—"Nah, it's my left leg, and my rig's an automatic"—and having driven the truck and trailer the seventy-odd miles home, with my good friend Margo following to make sure I made it all right. In hindsight, I see what went wrong—what little wisdom I've gained coming most often this way, as in, say, after the decision to take that job, or after the marriage has collapsed. Or as in this case, after the boot's been applied to the horse's side—I see now that the moment at the fence might have required a bit more tact. Had I been less determined to boot him forward, or had I given him freer rein, or had I circled the field one more time. My mother resurrects in me, and with her the superstitions that ruled her days: I'd been tempting fate. And I think of the evening before, over dinner, when, while joking with my fellow horsewomen about the usual riding mishaps, I'd said, "I don't dare get hurt. I didn't do my dishes at home."

But in all honesty, the plainest truth is that I'm not really built for this sort of thing. Five foot three. Barely enough calf to wrap around the horse's belly. Add to that the encroaching rigidity in what feels like selectively chosen joints—toes, ankles.

As a young woman working with horses, what I lacked in confirmation, I made up for with athleticism and flexibility. I straddled my mares bareback, rode roughhouse through the fields. It was natural back then, my body still adept at adaptation, and yielding to the demands put upon it—a brave measure of grace I took for granted.

Not these days. Now, I compensate with what I have—discipline, a determined belief in hard work, and a limber will.

When I arrived at the hospital parking lot, even the ability to crab-step had disappeared. I stood lock-legged, hanging on to the back gate of my pickup truck, waving to passing vehicles, until an ambulance driver, having just made a delivery, found me and wheeled me into emergency, where I now sat, picking at the backless gown, trying to figure out how to sneak in a shower. It had been three days of camping. Record heat. Riding horses. No showers. Washing out of a bucket at the end of each day.

I am belligerent and in the face of a bushwhacked nurse: "I want a shower."

"I can't let you do that."

"Listen, you know how your mama always told you about clean underwear? Well, that's the least of it. I've just spent three days in horse camp."

She gives me a tight smile, brings me a tiny basin with a postage stamp washcloth, a sliver of soap. An impossible task, given the scale of the job, but I lift the airy gown, dab under an arm, and quickly realize it's hopeless. When I look up, I see a doctor has entered.

She looks somber. "How did this happen?"

I shrug the gown back over my arm. "I was jumping my horse, who's clearly a better jumper than I am." It's a line I've used any number of times in the past hour. I wait for the requisite Christopher Reeves reference. She doesn't disappoint. She caps it with "It's people like you who keep us in business."

"I thought that was motorcyclists."

She's not amused.

"So, what did I do? Dislocate something? Tear a muscle?"

"You broke your hip."

It takes a moment. "You mean like a chip. Right?"

Her look suggests the level of my naïveté. "This is the sort of thing they do hip replacements for."

THE FIRST TIME I entertained the idea of jumping, it was a full two years earlier. I was at the Round Up Grounds, an indoor arena down on Tammany Creek road. I'd come to meet an instructor recommended by a trainer at one of the local stables. "You want to ride English? Tom Ordway's the best."

I sat in the bleachers overlooking the spacious, dimly lit indoor arena. The place was a curious mix of east and west: Center floor were the crisp white jumps, but against the far wall, a row of steer chutes and rodeo banners still decorated the walls. What little light there was filtered in from the large open doors. Pigeons flapped about in the rafters as a sparrow hawk coursed after them. The instructor was coaching two women on horses over a gymnastic.

I watched the full hour, intrigued, though I wasn't about to entertain the idea of jumping. At that point in time, given the turn my life had taken, riding was risk enough without adding that kind of foolishness.

I was still reeling from the discovery of my husband's betrayals, the news just a few months cold. It was my second marriage; we'd been married for ten years, and I'd believed our marriage was a good one. We shared a love of literature; we were both writers and taught creative writing at a small four-year college. We had a large community of friends; we lived in a good town, in a landscape that fed our art. It was, I believed, the life we'd both wanted and worked so hard to achieve. We rarely fought, and I took that as a sign of happiness, particularly following on the heels of my stormy first marriage. As much by our vows, I believed us bound by these passions, this history of work, friendship, and love.

And it all came undone in a matter of moments, a sunny afternoon's stroll across campus—when he told me about the affairs. He'd been caught by the woman's husband. The next few days brought with them new admissions, and each name was a new blow.

That the women involved had been friends made friends dangerous. I became reclusive. If I went out, the smile on my face felt a sham. I'd run into the women in the grocery store, at the gas station, at a coffee shop, my first reaction always being that pleasant flush of recognition, and a smile, and then the realization would hit again. I became withdrawn, refusing to go out. Other friends called, offered sympathy. They told me of their suspicions—"But I didn't really believe he'd do it," or "How could I tell you? I didn't want to hurt you." I stopped taking phone calls. After fierce weeks of anger and recrimination, Dennis and I agreed to try and work it out, to save the marriage, but I was having a difficult time cobbling together a relationship without trust. And trust was proving elusive. For what was left me? If everything I'd believed about our life together was illusion, then what did I have to rely on, if not my own eyes and heart?

And so I gravitated to what had saved me long ago, as a young woman in a troubled first marriage—horses. It was a handhold in slippery times, a means of regaining some measure of happiness, and, I believed, my best shot at recovering myself.

At the end of the lesson, I stepped forward. Asked about instruction.

Tom looked at me, and his eyes went weary. I could almost read it in his face—another middle-aged wanna-be rider—all want and no git-up. He was tall, about my age, with a shaggy head of dark hair. You ever ride before?"

"I used to have horses. Years ago. Tennessee walkers."

He winced.

"But I'm thinking of learning dressage. Do you teach dressage?"

He looked down at his feet a long moment. "Yes, I can teach dressage."

The two women strode past, leading their horses. I caught a whiff of hay and horsy sweat. The women were laughing, unstrapping helmets, stripping leather gloves from hands. They moved with such confidence, and I tried to imagine walking through the world that way again.

"You interested in jumping?"

I laughed. I couldn't believe he was asking me this. Couldn't he see that I was almost fifty? It was half jest and half in earnest when I said, "You gotta be kidding. Why would anyone in her right mind do that?"

He shook his head, said, "Because it's fun," then turned on his heel and walked away.

I MAKE SOME calls from the emergency room. First one is to Margo. When she's not riding, she works in intensive care at the hospital.

"Oh God," she says. "Say I didn't tell a woman with a broken hip to jump her horse." She recommends a surgeon.

I call my sister in Wisconsin.

"I knew it. I just knew you shouldn't be jumping horses. Face it. We're not at the age when we should be doing this sort of thing. I'll be right out. I'll grab a plane."

"Don't be silly. By the time you get here, surgery will be long over. It would cost you an arm and a leg, no pun intended."

"Then call me when you get out of surgery."

"It'll be three in the morning."

"I don't care. Well then, call me first thing in the morning. First thing."

I've barely hung up when the surgeon enters. He's a tall man with a step that's all business. His hair is silvered at the sides. I'm reassured. I'm always leery when faced with experts the age of my son. He's holding a set of X rays. "On a horse?"

I shake my head. "It was coming off did it."

"Trail ride?"

"Jumping."

He looks at me, says nothing for a long beat. Then: "Ever hear of Christopher Reeves?"

I squelch the smart-aleck in me; after all, he'll be at me with a knife in a couple of hours. Instead, I repeat what the intern said.

He pulls up a stool. "Nothing's as good as your own bones," he says. "We'll put a couple of pins in here." He points to the X ray.

I try to make sense of the picture, the bright rods of light in the bifurcated dark. He's pointing out the ball and socket, tracing the delicate bridge between femur and ball. Bones. My bones. I should feel more attachment to what it is he holds—that most intimate text—but it looks off scale, smaller than life, and dim in the fluorescent radiance.

He lifts it back down. "Of course, there's always the chance it won't work. Or there could be some residual bone death. But it looks good now. The bones didn't separate, and if the blood flow was good . . . And as young as you are—"

I laugh. "Bet you wouldn't say that if I was pregnant instead."

There's a moment of silence. A look comes over his face, and I want to write it off as confusion, but it's something more distasteful.

"You know—" I say, as if it needs explaining, "being called young? I don't hear that so often anymore."

He shrugs. "Well, you are."

I'm feeling relieved. Flattered.

"For this particular population. Most hip jobs are for the elderly."

The elderly. I'm trying to hide my pricked ego. It seems I've just entered a whole new particular population, and in doing so, I discover relativity hurts—I no longer fall on the upside of youth, but, rather, on the downside of age. I turn silent.

He gets up to leave but then stops in the doorway. "Why do you do it? Jump?"

I expect he wants something from me. Something revelatory, or profound. Something worth risking bones for. "Because it's fun," I finally say, and the answer comes off as a poor accounting even to me.

He shakes his head and leaves the room.

It's nearly ten o'clock at night. They will operate in an hour and a half. The last call I make is to my best friend, Kim, who lives thirty miles away in the small town of Moscow, Idaho. When she offers to drive down, I tell her not to bother. I ask if she will come the next day and make sure the boarding kennel can keep my dog an extra few days. I don't tell her how frightened I am. I don't mention the worries that are boring their way to the surface: How am I going to do my classes in three weeks when school starts up? How will I do recovery—living alone? The expense. And then there's the scarier stuff: I've ruined my health. The bone will die. I will die. I turn each thought over like a stone in hand and pitch it onto a growing cairn. Five hours later, when I wake groggy from surgery, Kim's waiting in the hospital room for me.

AS A YOUNG woman, I believed that in middle age things would become clearer, more . . . straightforward. As if the sheer bulk of the preceding years would provide the momentum to coast with grace right up to the end. Instead, I see risk everywhere, and middle age is clearly not the free ride I'd believed it would be.

Perhaps it is not merely my misconception, but an offspring of that sense of entitlement we seem, as a nation, to have developed—the one that seduced the dot-com generation into believing they'd actually earned their millions. Or, just as likely, it's a simple reduction of the economics—"You get what you pay for"; bank a pint of blood now, get a transfusion later.

Or perhaps I believed the wisdom gained from experience would steer me clear of missteps I so rashly took as a young woman. Or that I would have developed the stamina necessary to stay on task, whether it was marriage or career, and see it to its fruitful end. Or that aging was a metamorphic process, and in surviving youth, like a moth coming out of its larval stage, I would somehow transcend that most significant aspect of the human condition—the flaw, the inclination to sin and failure.

But most likely, I believed in this period of grace because I'd witnessed the generosity of my parents' declining years. My mother claimed it was the struggle that made them better: raising my brother, Dale, during the Great Depression, my father working odd jobs, taking a partnership in a two-pump gas station. Her miscarriages. The following thirty-five years, during which my father worked at Allis Chalmers on the enormous turbines that deafened him Wasn't it a natural, then—that quiet aging? Divine justice for the years of struggle? But others have been broken by as much. Or less. So what was it that determined the grace of aging? Hard work? Fate? Luck?

Dennis and I tried to keep the marriage going for a year, but by spring it was a shambles. It finally fell apart, as these things tend to, of its own weight. Dennis delivered an ultimatum. I saw a lawyer.

All during that year of struggle to reconcile, I'd been taking weekly riding lessons, and staying afterward to watch Margo and Peggy jump. I'd stand alongside Tom center arena, trying to learn it all, but faster.

The horses wheeled around me in a dizzying circle, then up and over the fence, and then around again, and up and over the fence, and there was Tom yelling, "Half-halt; don't let him fall on his forehand. Collect. You've got to bounce him up there. Do you see?" He'd turn to me and throw his hands up.

I watched Peggy circling her horse, a brilliant chestnut mare, before the jump. Peggy, a trim dark-haired woman, was nearer my age, only a few years younger, and shared some of my middle-aged fears . . . though we preferred to call it sensibility. Watching her take the jumps gave me heart, made me believe it was still possible.

I'd also had Margo coaching me between lessons on trail rides. It was on one of those rides when I brought up the possibility of my jumping. She was leading us down a beaten trail at Hells Gate State Park, a quarter mile of bluffs overlooking the Snake River. She rode her tall, rangy saddlebred Snick—a young horse, but with a steady eye that gave Scout the good example. Margo. A fit thirty, with long blond hair wrung into a braid down her back, still heady with youthful infallibility. She knew better than most how difficult a time I had keeping balanced, or getting my leg stretched down and around the young horse. She also knew how athletic Scout was. She quirked an eyebrow at the idea, mulling it over. She leaned back in the saddle, propped a hand on her horse's rump. "Give it a try," she said. "Start small. If you don't like it, quit."

Why not?

Why *now*?

Why start jumping at a time when risk should seem the least reasonable course, following hard on two years of chaos and the dissolution of my marriage, when everything was up for grabs.

Perhaps because everything was up for grabs. The world I knew and the place I'd made in it had vanished. My mother had recently passed away, my father had been diagnosed with terminal cancer, I'd just sold my first novel, and I was getting a divorce—all within six months of my having turned fifty.

I determined what remained, and what of that was precious. Family: my grown son, my brother and sister back in Wisconsin, nephews, nieces, cousins. A handful of friends. Writing. Teaching. My animals. Art. Music. This place. This landscape.

But other aspects of my life, I had changed dramatically. I purged with gusto, and it was surprisingly easy. Because much of the infidelity had, it turned out, taken place in our own home, bed linens were the first to go. A pillow out the car window at sixty miles per hour. Furniture that had too many memories. Dishware we'd collected. Photos. Clothes. Routines. Habits. I planned to make a new story of my life, and having, this past year, watched Margo and Peggy lofting over cross rails, verticals, and oxers, I determined to join them.

Tom took the news with a note of caution: Green horse, green rider. Worst-possible combination. He started us over a series of cavaletti exercises. We trotted rails, cantered rails, working on rhythm, straight lines, bending lines, and approaches. We stumbled over them, first because Scout was unused to them and then because he was bored. Weeks and then months went by. And so, even though I'd asked for it, waited for it, when it happened, it was still a surprise, watching Tom set up the first cross rail in the middle of yet another endless lesson on flat work. Margo and Peggy stood on the side, grooming their horses. I circled the arena at a nervous trot. He laid a series of ground poles ahead of the jump to set the pacing.

"All right," Tom said. "Trot him over the cavaletti and then the cross rail. No big deal."

Scout was already eyeballing the X and the standards. I moved him up into a trot, headed toward the cavaletti. I could feel him slowing, his hindquarters squirreling to one side and then the other. By the time we reached the X, we were at a walk.

"That's all right," Tom said. "Just walk him over it."

Scout turned his head to a side and eyed the standards. I pressed my heel into his side, clucked, and he stepped over the jump, scooting out the other side.

Next time over, he approached at a cautious trot. He gave a little hop. Margo and Peggy cheered from the sidelines. Scout perked up his ears, always the ham. I could hardly believe how easy this business of jumping was. Tom was back at the cross rail, fussing with the standards. He raised the rails a notch, then two.

"All right. Bring him around again."

Scout was into it now. We took it, easy. We went over it this way, and that way, back and forth, a little skip and hop. Tom changed it to a vertical.

At the approach, Scout slowed, came to a stop at this new complication. I let him look it over, turned him around, and brought him back. Scout trotted the cavaletti. One. Two. Three. Half seat. And then the small horse lifted, springing up beneath me, sailing over the jump, his tail and rump cracking up in the air at the end of it. He trotted away on the other side, tail cocked, head up: Look at me.

Off to the side, Margo was hooting. "That little boy likes to jump."

Well, yes. And no.

A DAY LATER, after surgery, I'm sent home from the hospital, having proven I can navigate on crutches without falling, fainting, or throwing up—all three of which feel close at any given time. The pain's kept at bay with the usual good drugs. For my first forty-eight hours, Kim leaves her family to their own devices while she rolls up scatter rugs, rearranges furniture, fills the fridge, does laundry, generally makes sure I'm able to take care of myself. After she leaves, the first qualms of being left alone are replaced by the grind of drugged sleep and waking frustration. Another friend, Jolene, nurse and hospice worker, stops in with a bag of goodies. Tools for the elderly, the infirm, but I've been humbled enough these last few days to accept them with gratitude, genuinely thankful for these acts of kindness, for her company.

A few days later, I'm in the truck, crutches stacked against the passenger seat, and I'm driving about town. Everything takes three times as long to do. Getting in and out of the full-size pickup is a chore in itself. Grocery stores are tough—toughest is fighting off the well-meaning clerks who try to escort me to the electric carts that the extremely elderly or morbidly obese tool down the aisles. I refuse to go there, insist on pushing a grocery cart, one crutch under the armpit, the other in the cart, along with the groceries. Clerks chase me with anxious eyes. It must look to others, outside of my moving slowly or gimping down the aisle of canned vegetables, that I'm a relatively able-bodied middle-aged woman. There's no cast, no gaping wounds, no outward sign of actual injury. People stare at me as if I'm a fraud when parking in handicapped zones, until I pull the crutches out and trundle away.

By the third week, I'm teaching on crutches.

A MONTH BEFORE the fall, I had schooled Scout cross-country for the first time. And Scout had been good. Mostly. By the second day, he had settled in and down. We'd been jumping well—the whiskey barrels knee-deep in grass, the small drop-off, the ditch. It was getting on in the afternoon, and we were coming to the end of the lesson. The visiting instructor moved us from one jump to another, walked the course ahead of us. I was mounted and feeling pretty confident about the day. Until I saw the last jump.

She pointed up a long slope. "You'll want to take this one at a canter. Get a good running start."

My spine went fluid and my buttocks clenched. I tried to relax.

Horses are reflections of their riders—lean and they lean, tip too far forward and they'll fall on the forehand in an out-of-balance run to catch up. Lean back and they settle on their haunches.

If I even lower my eyes before a jump, Scout feels that shift, the tilt of the head like a diminishing of spirit, and he slows, or comes to a stop. It takes that little—a moment of doubt, an instant, a blink, a hiccup in time. I have to remind myself that he's still a baby, a mere four years old, and at that age he's still learning balance himself, let alone having to negotiate the shifting weight that girdles his back. Add a jump, and imagine the complexity of his task. I looked up the long slope, trees branching high over the path, and the loggerhead at the top of it.

The wind was shifting in the trees, and the sun broke through the canopy in a splattering of light and shadow. The slope ahead stretched long and longer. I could turn him around. Now. I cued him with a kiss, and he jumped into the canter.

I PULL INTO Margo's driveway. Her car is gone and the house is dark. That's all right; I've come to see Scout. He's pastured with her horses while I heal. I think of her kindness. For someone who had given up on people, I have found myself delivered into their hands—this growing circle of friends—some old, some new, bringing food, offering help, teasing me out of my bad humor. It is curious how my entry into the world of horses has reimmersed me into the world of people. I slip the crutches out of the truck, lower myself carefully to the ground. I fit one and then the other of the wooden staffs under my arms. Push off. There's a stitching pain down the side of my leg, though there's no cut—just the two-inch scar farther up the thigh. I slam the door behind me, swing my way down the dirt path between the barn and fence, ease through the metal gate and into the dry lot.

The pasture grass is patchy, browsed close among long tufts of grass where the horses have spread their droppings. They are on the far side, and Scout's a bright gray among the more somber pair of bays. His tail flashes white as it flicks at the flies hovering about his flank. I watch him graze, and my gaze goes soft, drifts beyond this moment. I think about the many ways my life has changed, has caught me off balance. I shift my weight, feel the quiet ache in my leg, but I do not dwell on that. Instead, I think about bones knitting in my body, binding blood and marrow, building something new. I think about my life alone, and how it has pushed me out into the world in ways I might not have imagined otherwise. I think about risk, and accommodation, and, yes, even failure.

I call to Scout, and the young horse swings his head up out of the grass and answers. A high, lighthearted whinny that I've come to love. He comes at a run across the pounded earth and stops at the fence where I stand. He lowers his head, and I scratch beneath his forelock. I ease through the gate.

It's a clumsy maneuver, what with crutches and the gate's come-along, and for a moment I question whether I should be doing this. I get angry with myself, curse my hip, my age, and start my usual catalog of faults: what I might have done differently. If only I were younger. If only I were taller. If only I could trust him.

Scout raises his head. I think of the fall—the way his gaze found me, tracked my descent through the air. I recall how afterward, in ignorance, I'd mounted him again, and he carried me, broken but safe, over the last two jumps. Even as badly frightened as he was. It was a lot to ask.

And then I think of all that I am asking this young horse to do. Help me past the hurt of a marriage and friends fallen aside. To bring me to that place where I can believe once again. I drop my hand to my side. His eye is soft and dark. And deeply forgiving. It comes to me as quietly as his breath—there is no blame. Not in the man I loved, nor the women who were once friends. Not in my own inadequacies, nor the young horse's. It's not an issue of age, or trust. It comes to me this simply: We are meant to fall, as surely as we are meant to rise. Grace is not the property of youth or talent. We find that necessary measure where we need it most: in our own good humor, in the love of family, or in the kind act of a friend. In the four good legs of a young horse.

I turn my thoughts to that earlier time, before the fall, on the cross-country course, when I was so frightened, and, yet, how inexplicably right it felt to kiss the air and set him up the steep path. I think of the small horse, the way his sides drove beneath my calves, his breath blowing with each stride, and my arms following the plunging of his head as we galloped the long slope, funneled between the wood lines, up the narrow strip of green toward the dark mass of logs and bank. My gaze steady on the tree line above. And then how together, for one amazing moment, we broke free of the ground, soaring over the jump like a fierce exhalation into the wide eye of sky.

And I see that the difficulty is not achieving grace. The difficulty about grace is recognizing it for what it is. I set the crutch behind me, prop it against the fence, and sling my arm over his back, lean into his shoulder. On the road, traffic stills. Even the dogs have stopped barking.

It is warm for early fall, the sky cloudless overhead. In just a matter of days, it will be September 11, and the world will once again reaffirm how thin is the fabric of trust. In the time following, in the face of despair, when I feel my legs taken out from under me yet again, and I question whether any of us will ever find our footing, I will make my way back to this moment, and I will stand with my face pressed against this small horse's withers, in the good smell of sun on skin, and the tiny drone of flies, his flesh flickering in response, rippling down the length of my arms like heat lightning.

PART III

I HAVE A CRUSH
ON TED GEISEL

To nourish children and raise them against odds is in any time, any place, more valuable than to fix bolts in cars or design nuclear weapons.
— MARILYN FRENCH

•

[She] that has no children brings them up well.
— GERMAINE GREER

•

Most children threaten at times to run away from home. This is the only thing that keeps some parents going.
— PHYLLIS DILLER

•

The deep, personal material of the latter half of your life is your children. You can write about your parents when they're gone, but your children are still going to be here, and you're going to want them to come and visit you in the nursing home.
— ALICE MUNRO

•

Our grandchildren accept us for ourselves, without rebuke or
effort to change us, as no one in our entire lives has ever done,
not our parents, siblings, spouses, friends—and hardly ever
our own grown children.

— RUTH GOODE

Warning: Do Not Insert Your Head into the Towel Loop

LOLLY WINSTON

I *used to wear a bikini,* I want to tell the handsome, Gen-X anesthesiologist who just saw my bare forty-year-old rear, which has widened and drooped in recent years as though it has a slow leak. *I was twenty pounds lighter, I had a waistline, and I was* fertile.

Clearly, this is beside the point; here I am again at the hospital clinic for an egg-retrieval surgery for my second in vitro fertilization. My husband and I have already gone though three intrauterine inseminations (a date with my doctor, a vial of my husband's sperm, and a turkey baster–type medical device), and a string of other tests and procedures. I've had dye shot into my tubes to make sure they're open (I yelped "*Shit!*" in front of strangers), a hysteroscopy (some kind of hot-poker scope), and removal of ovarian cysts from too many fertility drugs (thank you, Valium). My husband had learned to give me up to four shots of hormones a day, which eventually made me want to hit him over the head with an iron skillet.

Now the young anesthesiologist says, "You just need to *relax.*"

Everyone wants you to relax when you're trying to get pregnant.

But how can I relax when the nurse just betrayed me? As she led me and my IV pole shuffling into the surgery room, she backed me up to the table and—*WHOOP!*—untied my gown. The fabric fell forward, revealing my backside to the anesthesiologist and his entourage: the embryologist, his assistant, and two other mystery strangers. It was odd how the group pretended I wasn't there, standing in a semicircle and chatting as though at a cocktail party.

I lie down and the nurse ties my arms and legs to the table. Why do they do this *before* giving you drugs? Meanwhile, Enya coos on a CD player. I liked Enya before doing in vitro, but they always play her music at the clinic—in the surgery room, waiting room, recovery room. While I used to picture Ireland's rolling green hills when I heard Enya, now I see needles.

"Hey, my—" I try to tell the anesthesiologist that the tube he just ran behind my head is looped behind my ear and yanking off my earring back. I can't lift my tethered hand to fix it.

"Count backward," he says, shushing me. The earring back pops off and I hear it clink across the floor. Then the ceiling melts.

THE IRONY, OF course, is that we spend all those college and early career years trying *not* to get pregnant. It was alarming to learn at thirty-seven that I couldn't conceive. I had waited until then so that I could go to grad school, get a decent job, find Mr. Wonderful, marry Mr. Wonderful, and buy a house with Mr. Wonderful. Meanwhile, gray hair sprouted on my head. No problem. There were highlights and weaves for that.

Unlike my mother, who'd gotten pregnant at nineteen and had to drop out of college to get married and have babies and clean house, I had choices. It never occurred to me that at some point I'd no longer be able to choose to have children. In my mind, children were always a given that I looked forward to. Two boys, preferably. The sweet smell of Johnson's baby shampoo, the *clack-clack* of little overalls tumbling in the dryer. Not baby lust so much as the desire to have a family. To set extra places at the Thanksgiving table when my kids brought home friends from college. To watch a son or daughter walk down the aisle at their graduation or wedding. Yes, and I know—all the hard stuff, too. The sleepless baby years, the potentially nightmarish teen years. Once,

I saw a cluster of tiny wheelchairs at the hospital and a pain shot straight to my heart. Having children means knowing that something could happen to them.

I wish I'd known more about infertility when I was younger. While there were plenty of waiting room pamphlets about monthly breast checks, annual Pap smears, and mammograms starting at forty, my OB-GYNs didn't talk much about age and infertility. I don't blame them. It's a personal topic. You might offend a patient by pointing out her diminishing chances.

The truth is, I've always been good at putting things off. I didn't get my driver's license until I was twenty-three and I didn't make a left turn until I was twenty-five. I was engaged to a nice lawyer back in my twenties, but I chickened out and canceled the wedding. News stories often report that women are having children later in life so they can focus on their careers. Yet none of my English-major jobs—proofreader, copywriter, public-relations manager—was worth giving up the chance to have a family.

After announcing to my OB that my husband and I were ready to "start trying," I stocked up on prenatal vitamins and drugstore ovulation sticks. They confirmed that I was ovulating like clockwork on the twelfth day of every cycle—as regular as the automated sprinkler system in our yard. My FSH (a hormone indicator of how viable your eggs are) was low. A good thing. Except—as my dad once quipped after seeing a movie he found dull—nothing kept happening. Meanwhile, friends were full of folksy advice: drink Robitussin before sex; schedule an "ovulation vacation" to Maui; lie on my yoga mat and rub soy milk in my third eye; JUST RELAX!

After a year of clockwork sticks and clockwork sex, my husband and I visited the OB. (I later learned that if you're over thirty-five, you should see your OB if you don't conceive after six months.)

"Are you ready to consider IVF?" she asked us.

IVF? Where was the bunny slope? "What about Clomid?" I asked. I had heard of this pill, which is supposed to rev up your system. There wasn't time for that, she insisted, because I was thirty-eight. My fertility would now decrease rapidly with age, limiting the odds for even IVF to work. She referred us to an infertility clinic, saying that she didn't work with patients my age. Sheesh. A year before, all I needed was folic acid, and now I was a lost cause? It was hard for me to share the doctor's sense of urgency simply because I'd celebrated another birthday. How could "old age" be a medical diagnosis when I wasn't even forty? Was it presumptuous and arrogant to think I was still young? Had I been duped by all that expensive hair color?

The doctor at the private clinic ran blood tests and examined my ovaries via ultrasound. He had a thick accent, which I found difficult to understand. He seemed to be relieved that there were no visible olives.

"Who can get pregnant with olives on their ovaries?" I joked, trying to remain calm.

"*Polyps,*" my husband said, growing impatient.

I hadn't expected polyps any more than olives, frankly. I hadn't known there were so many variables, that so many things could potentially go wrong. Except that, technically, nothing *was* going wrong. There were no polyps, and my fallopian tubes were clear, and my husband's sperm was fine, and all of my tests looked great, and we were normal as can be, except we couldn't conceive.

"Egg quality issues," the doctor finally concluded. "Eeets your age." He added that we did need to do IVF immediately.

I had hoped for some sort of fixable diagnosis from this specialist. Maybe a blocked tube or a weak cervix. Instead, we got the same news: *You're too old*. But wasn't forty the new thirty? Weren't women having babies in their forties all the time? Statistically, no, the doctor said. And many of the women had resorted to infertility treatments and donor eggs. It was misleading, because of the number of high-profile forty-something pregnancies in the news.

The words *egg quality* rang in my ears. I hated the doctor's *über*-modern glass desk and his stainless-steel trash can. The Bauhaus sleekness of his office. The high-tech surety of his statistics. I know it's irrational to choose a doctor based on his furniture, but I refused to go back to that clinic with the stupid armless chairs in the waiting room.

"Form follows function?" I steamed in the car. "I ask you, what function is there in a chair without arms?" I burst into tears.

"Don't shoot the messenger," my husband said.

"But I WANT to! I WANT TO SHOOT THE MESSENGER AND HIS ASSININE CHAIRS!"

We switched to a woman doctor at the Stanford Hospital clinic, someone a friend had recommended. Our new doc suggested we try the less invasive IUI before resorting to in vitro. We won the lottery on the first try: I got pregnant. According to an old joke, there's no such thing as being "sort of pregnant," but when you're doing infertility treatments, it seems there is. If your first blood test shows that you're pregnant, you have a second blood test two weeks later. If that test is positive, you have an ultrasound two weeks following, then another ultrasound at eight weeks. I made it through each of these hoops; my husband and I got to see our peanut's heartbeat twice. We graduated from the clinic and lined up a new OB. I bought toddler-size overalls with western fringe. They looked boyish, but I thought they'd be particularly cute on a girl. I pictured cowboy boots, two braids.

While I was pregnant, I found it nearly impossible to work. It was like drinking half a bottle of NyQuil and then sitting down at my desk. The hardest thing was giving up caffeine. In the mornings, my husband sipped his giant latte. I watched the foam collect on his upper lip, his eyes brighten, his day unwind in his head. Meanwhile, I was stuck with a murky cinnamon-apple brew called "Soothing Moments," which smelled like the potpourri at the car wash.

I felt guilty for being so preoccupied with this sacrifice. At parties, other pregnant women and new moms talked seriously about diapers. Disposable or environmentally friendly cloth? If disposable, what brand? I couldn't concentrate long enough to weigh the pros and cons. "Do you think I could have a little juice-size glass of Coke?" I asked. "A weak cup of Darjeeling?" The other women looked at me semisympathetically.

"I never missed coffee," one gal chirped. "I felt so *energized* by pregnancy."

I looked at the cheese platter, wanting to eat the entire thing. Or lie on the floor. Or throw up. The order didn't matter. When will the spaceship come and take me back to my planet? I wondered. Maybe I didn't *deserve* to have a baby. Lusting after Earl Grey!

Still, I liked being pregnant. I was finally off the infertility drugs. I took long walks through our neighborhood, gulping fresh air and talking to our teeny friend. "See, there's a park right by our house. We'll go on the swings there."

When I was almost through the first trimester, my husband and I went for our first visit with the new OB. I had an examination, followed by a discussion of whether we would do amnio. Finally, my husband and I followed the doctor into the ultrasound room.

"Let's look at the baby," she said as I lay on the table. These things were becoming old hat. "*Oh*," she said softly a minute later. "I'm so sorry."

For what?

"I'm so sorry," she said again, touching my arm. My husband cocked his head. "You've lost the baby."

"It's *there*," I insisted, not even worried. Those ultrasounds are so dang fuzzy, and the baby is so small. I honestly thought she just couldn't find it on the TV screen. "There's no heartbeat," the doctor said. My husband sat on the floor. "There are no limb buds."

On the way home, my husband and I weren't sure what to do. We cried and drove through a car wash. When we emerged through the spinning brushes into the bright sunshine, we drove through again.

I had a D&C, dunked my head into a vat of chardonnay, and lumbered back onto the infertility-treatment bus.

NOW, I AWAKE from the egg-retrieval procedure to the sound of my own voice calling out "I love you!" to the blurry image of my doctor down the hall. The "twilight" anesthesia makes me like a lush at a party, someone who thinks everyone is her new best friend. I do love my doctor, though. She's smart, frank, warm, open, and optimistic without fudging any of the details. She laughs easily and patiently answers all of our questions. She's a leader in her field and helps young cancer patients retrieve and save their eggs before undergoing damaging chemotherapy.

I particularly like that she'll tell you if something might hurt. Up until I met her, I hadn't been prepared for the pain of some of the tests and procedures because the doctors hadn't warned me. They kept saying that everything was going to be "like a Pap smear," which is sort of like saying that all crappy food tastes like chicken. "You might feel *pressure* or a *pinch*," meant a searing pain was around the corner. If you ask me, the medical community should nix the euphemisms and just say, "This might hurt."

At home after the surgery, I realize that the back to my diamond earring is gone. The stud hangs precariously from my earlobe. My hair is tousled, as though I've had sex on the beach.

In the shower, I compose a letter to the editor of the *Nonexistent Daily Register* on how the worst thing about medical treatments isn't the physical pain so much as the loss of dignity. Tying down your hands and legs and ripping out your earring. My hands shake with anger as I turn off the water. Remorse gives me pause. I should be calm and meditative. what embryo in its right mind would want to stay in this cranky campground?

I try to relax on the couch while waiting for the news on how many healthy embryos we have. Leaving your eggs and sperm at the lab is oddly like taking your car into the shop. You wait for a phone call to hear how things are going and whether more drastic, expensive measures need to be taken. With IVF, there are the options of assisted hatching or intracytoplasmic sperm injection—depending on the quality of the eggs and sperm. I feel inept, like one of those people who needs hired help for *everything*. When the nurse calls, she reports that this cycle is particularly promising; we have three grade-one embryos—the best quality possible. I feel a rush of excitement and pride. I want a bumper sticker: MY EMBRYOS ARE GRADE ONE AT THE STANFORD LAB!

Two days later, we return to the hospital for the transfer. I hold hands with my husband while lying in a semidark examining room as the doctor inserts the embroys (again with the Enya). Then I go home, put up my feet, and hope the embryos will implant—that they'll latch on and stay. At first, this is a promising, peaceful time. I stick the fuzzy ultrasound photo of our three little stars on the fridge and sing songs to them while rubbing my belly.

"I love you, embryos! Please grow some fingers and toes! I want to buy you clothes! My little embryos!"

My husband looks worried.

As the days between the transfer and the pregnancy test wear on, the cocktail of steroids and hormones erodes my sense of peaceful hopefulness. For me, the worst side effects are from progesterone, which gives you the same symptoms as pregnancy. It makes you tired, bloated, constipated, and nauseated. Then there are the PMS-like horrors—a sense of cataclysmic anxiety coupled with perpetually hurt feelings. I'm certain the world is going to end and I'm probably not even invited. When the baby elephant at the local zoo dies, it nearly kills me, too. I look at his picture in the paper—droopy eyes, big bristly ears—and wail.

I try to focus on my work, which, for now, is writing my first novel. I've decided to do two things before turning forty: try IVF—which has gone from a dreaded last resort to a final ray of hope—and complete my novel, which I've been whittling away at for four years. Even if the book sits in a drawer collecting dust, I want to finish it. Three days before my fortieth birthday, while still waiting to take the blood pregnancy test, I finish the last chapter. A friend's agent is anxious to read the manuscript. My husband, who loves any excuse to drive fast, races us to the airport FedEx office for the last delivery to New York. The FedEx clerk places my bundled manuscript on her scale, looks up, and pronounces, "Six pounds, two ounces."

I beam.

For my fortieth, we fly to New York. I celebrate with a champagne flute of ginger ale at the Waldorf-Astoria. I listen to every creak and tick in my body, and welcome a swirly stomach. "I feel sick!" I crow whenever I feel a wave come on. At the Metropolitan Museum of Art, I stand before Picasso's *Woman in White*, one of my favorite paintings. *"Please,"* I whisper to her.

We return home and I drive up to the clinic for the blood draw. I awake the next morning with a promising wave of nausea. Pregnancy, progesterone, or nerves? While I couldn't wait for this day to come, there's no way I can answer the phone when the clinic calls with the test results. My husband agrees that the nurse should call him at work; then he'll call me with the news.

Later that afternoon, my knees wobble and my hands shake when I see the caller ID for his office on the phone. "Hi," he says. His tone of voice tells me that we've had no luck.

From grade one to grade none.

I've already agreed to host Thanksgiving dinner for friends. I hoped I'd be celebrating with sparkling cider. I don't want to flake on our friends, so I start a shopping list: turkey, cranberries, FUCK! Deep breath.

After the holidays, my husband wants to take a break from the insanity of the treatments. But I'm caught up in the urgency of time passing, eggs aging, chances diminishing. I feel my already-small statistical pie slice closing in on me. Although I love our Stanford doctor, I make an appointment at a new clinic in San Francisco. I need a change of scenery. Whenever it's time to head up to the Stanford clinic, I quiver in the driveway like a dog that knows it's going to the vet. Besides, as with gambling, sometimes you just want to try another blackjack table.

The doctor at the new facility is as intelligent and compassionate as our Stanford doctor. He recommends we try one more IVF cycle with my eggs, then consider donor eggs. We agree. I'm surprised by how my husband and I have gradually become more open-minded about the different options for having a child. When I first started reading infertility books, I shuddered at the procedures outlined in later chapters, thinking, Thank *God*, I'll never have to resort to *that* crazy procedure. Egg retrieval, assisted hatching. As I reached those latter chapters in the books, each one was a little more complicated and difficult to read and comprehend—just like the more advanced aqua-and-silver SRA reading cards I'd had in grade school. That's the point to keep in mind when you can't imagine why people resort to the things they do. Usually, their actions are incremental. In our case, it all started out with a drugstore ovulation kit.

People often inquire about the cost of IVF—up to ten or twelve thousand dollars. When I picked up four thousand dollars' worth of drugs in a brown grocery bag at a pharmacy in Palo Alto, it did seem ridiculous and desperate. Yet it's no more expensive than adoption. And, as my friend Julie points out, we don't think twice about spending twenty or thirty thousand dollars on a car, which lasts maybe ten years.

After the San Francisco appointment, I schedule yet another consultation with a third leading Bay Area doctor. Despite the fact that our medical records are now as thick as the phone book (no writerly exaggeration here), he wants to run a slew of additional tests, including measuring my uterus and sending my husband's sperm to Idaho for analysis. What do they have in Idaho that we don't have in California, I wonder, except for maybe trout? All I can think of is this *New Yorker* cartoon in which a man is standing at his desk, on the telephone, looking over the pages of his day planner and saying, "How about never—is never good for you?"

While the two new doctors seem equally informed and competent, they vehemently disagree on the usage of a common infertility drug. It's as though my husband and I have gotten off at a wrong exit and we'll never find the freeway again. At a friend's recommendation, we visit a counselor who specializes in infertility and adoption. A kind woman in a sunny office with pretty antiques and comfy couches, she reminds me of my mom, who died before I got married. I want to go home with her and eat canned soup. Weighing the pros and cons, she helps us decide to take a break from IVF for at least three months. Yes, age is a factor, but three months isn't going to make or break our chances. We agree that we're too stressed, broke, and shaky to continue right now.

Soon after that, a Dear John rejection letter from the agent who requested my manuscript shows up in the mailbox. I've achieved both of my turning-forty goals, and they've both gone bust. The weight of failure makes it hard to get off the couch.

IN THE SPRING, my brother, a troubled alcoholic, whom my family hasn't heard from for ten years, drowns while trying to swim to shore from a party on a houseboat. After much searching, the police find a family phone number among his belongings and contact us. I have the odd, familiar feeling of losing someone whom I never really had. I'm mad at myself for not working harder to find him over the years. I'm mad at him for not contacting us. I'm mad at the people who let him swim to shore. I'm mad because I've already lost my father and mother, and now one of my three brothers, and I'm running low on family members, and can't seem to create a family of my own. I'm mad at the poor lady at the sandwich shop who serves me ham and cheese on stale wholewheat bread.

"This bread is STALE!" I bark at her, the plate shaking in my hands.

If I were her, I'd tell me to fuck off. Instead, she offers to make me another sandwich with new bread, give me my money back, or fix me a salad.

"Thank you," I mumble.

That weekend, I sit at our neighborhood swimming pool, overwhelmed by the number of children, the number of families. Kids splash and scream with joy. Sun slices through the trees. Charcoal smokes on the grill. The lifeguard's whistle shrieks. *Walk, don't run!* I think of my brother who died and wonder how painful drowning is. Isn't it sort of like going to sleep? Or is that hypothermia?

The next day, I have lunch with my friend Vicky at our local coffee shop. In the bathroom, there's one of those old-fashioned rotating cloth towel loop deals to dry your hands—the ones that always seem to be at the end of their tether, the clean towel all used up, wrinkled and spotted with dampness. Just a teeny triangle remains at the top. I pinch and tug at it. Nothing. I wipe my hands on my pants, reading the metal placard screwed to the towel dispenser. WARNING: DO NOT ATTEMPT TO INSERT YOUR HEAD INTO THE TOWEL LOOP. Well, why not? And who would? And what for? To kill yourself? Could you strangle yourself with a weird blue dirty towel contraption? Or might you be trying to dry your hair and just get tangled up and start choking? I can't stop laughing at this thought. Hysterical laughter. Then I can't stop crying. Hysterical crying. Is choking worse than drowning? Is drowning a kind of choking? I know someone's waiting outside the door to use the rest room. I also know that I need to try antidepressants. I've read enough articles. I've seen enough checklists in magazines.

In a book called *The Sell-Your-Novel Toolkit* I come upon a chapter called "Goodbye Rejection: Hello Redirection." A little corny, but this becomes my new mantra. Every morning, I climb the stairs to work. I trim, rewrite, research a new agent. Just chip away at it, I tell myself. An image of a sculptor takes shape in my mind, the *chink, chink, chink* of his chisel chipping away at a Rodin-like Thinker fellow. Meanwhile, I'm wistful for the groggy days of my pregnancy. At least I got to be in that most feminine of clubs for a while.

Finally, the rewrite of my book feels polished enough to send to a new agent. Less than a week after I send it to her, she calls to tell me that she loves it and wants to represent me. The pause in my voice makes her think I'm hesitating, have other offers. I'm simply overwhelmed by how good this news is—by the sheer *weight* of the news I've received this year: *Grade one. Not viable. Pregnant. No heartbeat. Found him. Bottom of the lake.* I'm afraid to be excited about this seemingly fabulous agent and her enthusiasm for my work. But she's for real. I sign a contract. That fall, she sells my novel in a two-book deal. I'm able to celebrate my forty-first birthday knowing my novel will be published.

My husband and I decide we don't yet have the spiritual, psychological, physical, or financial stamina for another cycle of IVF. Fortunately, our fear and loathing is mutual. I wonder if it's time for us to move on to adoption. People often ask why we didn't adopt in the first place. I try to explain that it's equally expensive, stressful, and potentially heartbreaking. I have friends for whom adoptions have fallen through, and one friend who adopted a baby, only to have the biological mother change her mind. In California, where we live, it's the biological mother's legal right to do this within six months of giving up her baby. Here's how one of my doctors, who has both an adopted child and a biological child, puts it: "For six months, you don't know if you're baby-sitting or if this is your child." By contrast, I know six women for whom IVF has worked. Six healthy kids. So my husband and I decide to hold off.

Instead, we adopt three kittens from the pound, Popoki, Piglet and Einstein. They sleep on our heads and ruin the furniture and make us laugh. I write songs for them: "Life's not too shitty, when you're a kitty!"

At parties, well-meaning friends with children dole out silver linings for not having kids. I'm lucky, they say, because I can sleep in late and go to new-release movies. *THAT'S WHAT NETFLIX IS FOR!* I want to holler, drinking my chardonnay a little too quickly.

"If it didn't happen, it wasn't meant to be," some people say. Or: "Everything happens for a reason." I've never understood these catchphrases. I don't believe that everything happens for a reason. The Holocaust, the events of September 11, a lump in a woman's breast, a flat tire. These things don't happen for a reason. Sometimes bum luck comes our way for *no* reason. Sometimes there are no silver linings.

Yet, I found one silver lining in doing infertility treatments. I could choose to stop them. I could quit going to the doctor and surrendering my dignity. This isn't true for my friends and family members who have cancer. Now when I get up in the morning, instead of going to the clinic, I can hike to the top of the hill behind my house and look out at the valley. I might have to run for cover when I'm surrounded by a mommy-and-me group at our local coffee shop now, but nobody's going to stick me with a needle. And I won't have to bare my ass to an impatient young doctor.

I visit my friend Shari, who's tried IVF, with no luck. After a year of negotiations and travel, she and her husband, Tim, have adopted an eighteen-month-old boy from Russia. She and her friends and gather in her living room drinking wine, laughing, and talking about books. Then Tim comes home with their new son, Michael. As soon as Tim sets Michael down, Michael shrieks "MAMA!" and flies into Shari's arms. Shari's face flushes with joy. When I get home, I want to e-mail her to ask if she'll meet me for lunch to share information about foreign adoption.

I always thought I'd write one book and have two kids. Now it seems I'll produce two books and own three cats. And maybe be a parent to one child. Someday. Somehow.

I Have a Crush on Ted Geisel

JULIA GLASS

For Paula Klein

M ine was a glib and easy youth. In the era when divorce became widely contagious, my parents stayed happily together. I lived in leafy historic towns and went to the best of schools, both public and private. I earned the best of grades. I read with thirst and passion. I sang, drew pictures, and acted in plays. In short, I flourished. From the time I was nine, my parents held on to the same house so that my girlhood bedroom was always there to go home to, my sentimental treasures allowed to rot gently away in the attic (Barbie's Dream House sits up there still, a turquoise cardboard suitcase, anachronistic but dignified). After college, I lived in Paris for a year. After that, I worked in an art museum. And then I moved to New York City to join my smart, creative, enterprising friends in a life that was intellectually, if not financially, privileged. At thirty, I married. (How old that seemed then; how young it seems now.)

Have you stopped reading yet? I wouldn't blame you.

Some people, it's true, lead lives that are charmed from beginning to end. I never believed I was one of the chosen; ironically, my bouts of trivial heartbreak (back then, they did not look trivial) sometimes loomed large enough to make me feel as if I were genuinely acquainted with grief. Indeed: as *if*.

In my mid-thirties, a trio of catastrophes struck—in part from within, in part from without. The first was divorce; I was the one to force the break, but not without cause and therefore not without despair. Before that year ended, I was diagnosed with cancer. Twelve days later, my only and beloved sibling—a charming and successful but emotionally elusive woman—killed herself.

A manic relay of rituals filled the next few months: seeking second opinions, packing up the remains of a life, going under the knife, executing final wishes, beginning radiation, writing eulogies, debating the pros and cons of chemotherapy, answering (or not answering) what came to feel, in my state of rock-bottom bereavement, like a fusillade of condolences. Friendships changed: Almost without exception, each one cracked or strengthened. My parents and I were a body from which an arm had been sundered, and we adjusted as best we could, there being no suitable prosthesis. Half of what we wanted, we could no longer reach for.

I liken the rhythm of that time to a square dance: being flung almost haplessly from chore to chore, a do-si-do with life, then death, then life again, spinning and ducking and skipping busily, if not at all gaily, about. One experience after another had the same loopy, hucksterish veneer as a guy in phony western togs standing on a bale of straw and hollering into a mike. Take the gismo dangling from my armpit after surgery, a plastic see-through grenade in which I was to collect and measure the seepings from what I had wrongly assumed would be the lesser of my two "excisions." The call from my sister's long-ago, faraway boyfriend, who, embarrassed but desperate, wanted to know if I could please find (and destroy) those naked camping snapshots he knew she would have saved. The making of my personal body mold for radiation therapy, a minor farce involving Hefty garbage bags and plaster of Paris. My daily disrobings for said therapy, during which the nurse would exhort me to keep my gown closed when we both knew full well that, any minute now, a brigade of interns might whip aside the curtain to use my breasts as a learning tool. The arrival of my sister's ashes from Florida, shipped by priority mail. The obscene Italian gesture my boyfriend, Dennis, made at the container of ashes (cremains!) after I placed it, mournfully, tenderly, in the window containing our one nice view.

The interleafing of these two ordeals—real death and the threat of death—was, shockingly but also comfortingly, sometimes funnier than I could ever have imagined.

Gradually, after many difficult decisions, the waters settled some-what. You cannot live your life at terror pitch forever. You achieve what the cancer pundits call "a new normal." (If there were suicide pundits, they'd use that term, too.) The hardest decision I made was to refuse chemotherapy, which I did only after involved research, arduous de-bates, and variegated medical opinions—not because chemotherapy made me skeptical or fearful but because it would almost certainly have left me, at my age, after the particular drugs I would have taken, infer-tile. And oh how I wanted a child—especially after losing my sister.

My cancer was caught early, and there was no evidence it had spread, so while my refusal of that precautionary poisoning was risky, it was not egregious. My doctors agreed that pregnancy itself posed little threat to my health, but they advised me to wait a couple of years. If my cancer was one of the nastiest ones, it would come back in that time. So I waited; or rather, we did, Dennis and I. And then we had that child: the son I had hoped for, because I didn't want a daughter to look at me, at my history, and grow up with that extra fear (especially if—and we did talk about this—I should have a recurrence and die). I was surprised to discover how many people, even friends, were openly critical of a deci-sion my own doctors did not condemn. The consensus seemed to be that my urge toward motherhood was rash, selfish, and possibly too late in the game—as if those who'd already had their children were guaran-teed longevity, as if their desire to have those children had been purely altruistic. I forgave them; the friends who stuck by me through those bleak years I will forgive anything short of betrayal. And honesty, when you ask for it, tends to come mingled with tactlessness.

The new-normal me was now eternally grateful (though to what or whom, this reluctant atheist could not be sure). I will never forget hold-ing that baby all night for his first hours of life, just staring at him, my Alec, with wonder and an acute fiery joy. Oh, you say, all new mothers do that. Yes, but rarely with the awareness of how close they were to quite another fate—and not just the fate of childlessness. How very, very far I had risen. The day that Alec turned eight weeks old was the day I turned forty: the most ecstatic birthday of my life. (What's the opposite of hitting bottom?)

At this lofty place, having struggled for some time as a not-too-successful short story writer, I felt brave enough—maybe also battered enough—to think about embarking on a novel. Four years went by, during which I wrote that novel in whatever time I could wedge between money work and mother work. I was healthy; my son and his father were healthy: Our lives were as ordinary as could be. My novel filled, almost autonomously, with births and deaths, family celebrations and losses, several kinds of heartbreak and survivals thereof.

I had never stopped missing my sister, but as I watched Alec grow, I missed her in a new and more upsetting way. Because she'd been five years younger, I could remember her childhood as fairly distinct from mine. What she'd been like as a baby and toddler came back to me as never before. She'd put an end to my onlyness, and I had resented her for it, but who in any family is immune to the fascinations of a baby? How unlike me this second baby was: That belief is still stitched into family lore—against my agreeable self, how stubborn and loud; against my cautious nature, how physically determined; against my bookish stillness, how mischievous and how terrifyingly intrepid.

As I read to Alec—who seemed, like me, agreeable and cautious—I remembered what I had enjoyed most about early sisterhood. Though my parents were perfectly literate, at a certain point I became the one who read to Carolyn at bedtime. I went to the library and chose the books myself. And here, now, to my own son, I was reading some of the very same books I had read to her. In fact, out of my parents' attic— the same attic that reverently holds my Barbie's Dream House—came my sister's own copies of *Make Way for Ducklings, Blueberries for Sal, Ferdinand, Horton Hears a Who,* and both *Cat in the Hat books.* In *The Cat in the Hat Comes Back,* Carolyn had taken a yellow marker and— as I, model child, would never have done—colored in all the white stripes in that famous hat.

Like every small child with a sense of humor, Alec was crazy for Dr. Seuss. We owned, in addition to the several Seusses from Carolyn's childhood and mine, Dennis's copy of *If I Ran the Zoo,* one of the author's more ambitious works, an epic parade of creatures so magnificently weird, they make the Cat and his cohorts look like H&R Block accountants.

It doesn't take much imagination to know that holding these books so many years later, turning their fragile pages, catching the scent of that toy-laden attic, was an experience so fraught with emotion—emotion careening in every direction, from anger to rapturous love to desperate sorrow—that it recast my loss of Carolyn in a different, slightly demonic way. All of a sudden, I was no longer content with what I had. I wanted, more than anything, a sibling for Alec, someone for *him* to grow up and read to.

It was hard, and not just biologically, but eventually I did have that second baby, that sibling—in December 2000, three months shy of my forty-fifth birthday. He was almost precisely five years younger than his brother, as my sister had been to me. Two weeks later, my agent sold my novel. "Good Lord," said a friend, "let's put you on the job of world peace."

Alec had already taught himself to read and, like the child I'd been, did so with thirst and passion. The week I knew I would go into the hospital for the birth, I bought the book that Alec had recently been begging for, and I made a recording of myself reading that book. It was *One Fish, Two Fish, Red Fish, Blue Fish*. This was a book I recalled reading to my sister, but our copy had vanished. I told Dennis to give it to Alec on the night I would be gone—and to play him my amateur books-on-tape version so that he could hear my voice and, just as he would have done if I'd been there, read along.

The next day, they came to visit me and tiny Oliver. Alec insisted on bringing his new book along. I have a picture of Alec, reading that book aloud to the brother—the lobsterish rubbery squint-faced doll held in the crook of my elbow—he'd met not five minutes before. (*Now* have you abandoned my story? Again, I wouldn't blame you.)

During the next four months, I made final revisions to my novel and nested with my two little boys. It was an average winter, neither too cold nor particularly mild. My only worry was a tiny pimple—or not-pimple, since it wouldn't go away—in my right armpit, along the scar where, seven years before, lymph nodes had been removed. My doctors dismissed it as an aftereffect of pregnancy. The surgeon who'd taken out my tumor told me it was an infected follicle. "Put bacitracin on it for six weeks," he said.

Six weeks later, there it still was, unchanged. When I insisted on having it removed, my surgeon sent me to a dermatologist. The dermatologist snorted (really) and said, "You want this off?" "Yes," I said. (Had I, finally, become a hypochondriac? Was I merely being humored?) As he went to town with his scalpel, the dermatologist sang along to his radio. He sang so abominably that I can still tell you what he sang: "Ain't Too Proud to Beg". Loudly and blithely, drowning out the Temptations, he serenaded my armpit. It took him only those few minutes, the time it takes to sing one desperate love song, to remove the granule of flesh that, as you can guess, turned out to be malignant. They agreed that it was a teensy, though not to be underestimated, recurrence of the cancer everyone thought had surely been vanquished.

I will skip the strange behavior of certain doctors (how, for example, my long-vigilant surgeon pulled a disappearing act). I will skip what it felt like to be swarmed by oncologists from different institutions, all fascinated by my peculiar case; likewise, what it felt like to hear the gratuitous opinions of doctors who believed, on the one hand, that my pregnancies had probably delayed this recurrence (and might protect me yet) or, on the other, that I'd brought this fate upon myself by daring to reproduce. I will skip the suspense of getting every scan known to modern medicine, watching the doctors pretend not to look for what they were sure would be a metastasis somewhere else, somewhere deeper and far more lethal than my armpit. Ditto the monthlong medical debate, like a leisurely game of badminton, as to whether or not I should have chemotherapy (now, at long last) and even as to why. "If you're going to get another recurrence, which would probably happen soon, the chemo wouldn't do you much good, so why go through it?" said one celebrated expert. (I've written about these particular trials elsewhere; I write about this time in my life again and again, because it was my crucible, because I don't want to forget a single detail, perhaps because I'm always hoping to glean from it further wisdom, as if that's my due. Again, as *if*.)

Come July, I decided, with the help of the only doctor in sight who seemed to have a sense of humor, that I should have that chemo. Over six months, she would give me large helpings of some pretty strong stuff. The first drug was cherry red, a Shirley Temple without the fizz; it came in a big shiny IV pouch, and when I watched it start its sinuous way into my left arm, I thought that my life had never felt so dramatically strange. They pour it into your veins slowly—sip by sip, like a rare vintage wine—over a couple of hours. To deaden the anxiety, they inject you with a soupçon of Valium, which enhances the sense of absurdity.

There I sat on my big green Barcalounger, along with all the other docile, dozing chemo patients in *their* Barcaloungers, all of us pale and still and chemically becalmed, like figures in a wax museum. "Hydrate, hydrate!" the nurses cajoled. Now eager to be the most obedient of patients, I drank glass after glass of water, which meant that I had to pee about every twenty minutes. Several times I would shuffle, along with my maraschino potion on its pole, to the bathroom down the hall, taking care not to tangle my summer dress with the loopings of the IV line. My urine was peony pink.

"Stay out of the sun and wear long sleeves," I was warned. If our winter had been mild, our summer was not, so when I had to go outside, I would cover my bald head with a Scarlett O'Hara picnic hat and, like a thief or a cockroach in search of an outlet, hasten along the shadowed sides of the very tallest buildings.

But all this, all this medical stuff, paled beside what I experienced at home with my precious (perhaps my very costly) second baby and my sweet bookish little boy, who was headed for kindergarten. First, I had to wean Oliver almost cold turkey in order to start the chemo. This ordeal in itself made me cry like there was no tomorrow, the same way I would also cry in the moments when I feared that there would be, one day too soon, *literally* no tomorrow, that I would leave my sons without a mother, leave their father to cope with so much all alone.

Because I was self-employed, and my employer could not afford to give me leave, I continued to work as well as I could. Sometimes I even worked at the hospital while I received my chemo. I did everything in slow motion. I could not bear to write fiction (who would want to invent more trouble than what I had right there at hand?), but I edited banking brochures, letting the monetary jargon lull me into an occasional, entirely welcome stupor while a baby-sitter took my children to the park (a sunny place, off limits to me for more than a minute or two).

People who haven't been through chemo focus with awe and fear on the loss of one's hair. Mine was long and blond—not lush, but not yet gray—so seeing it thatch my clothing and curl down the drain was hardly easy, but I came to enjoy creating arabesques of patterned silk on top of my head and later, when winter arrived, wearing a series of tasseled elfin velvet caps made for me by a seamstress friend (my favorite was neon orange). Loss of hair was the least of it. Loss of my enthusiasm and talent for the minutiae of mothering was the worst of it.

The sheer difficulty of tasks I had taken for granted—lifting and rocking Oliver, bathing him, merely carrying him on my chest to the store—was beyond depressing. It was a nuisance not to feel strong enough to carry two bags of groceries the four blocks from store to apartment; not to feel strong enough to carry my six-month-old son that far was torture. For weeks, I could not even put him to bed, because at that tender, difficult time of day, my lap was a cruel place for him to be. He would sob and push his face against my chest; my one functional breast, in sympathetic longing, would swell with milk. (Right before my first chemo treatment, I had to pump out milk in the hospital bathroom and flush it down the toilet.)

Alec no longer needed carrying. In September, I began walking him to kindergarten, then picking him up at the end of the day. I held his hand and heard about his new friends. He was old enough to hear about my sickness, if only in the broadest terms, and the bizarre effects of my medicine. (They didn't seem odd to him; he gave full credence to tooth fairies, Christmas elves, and movies about toys that had a social life, so why not a medicine that made you sad and tired and bald before it made you better?) If I was too weary to do something, he—unlike his brother—could understand. And I still had the everlasting pleasure of reading with him. Once again, having spent a hiatus with simpler books, we immersed ourselves in the world of Dr. Seuss. I found, to my muted delight, that his sensibility dovetailed now with my own perceptions of life. Miraculously, he restored the sense of humor I thought I had lost forever. Cancer had been inescapably funny the first time around, but the second time, when the fate of my children was involved, I could not crack an honest smile for months.

The loony clutter and carnival logic of these invented worlds—Whoville, Didd, Sala-ma-Sond—reflected life as I suddenly knew it. (Did Dr. Seuss ever realize that Whoville, with its careening stairways and higgledy-piggledy high-rise structures—like a pueblo on speed—bears an uncanny resemblance to the modern adult brain in all its hectic glory?) One evening as I cruised along the shimmering surface of his verse, I realized that Dr. Seuss's nomenclature might aptly be looted to describe my own symptoms: the Hoodwinks my naked eyebrows, the Yinks my most intimate sores, the Colliding-Collusions my slugs of bone pain, the Wily Walloo that numbness I had to shake off my hands every morning. The Grizzly-Ghastly would have to be a certain portion of my anatomy I'd never expected to see without hair, the Harp-Twanging Snarp a violent chill that sometimes passed through my teeth like a telepathic warning. For exhaustion as plush and dense as a fog, no word could fit better than Oobleck—and what is a Flummox if not a bout of the digestive gridlock one gladly accepts from the drugs that stave off vomiting?

I was hurled, like a boulder from a catapult, straight into menopause. (I had been waiting. This, after all, was the reason I'd refused the chemo seven years before.) No tenuous ifs, ands, or buts, no delicately petaled "peri" menopause (the topic du jour among my healthier peers). I woke up one night in early September to find my smooth head slick and dripping. My pillow was drenched right through and smelled like a chicken coop after a rainstorm. Rising to shed my sodden pajamas, I left footprints on the floor.

Hot flashes are the movie stars of menopause. Many distressing symptoms line up in the background, chorus girls all, but these personal volcanic eruptions, brazen as Bessie Smith, occur unpredictably—that is, wherever and whenever you dread them most. You break out in rivulets of sweat while being photographed. You drip on your baby as you hold him in your lap, trying to sing him to sleep. You drip onto a salad you are tossing. And then it begins to seem as if these outbreaks are triggered, full force, by any and all stimulants of stress—the rude cashier, the traffic jam, the whining child, the cranky spouse—or, conversely, by certain pleasures: a glass of wine, the rare turn on the dance floor, the rising curtain of the first play you've gone out to see in a year. (Are you dripping on the stranger to your left? Can he feel the heat you exude, like embers on the surface of your skin?) Sometimes you're sure that you will suffocate in your autoeffusion, that you must get free of everything around you: your clothing, your children, your home. If the ocean were nearby, you would run, stripping, and leap into the waves buck naked, as if you were on fire. But you are never by the ocean when it happens. No. You are in the subway, or a job interview, or you are helping your son with his homework, and it's all you can do not to issue a primal scream. And if you've had breast cancer, not even herbal remedies are considered safe. So you bear up. Packin' heat, I tell myself. Watch out, world, I'm packin' heat.

I confess to having become a menopausal gorilla three or four times in front of my children. I've apologized, assuring them it has nothing to do with them. But how do you explain hot flashes to a pair of small boys? Especially when you can barely explain these conflagrations to their father? All they can do is regard me with consternation; all I can do is hope that one day they will look back and shake their heads, that they can forgive me. (That huge walruslike creature with a great red maw and great white teeth, about halfway through *If I Ran the Circus*? The Spotted Atrocious? A hot flash incarnate.)

While I'm being frank, let me say that—except when I was yearning to be pregnant—I never minded having my periods. At times, they were inconvenient, or made me queasy, and I hated what they did to my skin, but they were like the declarations of a grandfather clock at the heart of a well-appointed home: now and then disruptive, but only in a fleeting way. For the most part, they reassured me that the household—the essential *me*—was running smoothly. When they ceased, I did not long for their return, but I also sensed that the household, without their calculated order, might begin slipping toward pandemonium.

The pandemonium I feared was not, at first, the pandemonium I got. In the midst of my chemotherapy, just after the hot flashes started, just after Alec started kindergarten, the planes flew into the towers. You could see them burn and collapse from the end of our block (though after the first one tumbled, after we brought Alec home from school, we huddled indoors, following Rudy's orders).

Neighborhood walls and windows filled up with posters of the missing. The bus shelters filled with candles and prayers. Our fire station, all its men but one now dead, closed to become a sidewalk cathedral. Emergency vehicles sped silently along our streets for days, even weeks, numerous as taxicabs. News crews colonized our sidewalks, taping down fat electrical cords, pitching tents, putting up tables piled high with doughnuts. Alec's school took in children displaced from classrooms beside Ground Zero.

I felt so much worse, yet I knew I also had to feel better. I had to feel better because I and my family were whole. I had to be an example of calm, of life going boldly on, if just for Alec. This became especially true when, the following week, Alec broke his leg in school. With no taxis in sight, I carried him on a rush-hour subway to his doctor's office. I don't know where I found the strength. No one offered us a seat, and I remember bursting into a florid hot flash, wishing desperately for a towel. Utterly exhausted as I was, I wanted a towel more than I wanted a seat. So much for my top-of-the-world good fortune of six months before; oh, and so much for *world peace.*

Still, my family was whole. Still, my book would be coming out the following spring. My doctor predicted that I would have just enough hair back by then to uncover my head without making a militant medical statement. After the chemo ended, in January, I realized that I had to adjust to a *new* new-normal (suddenly, didn't we all?). Now, for the first time, I felt like the proverbial older mother. About then, a stranger who saw me with Oliver said, "Awww, are you the grandma?" (A tip: This social gambit is worse than asking a large-bellied stranger when she's due. Don't ever utter these words.)

Almost as if I were watching one of those science filmstrips where tulips bloom and then wilt in a matter of minutes, I felt my joints grow stiffer, my middle grow softer. (In the three years since then, I've seen my height dwindle by an inch.) I began to wonder if I had asked for too much; if, on a larger scale, members of my immediate generation—those of us born in the ten years preceding the Beatles' American debut—have expected more than we should from life. I've noticed that the newest mothers around me seem younger and younger, as if they've watched us closely and learned from our hubris. Face it: Mother Nature has good reason for letting that grandfather clock wind down when it does.

After the chemo, my hair grew out, still blond, but curly for a change. Eventually, it straightened out again, and though I'm now nearing fifty, it still has yet to gray. I consider it a lovely souvenir of my glib, easy youth, but I've decided to keep it short. Last week, out of the blue, Alec asked me, "Mom, when will your hair get long again?" Startled, I asked if he could remember it long; he said that he could, and he liked it better that way. "But you remember how I lost it all when I had to take that medicine, right?" I asked. "No," he said, looking puzzled. He remembers the more youthful, longhaired mother, it turns out, but not the half year of hell she went through. Or he remembers, defiantly, the mother she'd have been without the chemo. Is that reassuring? What else that I assume he knows does he, in fact, *not* know, *not* notice?

As I feel myself age—and complain about it, and fear that my boys won't have a mother for as long as they deserve—I realize how lucky I am to be aging at all. Thirteen years ago, a dogged, fussy radiologist did not like the look of a perfectly routine baseline mammogram. I may be alive because of that man, a man I met only once. I curse the hot flashes I still have—but how can I not bless them as well? I might never have lived to find out just how crazy they can make me.

An older friend of mine told me, years ago, that you know you're entering menopause when you find yourself getting crushes not on the young hotties in the movies you pay a baby-sitting ransom to go out and watch with your husband—not on Matt Damon, Colin Farrell, or even Johnny Depp (who's aging, too)—but on Christopher Plummer in *The Sound of Music* and Dick Van Dyke in *Chitty Chitty Bang Bang*, the movies you plug into the VCR for the kids so that you can get something done around the house. Except that you sit down, oddly transfixed, and watch them, too . . . and become engulfed in their courtly, fusty charm. And you look at Julie Andrews or the bubbly blonde who never found stardom and find yourself thinking, Excuse me, missy, but you are way too young for him.

Well, my midlife crush is on Ted Geisel—Dr. Seuss to you, or perhaps Theo. LeSieg (author of *Would You Rather Be a Bullfrog?* and *Ten Apples Up on Top*). There are distinct disadvantages to this crush, I admit. That he's dead isn't really the issue, since he would be unattainable anyway. (If he were alive, he'd be one hundred years old right now—and if he *were* attainable, that would be fine by me. On certain days—like yesterday, which I spent sledding with my boys—I feel about a hundred, too.) No, the biggest problem is that there isn't much fodder for my crush. As I idle in grocery store checkout lines, I will never be able to snatch up a magazine revealing, say, the inside of Dr. Seuss's/Theo.'s/ Ted's stylish home, the bedroom suite decked alluringly with the hides of animals (of Sneetches? of Drum-Tummied Snumms?), where lately he cavorted with the likes of J Lo and Paris Hilton. Unlike Ben Affleck and P. Diddy, Ted Geisel, while he was alive and young, seemed to be something of a geezer (courtly and fusty). He loved only Helen, and after her tragic death, he loved only Audrey. If more went on behind closed doors, the tabloids will never reveal it.

About his work, by contrast, there is all too much conjecture. Critics prone to jealous spite speculate that Dr. Seuss's never having children of his own surely reveals that he never liked children at all and so must have led an emotionally stunted life. And we all know by now about the political agenda in his books; children who giggle over his drawings may not realize that the source of their amusement is nuclear escalation, deforestation, or anti-Semitism. Yes, I know that the Whos are the people of occupied Japan. I have even read that Ted's oeuvre simmers with intimations of child neglect, if not child abuse. I believe, however, that he wrote primarily, far above all, for the pleasure of his readers, children and parents both. To read Dr. Seuss aloud feels to me, a lover of language, as I imagine it would feel to water-ski like a pro (which I will never do, because when it comes to the physical, I am a consummate sissy). I adore him for that playfulness alone.

Let me throw in a few narcissistic interpretations of my own: First, *The Cat in the Hat* is about being treated for cancer. You may try to convince me that the Cat is General Patton or General Mills, the Soviet Union or a premonition of Bill Gates (would IBM be the house or the mother?), but seriously, take a close look at the Cat's persona: Likable yet arrogant, irresistibly bossy, well-meaning yet oblivious, assured yet sometimes alarmingly clumsy, he is, no doubt about it, the medical establishment. Thing I and Thing 2 are surgery and radiation. The recently departed mother is your breezy impunity, your assumptions that the best is yet to come. The narrator and Sally are your ego, cowed at first, then accepting, then angry, then finally assertive. The fish is your pesky id. (Pessimists, note the ultimate return of the mother.)

Which makes *The Cat in the Hat Comes Back* a parable about recurrence and chemotherapy. That platoon of tiny cats from A to Z are the drugs themselves, playing havoc with your body, staining everything peony pink—and in one great final explosion (you hope) cleaning up the mess they made *and* your cancer, too. Except that from here on out, for Sally and her brother, life will never, never be the same. After all, can they assume they've seen the back of that Cat for good? How silly could they *be*? All they can do is follow that neatly shoveled zigzag path back to their house; who knows whether the table will be set with hot chocolate and cookies or lima beans and Spam?

I love Ted because, like me, he took a few decades to hit his professional stride, to find the one thing he was meant to do. I love him because he looks a little like a penguin but also, in his youth, a teensy bit like Montgomery Clift. But I am *smitten* with Ted because he gives a perfect cadence to life as it escalates in both its absurdity and its beauty, to the relentlessly goofy observations that run through our heads all day but that we generally keep to ourselves. If once upon a time the rhythms of my life felt like those of a square dance, now they feel a lot like the dear doctor's madcap poetry, with its ragtime patter and its precociously Dylanesque rhymes.

Recently, I spent most of an afternoon in yet another new doctor's office (most of it, as usual, in his waiting room). I had just changed cities, which meant changing oncologists, and so, yet again, I telescoped my complex, unruly medical tale into a giddy, self-deprecating rendition: my illnesses, my choices, my vices, my triumphs. The history gets a little longer every time I tell it, but the central drama remains the same. I never know until I'm through telling it whether the new doctor will reveal, openly or not, approval or disapproval, surprise or amusement. Doctors are not supposed to judge, but often they can't help it. (My favorite was the otherwise-charming female oncologist who, giving me a second opinion on my recurrence, said, "Well, if you had been *my* patient when you were diagnosed, I'd have told you not to have those babies! But hey, you wouldn't trade 'em for the world, now would you?")

This latest doctor was attentive and kind, and he offered an optimistic outlook for the future of women with cancers like mine. I went away happy and relieved. Yet that night I had trouble going to sleep—because once again the hardest, murkiest part of my past had been stirred up from the depths, like the mat of blackened leaves that festers at the bottom of even the clearest pond. I felt the familiar uncomfortable mixture of sorrow, regret, relief, and gratitude. Unlucky me; no, *lucky* me.

That night, putting three-year-old Oliver to bed, I had read his two favorite Seusses. The first was our now quite well-used copy of *One Fish, Two Fish, Red Fish, Blue Fish*. In my own bed, in the dark, I gave myself over to the rhythm of its piecemeal ditties, composing a rope of verse about the state of my aging body and my complex feelings (grandiose, humble, resentful) about being that mother mistaken for Grandma. I went to sleep spinning this nonsense and, in the morning, greeting myself in the mirror, took up where I had left off. . . .

My face is lined.
My teeth are gray.
My chin's become a lump of clay.
(Just like my memory, did you say?
Wait a minute. Did who say?)

My thermostat's busted.
My wrists have rusted.
I can't remember when last I lusted.
My eyesight is shifty.
My bones are shrinking.
Having kids so late, what was I thinking?

Young mom,
old mom;
wise mom,

silly mom;
early-to-rise mom,
over-the-hilly mom.

That one has an SUV,
this one has a tricky knee.
That one has a yoga mat,
this one wears a chemo hat.
That one can give you a piggyback ride,
this one remembers the Dave Clark Five.

Say, would you like a mom who's an ingenue?
An ingenue from Timbuktu?
Or how about a mom who's a blushing bride,
a blushing bride from Telluride?

We have a mom whose hair is blue,
whose lap is the size of a war canoe,
who wears trifocals and an orthopedic shoe,
Who cries, "In with the old and out with the new!"
She can't play Twister, but we like our mom—
even if she looks like an old grande dame.
She's not always calm and she's not always sunny
(she seems to worry a lot about money);
but when times are bad—even bad and a half—
she still knows how to make us laugh.

All right, all right, I'll stick to novels. Dr. Seuss would never be so heavy-handed. Almost invariably, his life lessons come in wrapping paper as hokey as a square dance, frenetic as a subway station at rush hour, weird as a wax museum. The second book I read to Oliver that night was *Oh, the Places You'll Go!* Now that one does flirt with the preachy. But I love its shamelessly Odyssean themes, its grandfatherly tone, and I love the way that the book itself reveals, in its slightly vague and shaky drawings, how Dr. Seuss followed his passions until, at the age of eighty-seven, he died in his sleep.

This is currently Oliver's favorite book, and he makes me linger on the same three pages, always asking the same questions. "Whyzee wearin' roller skates?" he asks of a certain blue elephant. "He goes past 'em? He goes past 'em?" he wonders anxiously when the elfin boy hero confronts the "things that scare you right out of your pants" on the road between hither and yon. And finally, insistently, always stalling our progress by slamming a small hand down on the page he says, "*Those* are the Hakken-Kraks?" Here, near the very end, is where the boy's arms get sore and his sneakers leak, where the weather is fowl and where enemies prowl. "Yes, those are the Hakken-Kraks," I answer, and I like to linger on that page too. Sometimes I get a little teary. How well I know those Hakken-Kraks, and how glad I am to be able to look at them in the safely two-dimensional, in their deceptively pink and lavender viciousness, from the distance I've traveled. I've rowed that way before, at least twice, and I may well row that way again. And when I do, I will pack an extra pair of sneakers for my sodden feet, Tiger Balm for my aching arms, and hope that my sons, one or both, will read to me from the books of my beloved Ted.

An Apartment of Her Own

KIM BARNES

The aging Victorian sits on the corner of a busy downtown back street and rises three stories from a cobbled foundation of stone, cement blocks, and concrete. I step onto the wraparound porch that lists toward the yard, think it might once have been called a veranda. Instead of wicker furniture, it is crowded with bicycles, a barbecue grill, empty beer bottles, an overflowing litter box—sure indication that a once-grand mansion has been hacked and parceled into housing for the college students who make up half our town's population.

I do my best to quell my dismay as I enter the foyer and check my directions: basement studio apartment, number 9. Although no one is near, I fear that I might be caught in my appraisal, wrinkling my nose at the smell of cat urine, testing the locks on the door, scraping at the peeling green paint with my thumbnail. I feel out of place in my black blazer, dress slacks, silver bracelets, aware that the gray in my hair is indication enough that I am an outsider and don't belong. Some of the tenants might even recognize me as a professor of English at the university they attend. They may see me making my way down the dark stairway, the rental agreement clutched in my hand, and wonder what turn my life has taken.

The stairwell itself is larger than most, and I remember what I've been told—that this building had once been a hospital. A sanitarium, I think. It's a setting that Hitchcock would have loved: a dank maze of mahogany hallways; creaking floorboards; brooding turrets capping each corner of the house. The stairs spill me out into a lower entryway that opens into the alley—a prime place, I note, to be accosted. The door of neighboring apartment number 8 is papered from top to bottom with Budweiser labels. The adjoining wall holds the bared guts of the building's electrical configuration. I know enough to recognize the wrapped wires as dated by at least half a century. I imagine power failures, overloads, sparks setting the tinder-dry paneling ablaze. I close my eyes, lean against the doorjamb of number 9, and take a deep breath. The rental agent will arrive any minute, and I want to compose myself, make her believe that I know what I'm doing, that I am a middle-aged woman who has weighed carefully the choice she is about to make.

OVER THE LAST several weeks, I've found myself attempting to convince any number of people that, after years of foreboding and contemplation, my husband and I have made the right decision: to allow our sixteen-year-old daughter to move out on her own. Grandparents, aunts and uncles, concerned friends, even my hairdresser—all have reacted with some measure of disapproval. A few are frankly appalled; others offer their concerns cloaked in careful questions. "Are you sure you're ready for this?" "Have you drawn up a contract?" "What are the stipulations?" "What if it doesn't work out?" "How will you stand the separation?" "Can't you wait even one more year?"

I smile bravely, shrug my shoulders, try my best to look self-assured. I'm both anxious and excited, I tell them evenly. It's a huge move, but the right one at the right time for the right reasons. If things don't work out, we'll fall back and regroup. I cite the closeness of friends who live near the apartment building, stories of others who have had to let go of their children early and had all parties survive. What I don't tell them is how, some nights, I lie sleepless, rigid with terror, sure this decision will plunge my family into chaos.

They shake their heads, say they could never do it, could never let go this way. That they admire my courage. They understand that it's an unusual situation and wonder, sometimes, how their own lives might have been different had they had the kind of parental trust, encouragement, and support that we are demonstrating.

I think that what my husband and I are demonstrating is more desperation than determination. That our choices are not so free as they seem. That we are relying on intuition more than logic. That we are less in control than we are simply hanging on to what we can, for as long as we can. That it is all I can do not to beg, *Please, please, don't go.*

Footsteps echo down the stairwell. A jingle of keys. The rental agent appears, winded by her race from one available unit to the next. Another few weeks and the town will empty of cars, quiet into a kind of tranquil hibernation, but these last few weeks of the semester are when leases are cleared and redistributed. It is the season of U-Hauls and Dumpsters overflowing with stained mattresses and busted milk crates. It is the agent's job to leave no space vacant for longer than the twenty-four hours it takes to steam the carpets, replace broken faucets, mend the window shades. She brushes the long brown hair from her eyes, apologizes for her dusty jeans and sweatshirt.

"Doing a little cleaning as I go," she says. She keys the lock, hesitates. "Your Jordan's mom, right?"

"Yes, I am."

"This is small, but Jordan really liked it."

"I know," I say. "It's what she can afford."

She smiles. "You're really brave to be doing this."

I nod, square my shoulders, step into the underground rooms that will hold my daughter's life.

MAYBE WE SHOULD have foreseen the inevitability of this moment. The stories we tell of Jordan's childhood read like a billboard pointing down the road toward early independence, or those Burma Shave signs marking the miles toward some sure destination: IF YOUR DAUGHTER / HADN'T OUGHTER / KNOW SHE WILL / COME HELL / OR HIGH WATER.

She was born the fall after I turned thirty. My husband and I had waited seven years before conceiving, for several reasons: The divorce from his first wife and the emotional toll it had taken on his young son had made him wary, and he wasn't sure he wanted any more children; I wasn't sure I wanted children at all, until I did; after so many years of fearing pregnancy, I found that conception was something that must be courted, rather than guarded against.

It seems a portent that Jordan came into the world adverse to expectation: Her position in utero was frank breech (I think of the term more as the name of some forthright and stubborn character in Sheridan's play *The Rivals,* right along with Lydia Languish and Sir Anthony Absolute). Nothing the obstetrician could do in the weeks before her birth could divert her from her course. She was "contrary," he pronounced, even as he worked his fingers around the outside of my abdomen, pushing and prodding her toward transversal. After several minutes of fruitless manipulation on his part and a series of hard contractions on mine, he gave up. It was, he told us, his first failure at turning a baby around.

By the time her brother was born and she was two, Jordan had become adept at articulating what she would *not* do: wear shoes, which all pinched; wash her hair, which frightened her; respond to any kind of bribe, which offended her mightily. If I, as a child raised in a strict and authoritarian household, had uttered the word *no,* I would have been spanked soundly and sent to my bed to sob my regrets. Determined to give Jordan room for expression but determined to maintain discipline as well, we chose our battles carefully: We let her wear open-toed sandals when shoes were necessary, even in the middle of winter; we discovered we could let her go days between shampoos without having someone call Child Protective Services; we never bribed her, but explained carefully our rational for requiring that she change some behavior. She would listen, consider for a while, and then either acquiesce or offer a counterargument that often convinced us we'd been erroneous in our evaluation.

At five, she began waking us up before dawn with the repeated pronouncement that she was bored. Although she was a pleasant and respectful student, her grade-school teachers called us with their concerns: Weren't we a little alarmed that Jordan had become obsessed with crucifixion iconology? Fixated on Picasso's Blue Period? Entranced by stories of the Holocaust? That she wanted to convert to Judaism so that she might absorb via osmosis the talent to play the violin?

Instead of greeting Jordan's divergent interests with alarm, we applauded her autodidactic nature. Simultaneously, it seemed, I felt my own intellectual fires rekindle. Following the intense rearing of two toddlers while teaching as an adjunct, I was grateful for the hours allowed by their going off to school. After years of writing whenever and wherever I could—at the kitchen counter, a nursing baby in one arm, a pen in the other; in the bathroom, the only space with a locking door—I'd squeezed a desk into the corner of our small bedroom and begun to write about my young life growing up in the logging camps of northern Idaho. On days I didn't teach, I wrote fiercely, from the moment our children caught the school bus until the second they arrived back home. I didn't care that my elbows rested atop stacks of drafts, student papers, and bills waiting to be paid. I was desperate for time more than space, and the eight-by-eleven page in front of me was all the room I needed.

When my first memoir met with critical success, we were able to add a few rooms onto our nine-hundred-square-foot house. With the help of friends, my poet husband built himself a small study. I designed an office space off the master bedroom, and it allowed me more privacy and solitude than I'd ever known. When my writing day was done, I felt sated enough to focus on dinner, help with homework, read my children a story before bed, prepare for the next day's classes.

Yet, even as my own life was beginning to hum along with reliable satisfaction, Jordan's increasingly was racked with angst. Was it at eight that she began crying each night at bedtime because she couldn't be in Paris? A year later, it was Kosovo she wanted to travel to, believing she, if no one else, could talk sense into Milosevic. If she were only older, she grieved, people would believe she was capable, would trust her insights and judgments.

So often, the very things that have made others in the family feel lighthearted and gay have brought her to sadness. She would often mourn the pleasures she loved, simply because of her mounting awareness that they would not last. When we took our annual trip to the Oregon coast, one of her favorite places because of the gray skies and misty air, she wept each day because each day was passing. Over and over again, I have told the story of when Jordan was ten and we had gone to the nearby river to fish and wade in the shallows. As was so often the case, Jordan separated herself from us, went off to find her own little corner of sand and willow, where she would solemnly study the current. Every now and then, as I cast a watchful eye her way, I'd catch a note of the ballad she hummed and wonder how such a young child could be so serious, be so aware of experience passing into nostalgia, as though she existed at that portal between the present and the past. I saw that she had her father's pocketknife and was carving a piece of driftwood. Later, I would find it on the car seat: a thin root of twisted cedar, worn smooth by water, that I turned and turned in my hands, reading the message etched along its length: *I JUST WANT TO BE FREE.*

"Be patient," I'd say. "You have your whole life," and she would reply, "But I feel like there's so little time."

She's mature for her age, people have always noted. Older than her years. What my husband and I have wanted is for her to slow down, not grow up so fast, not take the world onto her shoulders, especially when those shoulders still feel like the hollow bones of birds beneath my hands.

I WAS AT my writing desk when, in 1998, I received a call from the grade-school counselor. Jordan wasn't being challenged enough, she said, and her learning style wasn't being well served by the curriculum and overcrowded classrooms. The staff had exhausted their limited resources. I should consider home schooling.

"But I'm an English professor," I protested, ignoring the irony. "And I write. I don't have time to home-school Jordan. Besides, she won't let me teach her anything."

"I understand," the counselor said. "It wouldn't be easy"—and here the counselor paused—"but I'm afraid if we don't do something, we're going to lose her."

I felt my heart racket against my rib cage. "Okay," I said. "We'll start on Monday."

I was forty years old, and I was hit with the sudden conviction that I had started too late, that I was too old to be doing everything at once. Many of the young women I'd gone to school with were now seeing their youngest children off to college, preparing for a son's wedding, attending the birth of a granddaughter. My mother had married at sixteen, given birth to me at eighteen, my brother at twenty. By the time she was forty, I was dating my future husband and finishing my first college degree.

"I don't have time," I repeated to myself, and I knew I meant not just hours but years.

I thought of the counselor's words: *we're going to lose her.* I hadn't asked what she meant because I knew. I was fourteen when my parents lost me for the first time, eighteen when they believed they had lost me for good. "What goes around comes around," my mother would tell me, but I'm determined my daughter will not suffer the same disillusionment and disconnection that I did. What I felt as I sat in my study, the blank screen before me, was a remembered fear, a sense of hopelessness and rage. What I felt the year I ran away from home. What I know my mother must have felt as she watched me tear away from her.

UNLIKE MY DAUGHTER, raised in an environment of tolerance, I was the child of parents whose ties to the Pentecostal Church dictated separation from the world and punishment for all sin, which included going to movies, dancing, bowling, drinking, smoking, swimming with the opposite sex, and listening to the devil's rock'n'roll. This was in the 1960s and 1970s, and, while my classmates donned miniskirts, fishnet stockings, and blue eye shadow, I wore my hems two inches below the knee and was prohibited from wearing makeup at all. Because I, like Jordan, had a mind of my own and was intent upon making my own way, it was, perhaps, predictable that I would rebel, that, by the time I was in eighth grade, my straight-A average had fallen to F's. That I would lose myself in the very things my parents feared: alcohol, drugs, music— all avenues that allowed me my escape, carried me away from my father's unsparing strictures and harsh discipline. The spring I turned fourteen, I made my run for freedom, headed to California with a friend and her older lover, until my father found me and forced me back home. I remember the suffocation of his strength and restrictions, my fear of his reprisal should I run again.

What Jordan has is fewer boundaries than I did, more intellectual and social stimulation, and no threat of a Hell that is not of her own making. There is very little that she has to push against, to define herself in contrast to, and that in itself may be a worry. We've known from the beginning that this is a child who must be allowed to take risks. We've understood how much better it will be if we can control and direct those risks. Instead of having her run away *from,* we mean to direct her *toward.*

When she was eleven, we arranged for Jordan to realize one of her dreams—to travel to Europe, a place that, as a girl, I never imagined I might travel to and still have never been. Her company was a group of senior citizens, one of whom was the mother of a friend, a retired schoolteacher Jordan had met only briefly but who generously invited Jordan to be her traveling companion. For three weeks, they toured, visiting Vienna, Auschwitz, Budapest. Jordan turned twelve in a foreign land, in the company of strangers, without us. I'd lie in bed, trying to imagine my young daughter half a world away, alone in her dreams, the night sounds unfamiliar, even the hours of her day gone strange. I feared she'd be lost in the streets of Amsterdam and never found. I feared that if something were to happen, my own parents would never forgive me my bad judgment. That I would never forgive myself.

Every few days, she would call, sounding weary but happy. Yes, she missed us, but she couldn't say she was homesick. Only when a virus grounded her with fever and chills did her words take on the slightest lisp of longing. "I wish you were here to hold me," she said, and I thought my heart would break. The next day, her voice was stronger than ever. "I'm fine," she announced. "Just a cold. Nothing to worry about." She came back to us lugging a suitcase full of souvenirs she'd bought for her family (including Hungarian paprika and Czechoslovakian vodka), but missing the items she had found most burdensome: Her calling card she had dropped into a charity box; her extra traveler's checks had been doled out to "the homeless." She immediately began making lists of other desired destinations. Japan, Australia, Kenya. She wanted to be anywhere it seemed, but home.

Just as Jordan's world was expanding, mine was becoming spatially smaller. Not long after Jordan's return home, my husband and I accepted jobs at a university sixty miles north. We sold our just-remodeled house, bought a smaller one with no office space. My husband set about building another studio; I moved my desk into a corner of our bedroom, once again surrounded by the distraction of domestic life: bills needing to be paid, laundry needing to be folded, dishes needing to be washed, and a daughter who, without the daily schedule of school, seemed in need of everything: intellectual and creative stimulation; my opinions of her friends; and, perhaps most importantly, my company. She was at an age when children demand both separation and comfort, and sometimes what she needed from me more than anything was fifteen minutes in my arms. And how could I turn her away? I'd leave my story midsentence, go to the couch, where she could curl up next to me, needing me to do nothing more than simply listen. This is not a sacrifice, I thought, but even as I murmured my empathy and encouragement, my mind was scrambling to hold on to words and ideas. Even though I knew that my daughter and I were both in a time of transition and, that if I held on and was patient, I would once again find room to write, I felt fragmented, unable to exist wholly in my role as mother, writer, teacher, wife.

After several years of self-schooling (it was true that we couldn't teach her, but she proved adept at teaching herself), when Jordan was fourteen, she sat me down, held both my hands in hers. "Mom," she said, "I love you and Dad. I'm grateful for everything you've done for me. But I need to be out on my own. I need to know when you can let me go."

I sighed. We were never far from this. She was forever researching places that might take her in like some kind of orphan, let her work in exchange for room and board: the World Organization of Organic Farmers; bohemian boarding schools states away.

"I'm not sure I can tell you that I'll ever be ready to let you go," I told her. She slumped and tears filled her eyes. "But, if you continue to make

the kinds of responsible decisions you've been making and keep pursuing your education, we might consider it at sixteen."

She brightened, hugged me. "Two more years," she said. "I think I
can make it that long."

THE DOOR OF number 9 swings open into a square kitchen that is
roomier than I thought it would be. The far wall holds a window large
enough for egress in case of fire. The cupboards are a conglomeration of
tear-outs scavenged from remodeling sites: Some are green metal;
others are wood coated with thick white enamel. The range is brown,
the refrigerator gold. The right paint, I think, might pull it all together.

Down the hall is the bathroom with its metal shower stall and corners furred with mildew. We turn left into the sleeping/living area. The
Murphy bed creaks as the property manager lowers and raises the mattress (only *slightly* stained) to show it is in working order. Another large
window allows light from the alley. I check fire alarms, faucets, and
baseboard heaters, ask about utilities and noise. I try to imagine my
daughter lounging with friends, maybe cooking a meal, and all the bells
in my head are ringing: She'll be able to do anything, anytime she wants.

As a teenager whenever I escaped my parents surveillance I drank
Annie Green Springs, smoked marlbors, and dropped mescaline in the
eerie glow of black lights. What will keep Jordan from doing the same?

But she's made those decisions already, I argue with myself as I make
another sweep, scouting for leaks and faulty lighting. Longing to social-
ize, Jordan had tried a semester of junior high, then a year of high
school, and finally surfed her way into college at fifteen. She has a job
at the bookstore, a car, and an impressive savings account comprised of
nearly every dime she's earned. Many of her friends are old enough to
drink legally, and most of them do; she's assigned herself the role of full-
time designated driver and preacher of moderation. She has no curfew
because she's never needed one. She seldom makes bad decisions, because she fears nothing more than having the freedom she has earned
taken away from her—by her parents, or by the law. I wish I had been
so aware when I was her age, that I had understood how much of my
own life I might control.

I turn to the agent, nod my head. "I guess we'll take it," I say. "I guess this will be okay."

"You'll have to fill out the lease because she's a minor."

I take the pen, sign my name and the date, fold my copy into my purse.

She walks me to my car, says, "I bet she's going to be just fine."

"I know she will be," I say, feeling the tears stinging my eyes. "It's not her that I'm worried about."

When I leave the apartment, I call my husband at his office. "Did you do it?" he asks and I feel like we've embarked upon some crime, that the details must be kept vague, our meaning coded.

"Yeah," I say. "I did it."

"Are you okay?"

"I will be." I take a deep breath. "We will be, won't we?"

"I don't want her to do this," he says, and I hear his voice break. "She's just a baby."

I feel my resolve come back. "No," I say. "She's not a baby. She's sixteen and a half and more responsible than most eighteen-year-olds. It's not like she's moving to another state. Just a few miles down the road."

"I know, I know," he says.

But I have to convince him again, make myself believe. "She wants to live in town so it's easier to get to her classes and job. It's her dream, what she's been working toward for years. She's doing this for all the *right* reasons."

What I don't say is how much I wish my own move from home had been for all the right reasons. That, like some of our friends, I wonder how different my own life might have been if my interests and intellectual goals had been nurtured and encouraged. My independent nature was the very thing most suspect, my maverick spirit what needed to be controlled, if not broken.

Those few years between my running away and my eighteenth birthday, I rededicated myself to my faith and did my best to stay within the fold. I attended church services several times a week, joined the choir, led prayer group and Bible study. Yet, other than my heavenly reward and the approval of my father, which, according to the Scripture I read, should have been enough, I was never sure what it was I was working toward. Our church's doctrine taught female subservience. The idea of a woman having a life of her own, much less a room, was considered deviant. My future seemed already determined: to marry, to bear children, to keep a clean house, to be content with my station. The night of high school graduation, after a final falling-out with my father, I made a fateful decision: I packed my bags and left for good.

I stayed with friends those first few weeks of independence. My plans had been to attend college and become an English teacher, but now I upped my hours at the pharmacy where I worked as a clerk and began looking for an apartment. What I found was a furnished studio on the ground floor of an older home across the street from my high school. Ninety-five dollars a month, all utilities paid. The living room was large enough for a couch, chair, and television. The wide hallway that led from there to the kitchen held my bed and dresser. No shower, but a bathtub that extended into the space beneath the stairway leading to the upper apartment: I loved the intimacy of it, my legs resting in a cove of equatorial water.

That apartment's kitchen was open and sunny, with a refrigerator that I stocked with frozen dinners, cottage cheese, and a tub of margarine. The cupboards held cereal, boxed macaroni and cheese, and saltines. The only housewares I owned were the few items that had been kept in my hope chest—Tupperware canisters, Tupperware tumblers, Tupperware measuring cups (my mother had once been a party leader). I had one set of sheets and the blanket that had covered my bed at home. Everything else came to me via the generosity of my boss's empathetic wife and her friends, who scavenged their own cupboards and gave me boxes of mismatched treasures: a set of lead-crystal salt and pepper shakers; a frilly red apron; a terry-cloth potholder; a large plastic mixing bowl—all items I still possess and cherish.

It wasn't until I started to seriously contemplate my daughter's "independence chest," as we decided to name her growing stash of household goods, that I realized how little connection I'd had to my own mother in those first few years of living on my own. My father shunned me for my disobedience, and my mother found herself torn between the will of her husband and the needs of her child. Perhaps she believed that, having found the strength to stand up to my father, I would find my way without her; perhaps, having never lived alone, she had no sense of what she might do to help. I think how much we missed of each other, how that time of transition can never be regained. No extra set of flatware passing from one set of hands into another; no recipes copied and shared; no housewarming party to celebrate such a coming-of-age event. Nothing but silence between us.

What I remember of those first years of living my solitary life is the absolute loneliness I felt. The break with my father coincided with the loss of every community I'd once known: I had separated myself from my family and my church; my school friends had left for college. I remember lying awake late into the night, no one to call for comfort. And though I never doubted the decision I had made, I felt cast adrift, no words of wisdom to guide me. What might have been freedom felt, instead, like exile.

I worry that we are somehow dooming Jordan to repeat my miseries. I'm worried that the wound of her leaving will keep me aching throughout the night, unable to sleep, unable to keep the fear from weaving itself into a cinematic nightmare of imagined scenarios: Jordan, always trusting, opening her door to a rapist. In my mind's eye, I wrestle them through the rooms of the apartment. I find things for her to fight with: the knife in the kitchen, the hammer in her drawer. I think I will call her daily and remind her to turn off the stove burners. I will warn her against candles, incense, smoking, leaving leftovers in the refrigerator for longer than a few days. I'll tell her never to mix reds and whites in the washing machine, ammonia and bleach in the toilet bowl, hot grease and water in the skillet. Because I know what feeble attempts at control they are, I write down my lists, keep them hidden in my purse or penciled onto the back pages of books, in descending order of potential consequence: at the top, "Never open door to strangers." Near the bottom, "Store flour in airtight container to keep out weevils."

What I know is this: as a young woman suddenly on my own, I survived the incidental tragedies of ignorance. I ate freezer-burned chicken, raw hot dogs left on the counter overnight, bologna that shimmered with bacterial decomposition. I drank myself into near-comatose states, accidentally fired a loaded rifle into my cereal cupboard (it made its way through Cap'n Crunch, frosted flakes, and Trix but missed my two friends, who stood only inches away), and drove my aging Chevy Impala at one hundred miles an hour down a twisting two-lane Idaho highway so as not to miss the kickoff of my lover's college football game.

I can present these stories to Jordan as cautionary tales. I can tell her, as well, that these dangers were not the greatest I faced, that it was the prolonged courtship of an older man that would nearly prove my undoing. But what can I list that would make any sense to her? Simply that he was older? That he drove a Corvette? That he wooed me with roses, fancy dinners, and exaggerated abstinence? By the time I realized what he wanted from me—complete submission, absolute control—it was nearly too late. I had lost my job, my apartment, my car—all my trappings of independence. I relied on him for my most basic needs—food and shelter—and still I found that some of that stubborn will remained in me. There came a point when I rose up and walked away, just as I had walked away from my father. And just as had been the case with my earlier leave-takings, I paid the price for my disobedience. Only this time, instead of being shunned and exiled, I was raped, left hungry and alone until a girlfriend took me in. With her encouragement, I began once again to rebuild my life. *This* life. The one I began to direct with a vengeance, working my way through three college degrees with the diligence of someone who believes her very survival might be at stake. Marriage, the birth of my children, the reconciliation with my parents, the fulfillment of my dream to be a writer—all had gone according to a miraculous and conventional plan I could hardly believe myself capable of. Some part of me has come to understand that I am not simply lucky but blessed.

Allowing my sixteen-year-old daughter to strike out on her own is not conventional. It goes against common sense, the caution of elders, and the way things are done. "Having kids is all about letting go," a friend tells me, then adds, "but this seems a bit premature." Parents of grown children say, "Make her wait until she's eighteen. By then, you'll be *more* than ready for her to leave." I think that two more years would give me more time to prepare, allow me time for transition. That I could adjust in increments, even as I realize that Jordan's demands on my time are not yet finished. I know she will call me when she's blue, that she will come and spend nights back home. She'll continue to ask me for guidance regarding her class registration and boyfriend selection. She'll pick up the phone when she can't remember how to make powder-milk biscuits or pesto. Always, Jordan has required an intense parenting, which has absorbed me with its demands on my stamina. I've held on by my teeth to my own creative and emotional life. The balancing act has won me the kind of accolades that mothers both long for and resent—the "I don't see how she does it" kind—which puff me with pride and make me frantic with fear that the whole charade will fall into shambles. I don't know how to prepare myself for letting go, not of Jordan and her brother, but of their dependence upon me. Having choreographed so carefully the requirements of their care, I feel as though I no longer know how to negotiate the rooms of my own life. I sometimes feel paralyzed and find myself standing alone in the center of the house, realizing that what I might have done next—pack school lunches, pretreat the grass-stained knees of play clothes, fill a bathtub with water—is no longer required of me. What, then, is?

I PICK UP Bob at his office, say I want to swing by ShopKo on the way home. I find myself trolling the housewares department, my cart filling fast. A set of pots and pans, clearance-priced. A toaster with slots large enough for the bagels Jordan loves. Spatula, whisk, measuring spoons, cutting board. A colander, grater, pepper mill, and spice rack prefilled with oregano, cumin, thyme. Bob is right beside me, judging the temper of knife blades, determining the merits of fire extinguishers. When we realize we'll need a second cart, he holds up one hand.

"Wait," he says. "I think this might be enough for today." He is wary, sensing that I'm on a mission and won't be easily dissuaded.

I tuck a few hand towels into the Corningware. I feel flush with two-dollar bargains and a wealth of utensils I didn't own until the second decade of my marriage. As we wait at the checkout, I imagine the colors the kitchen might be painted. Throw rugs at the thresholds. Drawer liners and new curtains.

"She wants to start a collection of Fiesta ware," I say. "Let's stop by the mall and pick up a couple of settings." Purple and orange, I think. She wants to mix and match the colors, but those are her favorites.

My husband nods, wheels the cart to the car, starts loading.

"We can put a wooden grate in the bottom of that awful metal shower—better than those rubber mats. And a peephole in the door. And a dead bolt." I check my shopping list. "We'll go to WinCo for staples. Sugar and stuff."

"Kim," he says. "Maybe we should slow down."

But I can't slow down. I'm suddenly sure that, with the right set of dishes and safety considerations, Jordan is going to be fine. More than fine. Better than she's ever been.

By the time we stop by the mall for Fiesta ware, forgo WinCo, and find our way home, my exhilaration is quickly turning to exhaustion. I tell Bob to leave the bags in the car as I drag my way up the stairs and onto the couch. Bob checks on our fourteen-year-old son, who's in his bedroom with his headphones on.

"Jace needs to do his homework before he meets his friends," he says, and pours us each a glass of wine. We sit together on the couch and look out over the lights of town. "She's out there somewhere," Bob says. "It won't be a lot different from the way it is now."

I try to feel the truth of what he's saying, but I know he's wrong. At some point this evening, she'll call, tell us her plans, how late she'll be out. We'll lie awake and wait for the sound of the garage door opening, fall asleep the minute she knocks to let us know she's home. I try to imagine our lives just like this: no children in our laps to read to, no toys knocking about our feet. No more smorgasbords of PB & J and celery with Cheez Whiz. Family movie night has already slipped away; each family vacation threatens to be the finale. The popcorn stash lasts longer than it used to, and everyone makes his or her own breakfast. I feel us separating from one another, like spheres in a weightless space that make momentary contact before bouncing off, headed out on a trajectory that knows no end.

I know that what I'm feeling is the beginning of the empty-nest syndrome, but that awareness does little to fill the physical void around me. I'm strung like a tightwire between my need for my children and their need for me. For so many years, their demands on my time have given me little room to think of anything else. Now, I feel myself in that strange land of transition, in limbo between hanging on and letting go. Between the past I have known and reasonably mastered and the future I have so little control over.

I look at Bob, my lover of twenty-three years—half my life. "I meant to get her a good skillet," I say.

"You will."

"She'll do this better than I did."

He squeezes my hand. I don't have to remind him of those dark years after leaving home, of the loneliness I felt, how it drove me from my apartment and into the bars, where the music and smoky din of voices kept my despair at bay.

"She'll do just fine," he says. "She has us close by. We won't let anything happen to her."

I think of the smoke alarms, the fire extinguishers, the dead bolts, and I know that such precautions only guard against what danger we can foresee. It's the dangers we can't predict that terrify me: men who might hurt her, physically or emotionally; a private sense of failure that might keep her from confiding in us if things don't work out; the temptations of drug and alcohol abuse that present themselves daily. How much more confident I felt standing watch over her as she played at the water's edge or lit our Fourth of July fireworks! I could keep my eyes open, my Band-Aids and emergency phone numbers at hand. I researched every childhood illness, kept meticulous records of immunication, queried the families of friends on the presence of firearms and poisons, weighed risk and benefit like gold in each hand.

Sitting on the couch, staring out into the darkening night, I feel the air opening around me, know it's both chasm and opportunity. There is a shift in the atmosphere, like earthquake weather, or the passing of a distant bank of clouds. I allow myself to consider how the space might be filled with all that having children has taken away: time to write late into the night, to read a book without stopping. Time to make love to my husband without locking the doors and whispering my pleasure. Time just to sit, as we are now, and look out over the land. Time to bring my own thoughts back home. I've even allowed myself to consider turning Jordan's bedroom into my office, with a futon she can claim whenever she spends the night. Perhaps the strong spirit that infuses her room will inspire me to lay claim to my own life once again.

"What should we have for dinner?" Bob asks. "I think it might be just the two of us."

I look into the kitchen, remember those evenings when we ate our supper at nine instead of five, took midnight walks around town. We can do that again, I think, even now, and I realize how much time I spend just *waiting*, feeling I might be called upon at any moment to administer to some need: hunger, boredom, fear.

"Do you think we can let her go?" I ask.

"I don't see how we can keep her."

I nod. Like me, Jordan is in a kind of holding pattern, biding her time, unable to move forward, no way to go back, waiting for permission to take the next step.

Bob pulls out a sauté pan, goes to the refrigerator for tomatoes and basil. "I just wish that when she asked how old she'd have to be before we could let her go, you'd have said twenty instead of sixteen."

I smile, pour a little more wine. "I think we'd have lost her."

"So do I," Bob says. "Why don't you cut up some garlic."

I add garlic to the list of groceries I'll buy to stock Jordan's pantry, then olive oil, linguine, and Parmesan. If nothing else, she can survive on pasta. I'm peeling cloves when the phone rings.

"Hi, Mom," she says. "Just checking in."

I nod at Bob as he holds up the mushrooms for my approval.

"Did you look at the apartment?" she asks. I can hear the hope in her voice, her desire that we work on this together, that we function as partners with the shared ambition of separation.

"I did," I say. "I signed the lease. It's yours."

There's a loud whoop that echoes from the phone out into the kitchen. I feel my own chest swell with glee, and I laugh. This is good, I think. This is the way it's supposed to be.

"Will you help me?" she asks. "I'm not very good at organizing."

I think of her room downstairs, the piles of clean clothes and dirty shoes, the dishes sprouting mold, the hairbrushes tangled with earrings and necklaces. After numerous flurries of frustrating excavation, folding, dusting, scouring the floors, I'd given up, shut the door, declared it a mess of her own. "Sure," I say. "That's one thing I'm good at."

"I think I'll come home early so we can talk about it."

I motion for Bob to put another handful of pasta in the pot.

"That sounds great," I say. "See you in a few." When I hang up the receiver, I'm crying again, and I never cry. Bob wraps his arms around me, pulls me close. "They'll always have a safe place to come back to," he says. "That's the one thing we can know for sure."

We wait for the sound of the garage door opening before filling our plates. She comes up the stairs flush with excitement. Our son, less inclined toward resistance and who claims he will live at home as long as we'll let him, has decided to forgo the movie with friends. He and his sister squabble and tease as they make their way to the counter. How is it, I wonder, that the ties that connect us can both loosen and tighten, tear us apart and bind us together? In this good moment, the future seems suddenly full of new promise, and I think I feel what Jordan must: the days stretching ahead like an open road, a sense of direction pulling her forward. She'll have an apartment of her own without penalty, and if it doesn't work out, she'll have this home to come back to—a place to reconfigure, to learn from her mistakes—a place from which to start over. Jordan's support network is extensive, her connection to family intact. Even my parents, more terrified than I am, have accepted Jordan's need to go it alone: My mother has begun rifling her basement for extra casserole dishes, her old iron.

What I feel is a sense of some part of me coming back—a remembered trill of measured freedom just over the horizon. More room, more space, more time. I realize I've never quite felt this before, that my own leap into independence was freighted with regret, veiled with shame. I wonder if what I fear most is my own impulse toward autonomy, that some part of me has been conditioned to expect punishment and repercussion in response to a woman's desire to be in possession of her own life.

I have to remember that it will not be this way for her. In this, there is no sin, nor, I must remind myself, is the slight trembling of anticipation I feel as I contemplate my own domestic liberation a transgression.

"I'm proud of you," I say to her. "And a little jealous."

"You can have my room for your office. It won't bother me a bit. I know that if it doesn't work out, you'll give it back."

I give her a quick hug, ladle pasta onto my plate. "Don't be so sure," I say, and turn away before she can see my face.

Where There's Smoke

JUDY BLUNT

Hospitals have these morphine pumps so patients can control their own pain relief after surgery. I wasn't good at them. Every shift change brought a new face to the side of my bed, another soft voice, saying, "Did you lose the clicker? Here, it's right here," and quick, cool hands would slide the gadget into my palm and close my fingers around it with a firm push, push, as though pressure were the key. Enough and the thing might stick like Velcro. Enough and I might recognize the echoes in my belly for what they were and hit that button without prodding. Instead, I lay awake in the gloom, breathing in hisses.

Like most forty-five-year-old American women, I had mastered a number of little farewells. I just faced mine earlier than most. Married at eighteen, I gave birth to my daughter within a few days of my twentieth birthday and then kept going until my husband and I joked that we had "one of each"—a girl, a boy, and an accident. What I had were three children in four years in a barely modern house on a working Montana cattle ranch seventy miles from the nearest small town. I was the 1979 poster child for tubal ligation, and I went willingly, gratefully, under the knife. I had no public rite of passage to mark the moment, aside from the zero-population lectures so popular at the time. Frankly, I had all the kids I needed or wanted—one of those dear moms who would give her life for any of her children but wouldn't give a nickel for another one. Still, I did not go blindly. I went with a young woman's awareness of how this procedure would change me, how it would alter something of who I was as surely as the onset of menstruation had done only a decade earlier. How exquisite to feel a pinch of loss, even as I became acquainted with my new baby son, how fiercely I fixed my memories of that last birth, that last fleeting of fertility as I waved to my husband and rolled away on a gurney to be rendered sterile at age twenty-four.

All my life, I had saved stories of those last moments like a miser vaults gold, storing them safely against time—perhaps because I was cast so wholly into motherhood, a sustained six-year immersion in the language of baby. In those years, my outsides had been remapped by stretch marks, lactating breasts, fluctuating weight, while my insides were probed, kicked, monitored, and profoundly, profoundly shared. There's no coming back from that. As I advanced through the years, I defined myself by roles: mother of three preschoolers, single mother, head of household, nontraditional student with three teens at home. Then, in the summer of 2000, I arrived at this new place: middle-aged, my three children beautifully grown, even as the part of me that grew them threatened mutiny, my medical charts a growing litany of unusual bleeding and bad Pap smears. Once again, I rolled through the doors with a nurse on either side. No little farewell this time. This time, I am delivered of my uterus and ovaries, a vaginal hysterectomy. I awake in recovery, obsessed by new definitions.

Through the afternoon, I persist in refusing morphine, stubborn, determined to feel how it feels, pain and all. The nurses persist with the pump clicking, puzzled, or perhaps worried that I'm not in my right mind. Perhaps I'm not. I think of my mother-in-law giving birth in the days of twilight sleep and forceps. Minutes before delivery, she was told what she had loved and anticipated as one baby was actually two. Such a revelation, at this last quick moment, she could barely wrap her mind around it. She resisted the gas mask, wanting to know how two babies felt in her belly, thinking at the last second that she must divide what she called her heart evenly so each would be born with a share. But it was too late. Nurses took her arms, one on either side, not unkindly, and held her to the table. The last thing she recalled as the ether closed over her head was the doctor's voice: "Come now, you don't want to be awake for this." At the brink of consciousness, she thought the words *but I do, I DO,* though she could no longer say them aloud.

Toward evening, I hold on to those words as I sink, finally, under the waves of opiate, colors and sounds blooming and receding as some gentle hand gives me a final push into free fall. Somehow the pain seems safer.

TWELVE HOURS LATER, I've moved from the hospital bed to my living room couch, still sweating and coughing out the anesthesia. My mother has driven to my university town from their ranch in eastern Montana, and she reads quietly in a nearby chair. My body feels like it's been beaten, the sort of all-over-hell ache that comes with the flu, but it's the emptiness that drags me up out of sleep. I tell my mother I have a hollow spot. I can feel my innards sloshing around. I sit up, wrapping my arms around my belly to hold everything in place. "You need a binder," she says, and I nod, relieved. We gave birth in the same small-town hospital twenty years apart, but shared the experience of being bound on the delivery table, our emptied bellies girdled by cotton sheeting, wrapped and cinched firmly in place. We make do with a flour-sack towel drawn tight and pinned around my lower stomach. I drift back toward sleep, feeling held in place. Safe. Mom settles back into her chair and picks up her book. I add to my bank of memories this growing awareness of my new self, a feeling I've associated with the heft of a newborn, the first flow of milk. This turning point looms larger and more final, a part of me not just emptied or made barren but gone. "It seems like it all went so fast," I whisper, or I think I do. I mumble something. "It's not quite three," my mother replies, and turns a page.

IN DAYS THAT followed surgery, I seldom left my Missoula condominium. Mom and I made a quick trip to the mall, where I replaced the dish-towel binder with full-length body armor guaranteed to suppress the most wayward of body parts. Soon after, she left for home. Within a

week, any pain I could point to had faded into something more nebu-
lous. In its place, a vague restlessness picked at me, a sadness that
seemed to grow with every dose of fake estrogen. I'd spent more than a
decade of summers in construction work, the sort of dawn-to-dark labor
that built muscles and calluses and savings accounts. Now I thumbed
through a postoperative protocol that might have been written in a foreign language—no lifting, no driving, no strenuous exercise. No useful
occupation, no purpose to my days. Every morning, I gathered the newspaper off my step and settled at my kitchen table with a wretched pot
of decaf and soy milk, already on the verge of tears.

In the news that summer, everyone was on the verge of something.
In mid-July, dry lightning storms and runaway campfires formed a raised
rash across the western Montana map—more than fifty forest fires
burning when I went to surgery on the twentieth, another couple of
dozen touched off in the days since. My first week home, temperatures
climbed into the nineties and blast-furnace winds blew fires out of control on every side. For a while, their number appeared to diminish as individual fires met and joined forces, merging into unholy infernos
thousands of acres across. By the end of July, the smoke rolled over the
Missoula valley and lay like a thick dark fleece. Overnight, the songbirds
seemed to disappear.

The day my mother packed her car to go home, I waved her off and
then stood in the parking lot under a light haze of smoke and listened
to the distant deep-throated rumble of motorcycles. From my upstairs
window, I spent the afternoon watching the headlights on Reserve
Street as two thousand. Hells Angels roared into town for a five-day
mountain vacation. The city police had been planning for months and
were squared off, ready to rumble. Borrowed officers arrived from Utah,
trained to control crowds and disperse mobs at the Salt Lake City
Olympics. That evening, the *whop-whop* of police helicopters joined the
continuous roar of slurry bombers and bucket copters overhead. Windows sealed tightly against the thickening smoke, I watched the pulse
of aircraft beacons far into the night, unable to sleep or even breathe in
the swelter of my second-floor bedroom until long after midnight. There
wasn't an air conditioner for sale within two hundred miles of town.

Mornings, I read the paper line by line, filling empty time. Fire camps and Red Cross evacuation centers had sprung up overnight, it seemed, and as residents poured out of their mountain communities, thousands of firefighters rolled in, hotshot crews from sister states and as far away as New Zealand and Australia, five hundred soldiers from Fort Hood, Texas, hundreds more from National Guard posts around Montana. Loggers coped with "hoot owl" restrictions that barred them from working during daylight hours. Tourists found cigarettes and camp-fires forbidden in national parks and campgrounds. Truckloads of farm animals and pets arrived at rescue centers set up at the Missoula and Ravalli county fairgrounds. Maybe I could help with the animals, I thought idly, help walk dogs or something. No pitching hay, of course. No hauling water. Any energy and motivation disappeared in a wave of self-pity. Stuck in the eye of the storm, I studied the photos of a world dancing on the edge. Downtown was crawling with bikers and hippie drummers and homeless people recently turned out of Poverello, the lo-cal shelter, as it underwent a long-overdue renovation. Thousands of members of the counterculture Rainbow Family had swarmed through Montana on their way to a gathering in the forest near Jackson, and when the monthlong gathering ended, some found their way back to Missoula, whether stranded or still vacationing, no one knew. Every evening, hundreds of local gawkers turned out to admire fancy motorcy-cles and barefoot dancers, or just trade the smoke outside for the cooler fog inside the city's taverns.

A WEEK AFTER surgery, I sat in Dr. Ruth Bellite's office, filling out an enormous State of the Uterus questionnaire. What was my reproduc-tive status? Stress level? Caffeine intake? When I got to the "Sexual Ac-tivity" section, I glanced furtively around the room. *Good Lord! Did anybody really answer these?* My fellow women of a certain age quietly tended to their magazines, which tended toward the *Smithsonian* and *The New Yorker*. The office exuded country charm, with tasteful art and quilted seat covers on the chairs. Dr. Bellite's practice focused on menopausal issues, and my perimenopausal friends raved about her naturopathic approach to hormone replacement. Perhaps natural medi-cine could replace what had been taken away without turning me into a tearful, brittle hysteric. I was ready to try anything. I turned in my paperwork and the office nurse showed me to an exam room almost immediately. She patted the table and lifted an eyebrow; I shook my head. "Just a consult," I said. I fingered the sheet of paper where I had listed my daily doses of vitamins and minerals. "We'll just leave this here in case you need it," she replied, folding a nice cloth gown on the exam table.

Dr. Bellite entered the room with a grim smile, my paperwork in her hand. Her response to my situation bounced between empathetic outrage and plain fury. Of course I was caught in a hormonal and emotional turmoil. *What did I expect after allowing them to castrate me?* I had come to her far too late to be helped, it seemed, and after a couple of lame attempts to defend my decision, I sat rigid and humiliated as she railed against the world population of surgery-addicted male gynecologists. Fifteen minutes later, I stood on the sidewalk with a fistful of handouts, searching through the smoke for my car. Back home, I dropped my estrogen pills in the garbage, followed by the handouts, the postoperative notes, and the pain medication. Then I drove back out to the grocery store for a pound of regular coffee and a pint of cream. *Fuck them all.*

Early Saturday evening, on the Hells Angels' final night in Missoula, townspeople and a few Rainbows led a march on City Hall, protesting the unprecedented police presence in our normally tolerant university town. All week, Angels had rumbled around alone or in small groups flanked by two, three, four patrol cars. A police helicopter circled overhead and officers walked the streets in pairs. A high school parking lot served as a command center for dozens of borrowed cruisers and cops. Not one gang member had been arrested during their five-day "run," which could have been a direct result of the police presence or evidence that the police presence was unnecessary, depending on which side you chose to argue. It was the protesters who made the headlines on the television news Saturday night. Police arrested forty-seven. The police chief withdrew from the cameras, betrayed by the townspeople he was trying to protect. Later that evening, police cordoned off Front Street for motorcycle parking, and the last-night party was on. When the bars closed six hours later, the Hells Angels put on a show for the lingering crowd, blasting down Front Street, popping wheelies through the intersections in a final raucous display of metal and tattoos. As their dust cleared and the smoke settled once more, the crowd that had cheered them on their way and the cops imported to quell them faced one another over the empty street. One moment shivered on the edge of reason; then all hell broke loose.

SUNDAY, NEWS OF the riot trickled in as the last of the motorcycles left the way they'd come. Monday morning, I gathered the newspaper as the coffee brewed, spreading it on the kitchen table in anticipation. A photo filled the top half of the paper, and I settled with my coffee to study the sea of faces in the panoramic shot of Front Street at 3:00 A.M. There in the center, arms braced in a classic defense stance, stood my twenty-four-year-old son, Jason, warding off baton blows from a policeman in riot gear. I reached for the phone and rolled him out of bed at the other end of the line. Trained in martial arts and boxing, he had escaped with a few bruised knots on his forearms, he said; his younger brother James had been doused with pepper spray when he stopped to rinse the eyes of a young man who had staggered, blinded, into the street and fallen. An hour later, I went back to the official versions of the story, coffee forgotten. Sixteen more citizens had been arrested, a couple of them dragged off their bicycles as they tried to leave, witnesses said. Injured civilians showed up at emergency rooms, along with one policeman, who had been bitten on the leg by a young woman he was detaining. I looked up from the paper, conscious of the dull ache in my belly. Unable to sleep, I'd spent a day and a night rolling the word *castrated* around on my tongue while I slowly cleaned, first everything in the house and then the house itself. Inside, the air smelled faintly of bleach, the rooms a patchwork of safe lines, all starched and pressed. Outside, smoke eddied around buildings and hung in the streets; outside, the world had gone mad.

ON THE FIRST day of August, President Clinton joined our governor in declaring all of Montana a major national disaster area. Residents of Missoula couldn't have agreed more. The city council was demanding an investigation of police actions during the Hells Angels riot. Public hearings were jammed to the rafters, the testimony nearly as rancorous as the riot itself. In the valley, witnesses described the Bitterroot fires as "apocalyptic": 280 homes evacuated, at least 50 lost to the blaze. New fires burned undetected, veiled in the smoke of others. As visibility disappeared, the slurry bombers taking off and landing at Missoula airport were forced to move operations to airports hundreds of miles away. Public health officials monitored the pollution levels and posted updates on the air quality hot line every few hours. Emergency rooms filled with those suffering from respiratory distress, asthma. The late-summer sunsets bathed the western sky bloodred, but only when darkness fell could I see the muted glow of fire on the horizon.

Wednesday, I woke before dawn, damp with sweat, the temperature already in the seventies. Coffee. Newspaper. Dry lightning forecast for later that evening. Irritable and restless, I thumbed through the fire reports and stopped at a headline about the homeless shelter. VOLUNTEERS, DONATIONS SOUGHT. During renovation, workers had discovered asbestos, which added days to the remodeling project. With their kitchen and dining room shut down, Poverello staff could offer only one hot meal a day, prepared and served from the basement kitchen of a nearby church. They fed around two hundred midday, fixed one hundred bag suppers. They desperately needed sandwich fillings and cold salads. I read the article again. My first job in Missoula had been as manager of a salad bar. I can do this, I thought, even as my stomach tightened with nervousness. The most visible of the homeless population were the panhandlers, a scary assortment of transients, typically ill-dressed men with ratty beards and large, dirty backpacks filled with God knows what. Before I could lose courage, I dragged out my stockpot and boiled up the twenty-pound sack of potatoes in my pantry. While they cooled, I headed for the grocery store, automatically ticking through the recipes and ratios I carried in my memory. Two bunches of celery, five dozen eggs, a gallon of mayonnaise, eight pounds of macaroni. By 10:00 A.M., two five-gallon cauldrons of chilled salad rested on my counter, ready for delivery. I considered them, their heft and bulk, against the doctor's directive—"*Don't lift anything heavier than your handbag for six weeks*"—and stood there weighing my odds. To hell with it, I thought, grabbing the tub of potato salad. If I get them to the car, somebody will be there to help me unload them.

Two trips to the station wagon left me wrung-out and winded, and I leaned against the car door with sort of a dawning horror. The twinges in my midsection were survivable, but the body I had fine-tuned to work construction was gone, and ten days of lying around had added wobbles and quivers I'd never experienced before. Knees dancing under the dashboard, I dug out my city map and rested a moment before heading downtown. Between the hospital and the courthouse, the great spire of St. Francis Xavier rose above the boulevard trees, visible for blocks, like a billboard pointing the way to salvation. Today I would need a street map to find it. I switched on my headlights and motored through the eerie gloom, the glow of one streetlight appearing ahead just as another faded in my rearview mirror. The smoke was worse at the center of town. People hustled along the sidewalks with handkerchiefs pressed to their mouths, ducking quickly into stores. As I neared the hospital, surgical masks replaced handkerchiefs. Pulling up in front of the church, I waited with my hand on the key for a local radio station to finish reporting a stage II pollution alert, warning everyone to stay indoors. Word hadn't gotten out around St. Francis. Under the broad maple trees and along the west wall of the church, the homeless had gathered quietly, waiting for the noon meal and keeping to themselves. I aimed for the basement entrance, stepping around packs and over the legs of those already in line.

A surprising number of the men and women were young, or at least younger than I'd expected them to be. One couple sat on a wool blanket with an infant between them, allowing their barefoot toddler to explore the grass as they marked his space with steely sweeps of the eyes. A gray van in the parking lot was the center of a colorful knot of tie-dye and hemp, long skirts and dreadlocks—the resident Rainbows I'd heard about. I edged around the line of waiting men and down a wide flight of stairs to the bottom of a deep cement stairwell. The back of my neck crawled with the sensation of eyes watching, hands reaching out to touch me as I passed, but when I reached the door and glanced back, the row of men slouched along the foundation wall and up the steps hadn't moved. Not a head lifted as I rattled the doorknob. Keys clutched in my hand, I tapped nervously on the locked door, waited, then knocked more loudly. Nothing. I glanced around, and the man on the steps nearest me roused from his reverie. He tipped his straw hat off his eyes and pointed with both hands, directing me up the stairs with one and north to the back entrance with the other. This door was kept locked until food was ready, he said. I nodded. He smiled and settled his hat back down his forehead.

The back door stood open, and I stepped down into a narrow passageway crammed with four- and six-tier rolling carts. Baked goods and pastries in commercial packaging filled most of the portable shelves and overflowed onto the floor. Bus tubs of limp carrots and assorted garden truck were stacked along one wall. A few sacks of moldy wheat bread lay by the door. As I stood waiting for a sign, another sack flew up and over a cart and landed on the floor in front of me. I nudged it toward the pile with one foot and shouted, "Hello." A slim dark-haired woman popped up, a fuzzy loaf in either hand, and greeted me. I recognized Laure from the television news. Hired at the beginning of the summer to head the staff of Poverello, she was nearer my age than not, I suppose, but where I stood frowning pensively in the doorway, wanting only to off-load ten pounds of salad and make good my escape, she burst from the bread stacks, radiating cheerful energy and profound gratitude.

This is *so* nice of you, you can't imagine how hectic trying to work out of this kitchen not nearly big enough and then today's the last straw— God knows where the cook's off to and I have a board meeting, we feed in an hour, but if it's late, it's late and it can't be helped. We're *so* glad to have the salads. This is Joe. Here're the aprons. Joe will show you where things are.

I stood aside, dazed and reunited, as Laure disappeared out the back door, scooping an armload of blue bread into the garbage on the way to her car. What the hell just happened? I wondered.

Joe and I shot a glance at each other. Joe had hard eyes, and he already looked pissed. I didn't bother to ask, just carried the salads one at a time around the building to the kitchen, setting them down every so often to rest. Returning to my car, I sat in the blistering heat of the front seat for a moment, thinking, then rolled up the windows, stuffed my wallet under the front seat, and locked the doors. I walked back to the

chaotic kitchen and tied on an apron. "So what's for lunch?" I asked. Joe
stood with one lean haunch propped against the stove, arms crossed,
hair neatly combed. At least he looks clean, I thought warily. Joe measured me through half-lidded eyes, his dark Italian features weathered
like ten miles of bad road. When he spoke, his thick gray-on-black mus-
tache twitched, but his eyes never flickered. "Goddamned if I know," he
replied.

I L E A R N E D   M A N Y things in my first hour at "the Pov," among
them that Joe was not the cook—the real cook had caught a freight
heading east the night before—and he really didn't know what was for
lunch. He did know everything else, though. He had lived at the shelter
for months, earning his keep by working in the kitchen. Serendipity was
the real cook, and she came through around 11:30 A.M., when the
kitchen's phone rang. Joe pointed to it, and, taking my cue, I answered.
The caterers at a big fire camp outside of Missoula had a couple hundred omelettes left from breakfast; did we want them? Yes, indeed we
did. Joe's eyes widened with something close to joy when I told him the
news, his reaction one I could understand if someone had dropped off
a big prime rib. "What's so great about eggs?" I asked. He hesitated and
I waited, curious. "They're easy to eat," he said finally. I had to be satis-
fied with that.

Waiting for them to arrive with the entrée, Joe set out trays of day-
old bread and used the lone butcher knife to cut a dozen pies and cakes
into huge wedges, arranging them at one end of the long serving
counter. Soon another enormous tray joined them, this one piled with
stale doughnuts and pastries. I scooped the potato and macaroni salads
into serving bowls the size of sinks. While I got the urn of coffee perk-
ing, he pulled milk from the cooler and held each gallon up to the light,
rotating it to see if it was still liquid. Every few minutes, someone tried
the doorknob and Joe glanced at the clock. Fifteen minutes after the
call, a truck pulled up at the kitchen entrance and two ash-covered men
tromped in with heavy buckets in each hand, each insulated pail holding around fifty cooked and still-warm ham and cheese omelettes. Joe
opened the door and the dining room began to fill. I cracked the seal on

the first bucket as Joe slid on a pair of sanitary gloves. He fished out omelettes with both hands and plopped them onto the stainless-steel food trays as people moved along the counter. A murmur of oohs and aahs trailed back down the line as word about our offering got around. I gave up trying to puzzle it out. As a ranch cook, I'd have been fired if I'd fed my meat-and-potatoes crew eggs for dinner. The answer dawned on me as I stood at the counter dishing out salads, Joe bantering with the grizzled old men as he dished up their eggs, sharing a laugh. Of course eggs were better than roast beef for these men. There wasn't a sound tooth or a complete set in the lot of them.

FOR THE FIRST night in two weeks, sleep came easily, and the next morning I stepped over the newspaper on my way out the door, already pondering how I could stretch twenty pounds of chicken into two hundred servings. I stewed them, removed the bones, and cut the meat into small pieces, then thickened the stock and added vegetables. While that simmered, I rounded up two volunteers from the group loitering by the back door and set them to peeling potatoes. Joe hung around the kitchen while they worked, watchful, and when their language grew coarse, he stepped over and spoke quietly to them. So Joe's got my back, I thought, smiling at his chivalry, but I began to relax. Dinner that day was a thick chicken stew ladled over mashed potatoes, and the trays came back clean. By the end of the week, Poverello's remodeled kitchen was up and running, and when Laure showed up with a crew to move everything from the church basement to the shelter, I trusted along.

My strength and my sense of humor returned at about the same pace, and as the days passed, I became more aware of the new world I had entered. With the showers and laundry facilities back in order, the general look of the diners improved. In a transient population, it doesn't take long to become a regular. By the end of the first week, I had a fan club. Once moved into the new kitchen, the staff took over some of the meals, and occasionally a traveler with kitchen experience stepped in for a day or two. When it was my turn to cook, the kitchen filled with resident volunteers. Elbow-to-elbow at the deep sinks, we washed, sorted, and trimmed tons of vegetables past their prime. They told their stories in a rush, with little preamble, as if accustomed to listeners who turned away. Their stories were occasionally funny and often sad, and I suspected a fair number were bald-faced lies, but they were always interesting.

I MADE CHILI and corn bread with the help of a young fellow who hobbled around in a pair of dirty wool socks. He'd hitchhiked to Missoula to find work fighting fires and spent the last of his money on a pair of heavy lace-up boots. To qualify, he had to hike three miles carrying a forty-five-pound pack in less than forty-five minutes, which he did— wearing his new boots without socks. I nodded when an older woman confided over a cutting board that she'd quit cutting her hair when her daughter died, and I didn't press because her hair was still pretty short. I rolled enchiladas and listened to the Rainbow group as they organized their workday, sitting around a dining table over juice and pastry. Which freeway exit, which cardboard sign, which time of day produced the best result. They seldom volunteered at the shelter, but I found a chance to visit with Molly, a woman near my age, and she talked of their life very matter-of-factly. They worked as earth's scavengers, she said, like the magpies and the coyotes. They ate what people threw away, wore the discards of a wealthy nation, and lived on the land. I thought of the checks I'd written to buy food the Poverello didn't have or had used up. We were always out of mayonnaise for salad dressings, and butter and oil were like gold. But I held my tongue. It was clear that she believed her own story. In a way, I admired their lifestyle for its absolute practicality. Only the women in the group worked, having discovered that donations fell off when the men were with them, and a preteen girl took turns standing with each of them on different days. Younger children beside the road drew police officers and social workers, so the little guys stayed with the men. Every morning, they gathered their signs, climbed into a van, and were dropped off at their various posts. Every hour, the van circled back and checked on them. On a good day, she made thirty dollars an hour, seldom less than twenty dollars, Molly said, and as soon as they had enough to buy what they needed—beer, cigarettes, soda pop and gasoline for the van, I was guessing—they stopped working. They were not greedy. They did not believe in capitalism. They prayed for world peace.

On the final Sunday before my university job started up, I donated one hundred pounds of hamburger and made two huge roasters full of meat loaf. Joe leaned against the steam table as I kneaded the burger with onions and bread crumbs and herbs, talking in his low, quiet way. What the doctor had said about Rocky's diabetes, that Wendy and Tom finally had enough saved for an apartment, that Dennis got caught stealing out of the walk-in cooler and was thrown out for a week. I smiled and shook my head, feeling the tug of new muscle in my forearms and back. I'd be sorry to leave, I told Joe, and he shook his head and called me a "crazy lady." Most people couldn't wait to get out of Poverello and back to a real life. We served the meal as we had the first day, working in companionable silence, and as the cleanup crew washed dishes, I stepped out on the porch and let the breeze fan my face.

Emmet, a wizened World War II veteran sat on a low bench along the shelter's shady side, staring toward the bulk of Mount Sentinel as though he could see. I greeted him, and he turned his head to find me. His eyes were nearly occluded by cataracts, and he'd broken his glasses. His face looked naked without them. I touched his arm and asked what he was thinking about so hard.

"Oh, cook lady," he said, "I wanted to talk to you."

"Sure," I replied, sitting on the bench beside him. "What can I do for ya?"

His mouth opened and closed, like he was having a hard time getting started, so I spoke first, trying to jump-start his thoughts. "Did you like the meat loaf?" I asked. He nodded his head and then shook it, distracted, and I settled in for a wait.

"You made that sausage gravy that time," he said suddenly, half-questioning, and I said, "Yes." I'd made biscuits and sausage gravy for supper a few nights before and we'd served it with scrambled eggs. In a place overrun with expired bakery goods, anything baked fresh was a rare treat.

"Well, that's what I want to tell you about." he said, and his voice pitched higher. "My mother . . ." He faltered, his tongue working the sides of his cheeks, "She made biscuits," he managed.

"I'll bet they were great," I said, picking my way carefully along. Emmet turned to me, his terrible old eyes awash. "I wanted to thank you for them biscuits," he quavered. "Them were mighty good biscuits."

ON AUGUST 20, an even month after surgery, I drove home with the window down, pleasantly aware that my clothes smelled of onions and hot grease. The air had begun to clear as sharp mornings and short days did what no number of firefighters could do, and in the valley, smoke took on a wispy, vaporous look, as though the earth itself were cooling. Fires still flared deep in the wilderness, as they would until snowfall. But those nearest our town gradually, grudgingly changed status, from out of control to what the fire commanders called "contained." Hundreds stood shaken in the aftermath, picking through the ruins of old lives, saving what they could. The town emerged from the dark days with a gasp, as if waking from a bad sleep, and volunteers and donations poured into the Pov, making up for lost time. Mike, the new full-time cook, came on board, and I was secretly pleased to see Joe give him the evil eye for the first couple of days. They'd get along fine. In a week, I'd step into the classroom as though I'd never left, and the summer would give way to the business of autumn.

All my life, I've saved stories. In the stories from the summer of 2000, I'm drawn to my first day in the church kitchen, the feeling of stepping into a vacancy and filling it all the way to the edges. That, of course, is the heart of all of my stories, the chronicle of a wife, mother, woman. In the years that followed, I returned to cook weekends when I could, summers when Mike needed a break, until finally I returned a stranger. I've made my peace with that. They still love my meat loaf. Being wanted is never the same as being needed, but it's not bad. Not bad at all.

Grandmother Land

ANNICK SMITH

Nous sommes arrivés! I announced as we passed Rodin's statue of Balzac, which guards the intersection of boulevard Raspail with avenue Montparnasse. Jessy sat forward in the backseat of the cab, looking out her open window and breathing the fumes of jockeying cars. It was a morning in June and the streets of the old city were replete with odors of fresh baked bread, water running in gutters, fish on ice being unloaded in crates at the back door of the Dôme restaurant, and the ever-present musk of oysters from the shuttered *huitre* bar on the corner.

After a madcap ride in the rush-hour traffic from de Gaulle airport, detouring in a maze of back streets with a cabbie who succeeded in driving the fare toward seventy dollars (I refused to tip the cheating bastard), we arrived at the studio apartment I had rented from a friend of a friend on the rue Delambre. This is a street I cherish in the *quartier* I know best, literally next door to the Dôme in the heart of Montparnasse, the artists and writers district where I had been born sixty-eight years before.

I am French in my mind's romantic byways, but by blood I'm Hungarian and Jewish. My mother, who is ninety-nine now, was born and raised in Transylvania. My father was from Budapest. They met in

1920s Paris, where he had come to be a sculptor, and where she had fled with her mother and brother from Rumanian occupation after her father died. Mother was a photographer for Paris *Vogue* when she fell in love with my father. She taught him the crafts of camera and lighting and they opened a studio across from the Parc Montsouris up on the hill of Parnassus, where my grandmother wheeled me in my buggy every morning of my first seven months. And then we emigrated to Chicago.

I returned to Paris with my family when I was sixteen, and the surge of recognition that assaulted me as I stepped out of our taxi on the place dela Bastille is a moment more felt than remembered. "Home, I knew it entering," wrote the poet Richard Hugo on entering the Dixon Bar in Montana. Entering Paris, I knew I had come home. Now I hoped to pass a similar experience to my eighteen-year-old granddaughter.

We dragged our suitcases into an elevator designed for sardines and rode, pressed close and sweaty, up to our fourth-floor apartment. The place was tiny, appointed in red, with a Pullman kitchen, high open windows looking down to a courtyard, a blessed ceiling fan, two beds, a TV, and a modern "American" bathroom with a tub and shower, and a shower curtain that fell down every other time one of us opened it.

"You're lucky," I told Jessy, "you're my only grandkid. If I had more, I couldn't spoil you like I do."

JESSY IS MY son Alex's daughter—the great good luck of my life past sixty. I did not know she existed until she was ten, or meet her until she was twelve. Now she was ready to step into womanhood, and this trip would be an initiation into the intimacies of female relationship that we had never had with each other—a relationship I could not have with my four sons.

The day I found out she existed was New Year's 1997. The sun shone weakly and pale shadows on the snow were more suggestions of form than form itself, the long one striding ahead, the smaller trying to keep up. Alex, back in Montana for the holidays from graduate school in Texas, had said, "Mom, let's go for a walk. There's something I need to tell you."

Walking is how our family connects. We head for the woods and anx-

ieties dissolve in mountain air. We walked with our German shepherds
on the logging road above our meadow, amid ponderosas and fir and the
tall barren larch whose needles lay like a yellow net under the snow.
Bear Creek had blasted a new course along a gravel bar laid down when
an ice jam melted, and the bears it is named for were denned in higher
country, as invisible to us as the cougars whose linear tracks along the
creek—one round paw in front of the other—warned us to watch our
backs.

I should have been happy to walk with my six-foot-four, lean, and
dark-haired son, but I was not happy that day. AIDS, I thought. He's going to tell me he is HIV-positive. Alex is not gay, but he is handsome and
loves women, and stories of sexually active young people contracting the
disease had recently made headline news. Waiting for the true subject
of our walk to emerge, I filled the winter silence with the complaint my
mother voiced so often, only party ironic on my part, the plaint of a
mother nearing sixty raised in a Jewish family and having only one son
married: "When will one of you give me a grandchild?"

Alex smiled a bemused half smile. "Do you know what I'm going to
tell you?"

"What? Do you have some awful disease? Do you have AIDS?"

"No. Not at all."

"Thank God!" I reached up to give him a big hug.

"What I've got is a daughter," said Alex, pulling back.

"A daughter?" Then, according to Alex, I said, "A child is good. A
child is life." He lifted me off my feet.

"Where is she?" I asked.

"I lost track," he said, but friends had informed him that his daughter lived in Lincoln, a logging hamlet seventy miles up the valley famous
as the Unabomber's hideout. Her name was Jessy Rose, and she was
ten. I asked who the mother was, and he said Robin, a person I had
never heard of.

"Did you just find this out?"

"No. I've known from almost the beginning."

As we walked back to the ranch, Alex told the story he had never told
me before. He and Robin had gotten together at a party up the valley
the summer after graduating from high school. They rafted the Black-

foot during a one-week affair, and I like to believe Jessy is the river's gift
to us, conceived on a July day when a young girl and a younger boy
drifted green waters, swam deep pools, and ran the rapids with rainbow
trout. The Blackfoot is my home river, my sacred place, and I believed
nothing but good could come of a union on its shores. But a baby was
not the gift those heedless teenagers wanted or expected.

When he came back for Christmas from Berkeley after his first semester at the University of California, Alex ran into Robin at the Stock-
men's Bar in Missoula. She was five months pregnant. "Who's the lucky
dad?" quipped Alex. "You," said Robin.

I doubt if Alex kept silent that Christmas because he feared I would
insist that he and Robin get married. Still, he must have felt life was
about to close down on him at eighteen instead of opening, so he swore
his twin brother, Andrew, to secrecy and told no one else. Alex knew that
Robin's life would be changed utterly; but she had kept the pregnancy
secret and the decision to bear the child and become a single mother
had been hers alone. Robin was Catholic and proud, and she would not
consider an abortion or give the baby up for adoption. She told Alex she
wanted nothing from him.

"How could you know for ten years," I asked, "and not tell me?"

I felt betrayed. The trust I expected from my children—especially
from the twins, whom I had raised almost single-handedly—had been
broken. But trust is a tricky concept, and even past sixty (perhaps especially past sixty), women like me feel impelled to stick to the myths we
have invented for ourselves. Only now, examining our lives as coldly as
I can, has it become possible for me to understand that I am no innocent party in the matter of trust. From their babyhood on, I had put dis-
tances between the twins and me, and to a lesser extent between myself
and the older boys by tending my sick husband while sending the kids
off to my parents or sister, or hiring caregivers. After Dave died, I would
go away for days or weeks to work on various projects, leaving the boys
in the care of relatives or friends or strangers—some of whom they
loved, and some of whom they could not bear. I would return home all
warmth and presents and kisses, then leave again in a month or two as
I doggedly pursued making a minimal living as a freelance filmmaker,
and after that as a travel and nature writer. I could have chosen a nine-

to-five job, or returned to teaching high school, but I wanted to live on my own terms as the artist I imagined myself to be, not fully aware of the costs to my kids, costs that eventually circled back to me and my granddaughter.

IN PARIS, JESSY and I awoke from a jet-lagged nap while the sun was still high. Feeling the urgency of time as only a woman of a certain age can, I prodded my sleepy girl into her shorts. But before setting off on the first of many walking tours, Jessy took out the pop-up map that Alex had given her.

"Where to, *chérie?*"

With no hesitation, Jessy said, "Notre-Dame." She had studied French for three years, had just finished a course in European history, had read our guidebooks on the flight, and knew exactly what she wanted to see. We set off through the Luxembourg Gardens, where well-mannered French children rode sweaty ponies and sailed boats in the pond. Lovers kissed under leafy chestnuts, and in the formal gardens, women in scanty dresses sunned themselves on wire chairs; it was cliché come to life in sentimental splendor, and Jessy and I bought the package whole.

Crossing the Seine to the Ile de la Cité, we detoured to see the Sainte Chapelle before closing time. "This was my father's favorite cathedral," I told Jessy. "Small, but gorgeous. I think that's what he loved."

"Perfection?"

"Yes, perfect beauty." My companion, Bill, and I had come to this chapel one June dusk several years before to hear a Czech musician play Bach's haunting suites for cello. We did not know those somber notes would be the music my father requested be played at his funeral only a year later. I mourned for my father as Jessy and I entered the heavy doors. How he would have loved introducing this girl to the glories of art! Late-afternoon sun shone jewel bright through the chapel's storied stained-glass windows. Tourists sat on benches against the wall and crowded the vaulted center. Jessy, in her shorts and worn gym shoes, was obviously an american, and, more to the point, an athlete. As she stood in the doorway trying to absorb the scene, she was greeted by a couple of teenaged boys. They traded credentials: "Where you from?" "Wha' d'you play?" Jessy's ponytail flipped above the head of a short red-haired kid, and I smiled.

When we reached Notre-Dame, the tourist crowd had thinned, yet the line for the ascent to its gargoyled tower was still half an hour long. I had climbed this tower when I was sixteen with my father and little sisters. My father had taken us into the church to see the original carved pews. He told us that if we looked carefully at their undersides, we would see they were signed. Building the cathedral had been a centuries-long communal enterprise, but even in that medieval age, artisan sculptors like my father knew their contributions were worth putting a name to.

Our turn arrived and we stepped up the dark, curving, and narrow stairway, emerging into the netted confines of the high balustrade just as the sun neared its fall, gilding the rooftops and chimneys of Paris, molting the Seine's flat waters to bronze, and tinting the white domes of Sacré-Coeur a rosy pink. Here, to Jessy's delight, was the great bell where the Hunchback had swung. Here, pocked marble angels blew trumpets down the ages and beaked monkey-faced demons laughed at the toiling humans below; and here we were, too, among the mythical beasts.

THE DAY I met Jessy, Alex had bought helium balloons—red, white, and yellow—which he fastened to the porch railing of our hewn-log house as a birthday welcome for his daughter, who would soon turn thirteen. She wore jeans and a maroon Montana Grizzlies jacket and stood nearly a head shorter than her present six feet. Robin walked behind, a compact country-and-western gal with long hair and a rosebud mouth, a bit defiant and hopelessly independent—a woman with whom I immediately connected. Jessy's black Lab, Tucker, jumped out of their Dodge pickup and got into a growl-off with our protective shepherd, Betty. Jessy smiled her trademark smile and I went to her.

It was love at first sight: *Hello. Here you are. I've been waiting for you so long.* Jessy let me hug her, not backing off as I might have done, but warm and innocent, embracing whatever was to come. When I took her hand, I had to hold back a gasp, for it was like taking hold of a miniature of Alex's hand—the fingers extra long and tapered, duplicates not only of his fingers but of his father's. I noticed that her feet were also long and narrow, like Alex's and Andrew's and like Dave's—the paws of a pup who will grow into a big dog. Then Jessy moved her hands in a characteristic gesture and my forearms broke out in goose bumps. These were Alex's gestures, which are mirrors of his father's. It was a Proustian moment, setting off memories of Dave so vivid they were almost hallucinogenic. Odd how gesture identifies us. We mimic the gestures of people we aspire to be like, or people we mock, but I had never before realized that gestures can be inherited.

Good God, I thought, Dave's ghost has returned in the hands of this sweet-faced granddaughter who replicates not only his gestures but his history. For Dave, too, had been an illegitimate child in a small town, and though he knew who his father was, even went to school with his twin half sisters, his father's Swedish farm family never acknowledged him. Dave's teenage mother, Virtue, was not as tough as Robin. She had a nervous breakdown soon after his birth, perhaps under the strain of shame and motherhood, and suffered from mental illness off and on for the rest of her life. So Dave was raised by his rigidly Baptist grandmother and aunts, and, like Jessy, he became the family's star honor student and basketball player. In fantasies of what could have been, I see the two of them charming our hearts. If only he had lived to know her.

Alex himself had met Jessy only a few days before. He was living at the ranch that winter, house-sitting and writing while I was off in some sunny land with my companion, Bill, and he had managed, finally, to get hold of Robin. They faced each other across a booth at Trixi's Saloon up the Blackfoot's valley in Ovando and talked about their child, and about Robin's struggles as a single mother, and Alex's attempts to write and direct movies.

"She's known you're her father since she was old enough to understand," said Robin. "If she wants to see you, it's fine with me."

"I have to be leaving soon for Los Angeles," said Alex. He wondered if they should wait. "I'm afraid she'll think I'm running away again."

Robin took out her cell phone and dialed Jessy. "She says she wants to meet you *now*," Robin reported, "in case you don't come back for another twelve years."

Funny girl, I thought. So much irony, so young. I tried to imagine what it might be like to be making such a life-changing decision at the age of twelve. Years later, when I asked Jessy permission to write this essay (I had already gotten the go-ahead from Alex and Robin), I told her I did not want to invade her privacy, and I would respect her right to tell me no. She smiled, but her almond eyes had a serious cast under their long mascara black lashes. "Sure," she said, with easy candor. "It's okay with me."

We were having dinner at Applebee's in Helena, where Jessy is a student at Carroll College on a full volleyball and academic scholarship. Jessy picked at her Oriental chicken wraps while I munched a Caesar salad with shrimp. "When it came right down to it," I asked, "how did you feel? Didn't you resent the fact he'd never made a move to see you? Never acknowledged he was your father?"

"No, I understood that all right." Jessy was silent a moment. "I only resented him on my mom's account," she said softly, "for not helping when she needed it. Raising me, you know. I didn't think it was right."

Jessy thought back to her seventh-grade self. She said she'd pondered what to do for several days, but her decision was never in doubt. "I just wanted to meet him."

And so their rendezvous took place in a little steak house called the Cozy Corner (Jessy's choice), which sits on a game preserve where elk come down from the Bob Marshall Wilderness to winter. "It was like the biggest date of my life," said Alex. "I changed my clothes three times, and still didn't feel right."

There is a photo Robin took at that dinner that sits on the oak dresser in my bedroom, where I see it each time I stare into the blotched old mirror at my blotched and aging face. The photo tells me it is not merely all right to grow old but damned fine! No smooth-browed chick could know how it feels to have swallowed the troubles I had been fed during my young womanhood, or to rejoice at the dessert those long years had served up. I have placed my precious photo in an oval frame decorated with bunches of grapes, red apples, pale green pears, cherries, and strawberries. Jessy's head does not quite touch Alex's shoulder. She is rosy-cheeked, with shiny brown bangs curled over her forehead, and wears a see-through white blouse and a long skirt patterned with tiny blue, yellow, and white flowers. Alex stands erect with his right arm around her, his left thumb and forefinger poking out of his pants pocket. His smile is identical to her smile, the same flexed bow of mouths, the same configuration of cheek and chin. There is no doubt whose child she is.

SO THIS IS where we stand. I am sixty-nine, Jessy is nineteen, and Alex is thirty-seven. As a grandmother, I find myself with more time on my table, less ambition, and more interest in rituals and family ties than I had as a single mom. Life is bigger and more complex since Jessy came into our lives, for it includes Robin's clan, which is an extended Catholic family of Irish and Danish forebears with roots in the plains of eastern Montana. Jessy's grandfather is a retired lawyer, her grandmother teaches Russian, her great-uncle is a priest, and her great-grandmother is a wheat rancher. Robin's three brothers—two doctors and an engineer—tended Jessy when she was a baby, and she is a big sister to their children, as she is to the family of her adoptive father. In this expanded circle, Jessy's graduations and birthdays, her basketball and volleyball games, along with summer barbecues and Christmas parties, have been added to our family's festivities.

Jessy's world is also bigger now, and more complex. She has met my sisters when they were visiting from Boston and San Francisco, and their offspring, whose Hungarian Jewish blood seems to dominate (at least externally) their Protestant fathers' more discreet contributions. Actors, artists, writers, teachers, and film people, they are an urban cast of characters, radically different from her back country grade-school pals in Lincoln and Seeley Lake, her Catholic friends at Loyola high, and her Montana clan, which includes a champion bronc rider. Sometimes I wonder how Jessy feels about us Smiths and Deutches coming to claim her. I know we have changed her story of herself, but I do not know if we have complicated her life more than she desires. These are subjects I have not yet broached, but she seems to accept us as she accepts Alex—bemused, a bit distant, and affectionate.

My mother, who visits from Chicago each summer, has formed a special bond with Jessy. They are a Mutt and Jeff pair, the tiny hunched old woman and the tall strapping girl. Jessy is entertained by Mother's Hungarian accent, and admires the humor and spunk that still defines her at the age of ninety-nine. The admiration is mutual. In my mother's universe, beauty ranks highest of all virtues, and Jessy fills the bill.

On our way to Paris, I decided to stop in Chicago to see Mother. I knew she and her French friends could prepare Jessy for her encounter with the Old World by offering personal connections beyond any story I could tell or any information she might find in books. And I knew it would give the old ladies great pleasure to pass some of their knowledge on to this girl. Alex drove us to the airport, Jessy in sweats, dragging her duffel, and me with my big black rolling suitcase. He would have loved to come with us, but this was a woman's trip.

We arrived to hugs and kisses at my mother's thirty-second-floor apartment overlooking Lake Michigan; it's in a fashionable, death-ridden old folk's high rise, where an eighteen-year-old girl is as welcome and out of place as a whiff of Montana air. Next afternoon, we visited our friend Marie-Jeanne, a widowed French woman from Lyons who has retired from the French embassy. She prepared a typical *déjuener*: eggplant quiche, a platter of *saucissons, salade verte*, a creamy fruit tart, and the obligatory cheese plate. Before eating, we sat on her balcony, delighting in the breeze off the lake and listening to my mother's best friend, ninety-three-year-old Victoria, talk in her high, whispery French voice about growing up as a French Jew in Cairo, being deported to Paris after World War II, and finally resettled in Chicago with an elderly husband and two sons, none of whom spoke English.

At table, Mother recalled stories about arriving in Paris from Transylvania at Jessy's age, having the time of her life with her French friends, learning to ski and canoe, and dancing at *bals musettes* with low-life Frenchmen called *apaches*. She talked about my intense and artistic father, and how we left Paris for the United States in 1937, escaping the German occupation; and about her sadness at leaving the City of Light for grimy Chicago in the midst of the Depression. And she reminisced about her brother Jean, a biologist who stayed in Paris during World War II, hiding from Nazis in the hills of Auvergne, where his wife, Jeanne, came from; and about their daughter, my cousin Hélenè (named for my mother), also a biology professor, whom we planned to visit in France.

Marie-Jeanne lifted her champagne glass in a toast, and Jessy gulped hers down, as she had politely braved the eggplant quiche and soft cheeses. Looking at Jessy, so uncomfortable with new tastes, I realized how different we are—the differences residing in nurture, not nature, and I felt a sharp pang of regret. Jessy is more conservative than my family—especially in some of her values and dietary habits. These are things I might have influenced if I'd been a grandmother to her from birth, but I came into her education late, as did Alex, and we have no right to insist on our ways, although we try to open doors that were never opened to her before. No question, Jessy is a fine person, brought up with love and good intentions by her mother, her adoptive dad, and her grandparents. Still, if I had my druthers, my girl would care less about sports and more about fine arts, literature, and politics. She would eat more veggies and chicken paprika and less pizza, drink fewer cans of Mountain Dew, and not make faces at good wine

Now that she is in college, majoring in childhood education and volleyball, I urge Jessy to study more challenging subjects, to test her mind as well as her body, and then I remind myself the girl is only eighteen. She has years to make the choices that are right for her. Jessy is not going to throw herself into early marriage, as I did, or be a single mother like her mother, or join the marines as some of her friends have done. She doesn't even have a boyfriend. "I'm attracted to men," says Jessy, "but I don't really *like* them."

O U R   F I R S T   A F T E R N O O N in Montparnasse, Jessy and I lunched on the sidewalk at He Séléct, eyeing the passersby, distinguishing French people from tourists. All week, we raced from one landmark to another—Jessy's picks, for the most part: the Louvre; a train trip to Chartres; climbing up to Montmartre; Rodin's museum (where she was entranced by the story of Camelle Claudel); Napoléon's tomb; the Champs-Elysées; the Eiffel Tower, and a tour of Versailles led by an actual monarchist—where, miraculously, among thousands of tourists, we ran into her history teacher and his family.

Jessy became master of the Métro and bus lines, guiding me when I got lost. Sometimes she was annoyed by my confusion, and sometimes I was dismayed by her cool, but we never quarreled or exchanged harsh words—a good trick for women of strong minds, disparate ages and backgrounds, closeted with each other day and night for two weeks.

We dined late at La Coupole and Therieux. We clinked kir royales to each other's health, and, during afternoon rest stops at sidewalk cafés, I downed espressos while Jessy gulped six-dollar Cokes. She tasted her first lamb roast (which she liked) and foie gras (which she gagged on). Mostly, Jessy ate chateaubriand and french fries, green salads, and fancy desserts, and was ogled by waiters young and old, while I shocked her by ordering steak fartare and oysters, pâté, artichokes, cassis, and cassoulet. Mornings, I'd run across the street to bring home fresh croissants and *pains au chocolat*. After dark, when we returned to our little apartment, footsore and exhausted, I read myself to sleep while Jessy watched *Pirates of the Caribbean* on the portable DVD set she'd received as a graduation present. At first, I was appalled at her obsession, but then I realized the movie was like a lullaby for her, a reminder of home and who she was back there.

For me, the spice of our trip was introducing Jessy to French friends and relatives—to life inside the culture. We had Sunday lunch with Bill's editor, his translator wife, and their little boys; went with them as they voted for president of the European Union, and walked in the forest of Vincennes. We took tea with an expatriate novelist friend who lives in a countess's apartment on the rue Jacob, and sipped an aperitif with our landlady's Russian-French-American family in Montparnasse. But the high point was dinner with my cousin Héleène, her husband, Henri-Paul, and their engineer son, Nicolas, who is thirty-one and fluent in English, to Jessy's relief.

My French family lives in a suburb of Versailles, in a house full of art, surrounded by a rose garden, which looks down on a pasture where a white horse runs. Jessy was impressed by the house and her warm welcome, and I was glad, but also sad that my mother was not with us, or Hélène's mother, Jeanne, who died last year in full mind and body, at the age of 103. As I prepared to commemorate the occasion, I studied Jessy through the lens of my camera, seeing a large girl in white surrounded

by smaller, dark-clothed French people. I thought how odd it must seem
to her to be in this foreign house with these new relatives. But she acted
as easy and sweet as if she were in my house, perhaps realizing, as I do,
that she and I, my family and hers, are united in ways we both can and
cannot control: by blood and culture, and by the element that tran-
scends both: desire.

Which brings me to the end of my voyage with Jessy, and to the present she gave to me last Christmas. It is an enlarged and framed photograph taken from her digital camera. The two of us stand outside an
Iranian restaurant off the boulevard Raspail, where we have just finished our last meal in Paris. Cousin Nicolas has dined with us, and it is
he who clicks the shutter. I wear a knee-length ruffled black skirt patterned with white rings, and my unruly white hair is pulled back with a
clip. Jessy's shoulder touches mine. Her hands are clasped over her pink
skirt, the puka-shell necklace I bought for her in Hawaii rings her neck,
and her dark hair falls over her shoulders. We look into the camera,
smiling, happy. Perhaps it is the midnight light, or perhaps Jessy has deliberately printed the image with a sepia tone, but its faint brownish colors indicate times gone forever and, at the same instant, timelessness.

The picture tells me I have come full circle, and it tells me circles
never end. Spiraling toward infinity is, for me, the ultimate joy of growing old, and as close as I can get to imagining heaven. I realize that I
have become what I never dreamed of being, a doting white-haired
grandmother like my mother and her mother, come late to the role,
which makes it more enticing. My heart is filled with gratitude. Thank
you, Alex. Thank you, Robin. Thank you, Jessy. It was twelve years
a-coming, but arriving at last in grandmother land has been worth the
turmoil, the heartbreak, and all the lost days of our journey.

PART IV

WHAT WE KEEP

Being a grownup means assuming responsibility for yourself,
for your children, and—here's the big curve—for your parents.
— WENDY WASSERSTEIN

•

There is a fountain of youth: it is your mind, your talents,
the creativity you bring to your life and the lives of people you
love. When you learn to tap this source, you will truly have
defeated age.
— SOPHIA LOREN

•

I believe the true function of age is memory.
I'm recording as fast as I can.
— RITA MAE BROWN

•

When you get old, honey, you realize there are certain things that just don't matter anymore. You lay it all on the table. There's a saying: Only little children and old folks tell the truth.

— SARAH LOUISE DELANY

Lipstick and Bindi

The Middle Way

BHARTI KIRCHNER

The summer I turned eight, my mother decided to throw a ladies' tea party. We lived in a small town in eastern India then and she knew just about everybody in the neighborhood, where, commonly, households consisted of three or more generations. Mother's guest list exceeded fifty and included friends of her age and their children, as well as their mothers and grandmothers.

She even invited a sharp-tongued elderly neighbor, Radha, a newcomer to the area. The stoop-postured lady, quick to flare, would often point a wrinkled finger at some cowering adolescent while admonishing her for some perceived misconduct.

Early in the morning on the appointed day, I saw Mother slip into the kitchen. I sneaked in and stood silently in a corner to observe firsthand the culinary magic she would perform. The train of her workaday cotton sari tucked around her waist, she arranged chunks of charcoal on a bed of kindling in a clay stove and started a fire. A thin haze of smoke settled above our heads, but it was soon dissipated by a breeze blowing in through an open window. Before long, the coals glowed with just the right intensity, the right *aanch,* in Mother's word, for her to proceed. She chopped vegetables and pulverized cardamom seeds, glancing frequently at the ocean of milk simmering in a pot on the stove. Occasionally, she allowed me to stir the pot so the milk wouldn't foam over. As the sun rose higher in the summer sky, the air in the tiny kitchen grew stifling. Yet Mother remained cool and focused.

By early afternoon, savories and sweet nibbles filled one serving platter after another—rice dumplings in saffron-infused cream, milk fudge in sugar syrup, and triangular pastries stuffed with potatoes and almonds. But that wasn't the end of it. She sliced red-ripe mangoes, pitted white-fleshed lychees, and sectioned off yellow-green guavas. Even as I took in the mélange of fragrances, I noted the lines of fatigue around the corners of her eyes, the sheen of perspiration on her forehead, and secretly worried she had overworked herself.

Come four o'clock, the ladies began to arrive, their sandals musically slapping the tiled floor. Mother, dressed in a gold-brocaded sari and choker necklace and looking as fresh as a bride, welcomed them. The ladies were attired in silk, crepe, or georgette saris in green, orange, and peacock blue colors, and adorned with gold and silver jewelry. The widowed and the elderly were resplendent in their white clothing. Married women were distinguished by a red vermilion dot between their eyebrows, in accordance with ancient tradition; the young singles sported rainbow-colored bindis on their forehead, as was the current fashion.

More than a few kajal-lined eyes shot curious sideways glances at Aunt Radha as she walked in. She lowered her face.

Everyone was seated on a cool reed mat in our spacious drawing room, with me occasionally standing up for a better view. Curiously, no child, myself included, had any urge to go play outside. We felt comfortable in the company of the adults, and altogether part of the proceedings. Mostly, we were dazzled. The women seemed all-powerful, all-knowing, and so charmingly catty. They sipped rich, pungent chai, nibbled on delicacies, and gossiped, occasionally adjusting their voluminous saris. Uninhibited by the presence of men, many dropped the veils from their heads. They talked about their husbands in reverential terms, not referring to them by their first names, which would be disrespectful, but as "He" with a capital *H*. One grandmother smilingly spoke of her consort as "my boss," "my *karta*," though everyone knew who the real *karta* in that house was.

Then one woman broached a topic of current interest. "Did you hear Nehru's speech about national unity on the radio? He addressed the listeners as 'Brothers and Sisters.' I felt honored and included."

"We are an independent nation," countered another woman, "and now Nehru dares to raise the price of sugar? How will I manage? My children must have sweets in their tiffin boxes."

And so it went, a lively political debate, for over an hour. At this point, Aunt Radha, who'd been mostly silent, cleared her throat and straightened her posture. As the eldest present, she occupied a position in the center of the group. Mother's tacit seating arrangement assured her of this honor. The white sari she had draped around her smelled of new cotton.

"You just know how to make these singharas." Aunt Radha smiled at my mother, revealing a few missing teeth. "Never in my long life have I tasted such perfection."

Her sweet words shocked everyone. My mother, ever the poised one, smiled back and offered her another helping of singharas. Aunt Radha accepted, then proceeded to heap more praise on her hostess. Before long, she was regaling everyone with stories of her youth: "What childhood? My puberty came at ten, and at fifteen, I was married." She spoke of her marriage to a "puny man, twice my age, now dead," and also of her various maladies. The women seemed as intent on her as they'd been on politics, and she basked in their attention. If her eyes became misty, her voice still rang with conviction.

As the afternoon wore on, Mother ran out of food and had to send a domestic helper to the town. He returned with a basket of mangoes. By now, evening shadows were creeping across the floor, and it was time to light the kerosene lanterns. The room only became more animated as the mango platter changed hands and women shared their personal stories.

After the party was over and the guests had departed, Mother lingered with a close friend. Surrounded by the detritus of the party—stained teacups, empty plates with strings from mangoes clinging to them, and echoes of conversation—they took a few minutes to relax in easy chairs and listen to the music of myriad insects outside.

"I've never seen Aunt Radha so pleasant, so talkative," Mother mused. Her almond-shaped eyes, set deeper now, still burned with excitement. "We never knew the person inside her."

"She just needed the attention," her friend replied, "and a stage. And you gave it to her."

A stormy wind rattled the mahogany tree in our yard. Soon they rose from their chairs and puttered around the kitchen, this time dwelling on the subject of reverence for old age.

"Old is gold," Mother quipped.

"When I first got married," her friend said, "and I had to yield to the wishes of my mother-in-law, it was difficult. Some days she'd be unreasonable. I'd silently curse her. Now I realize she's old, but she's wise, and it's my duty to take care of her. I wash the dust off her feet, serve her first at mealtime, and ask her opinion before I make a major purchase."

As she went on, the list of obligations grew long, even hopeless, and began to sound oppressive to me. I slipped out the door.

Years later, I came to understand the full significance of Mother's inclusiveness, the benefit of sharing the mat and mangoes with friends of all ages. Growing up in a multigenerational household, I'd taken this important feature of our ancient society for granted. It seemed entirely natural at the time that everyone you encountered would become an aunt, mother, sister, or grandmother. They formed a web around you, gave your life a context; in turn, you added a missing thread to theirs. Age didn't get in the way of relating, nor did it build fences separating the generations. An older woman, even a curmudgeon like Aunt Radha, had a place in the scheme of things, in the living room of a neighbor, in the partaking of singharas. She wasn't shunned because she had missing teeth, a stooped posture, or an unpleasant personality.

In India, a country of a billion people with a meager per capita income, such a network of relationships helps mitigate the burden of advancing years and keeps one's spirits up.

Aging, as Indian scriptures dictate, is actually attainment. Life is divided into four phases, beads on a necklace. The *brahmacharya,* or student phase, in which you study with a teacher; the *grihastha,* or householder phase, in which you fulfill your obligations to family and society; the *vanaprastha,* or devotional phase, in which you turn your attention to spiritual pursuits; and finally the *sanyasi,* or renunciation stage, in which you give up worldly attachments and prepare to move on to the next life. Originally believed to apply to men only, women, too, are now perceived to be pursuing a similar blueprint of life.

If youth, which comprises the first two phases, is not particularly glorified, neither is maturity, exemplified by the last two, denigrated. You embrace each phase in its turn with quietude, adjusting your mind's focus as you do so. And therein lies the secret to gaining peace.

Not long after the tea party, my mother shared with me her personal philosophy of aging. In her early thirties then, she was standing in front of a long oval mirror, her lustrous black hair hanging down to her back. One slender finger pointed to a section of her center part, where she'd noticed a few nascent gray hairs. "If you pull them out," she said, "they won't multiply. But I'm not going to do anything of that sort. Hair doesn't matter. This body is just a shell anyway."

If one's body is a frail vessel liable to shatter at any time—here Mother might have been trying to insinuate a higher truth into my young mind—one's spirit, the content of the vessel, is immortal. And that's what counts.

When I reached my teens, our joint family gained another member: Aunt Nivedita—Uncle Kachi's new bride. Young, modern, just out of college, and dressed tastefully in pastel colors, she swapped the fashionable green-gold bindi on her forehead for the red vermilion dot of a married woman. She traded the comfort of her parent's home to live with her husband's relatives. If there were difficulties in adjusting, as there must have been—she couldn't visit her family as often as she'd have liked, for instance—she never showed it. Her face always radiated a serene expression, which put whoever was in her presence at ease. "Who wants to go shopping with me?" she'd ask in a gentle tone, and instantaneously all the children would clamor to accompany her.

An expert shopper, she knew just how to choose the right gift for each family member. And this talent, I later realized, came from her innate consideration for others. She spent her days teaching school and still found time to entertain, although, being of a younger generation, she took a new approach. She would take us—all three generations—out to dinner at a noisy high-ceilinged Chinese restaurant. Intrigued by the smells of soy sauce, toasted-sesame oil, and ginger, we boldly ventured into new terrain, sampling unfamiliar dishes, ones that our Indian taste buds joyously welcomed. Afterward, we would stroll in the park.

During these walks, invariably in close proximity to a vendor roasting peanuts under a shady tree and calling out to the passersby, Aunt Nivedita would often confide in me about how much she missed the close-knit family she'd grown up in. Her eyes would briefly cloud over. Then she'd direct her gaze at the vendor, at a flowering *mohua* tree, at a child crawling on grass, and that familiar calm expression would once again settle on her face. A moment later, she'd smile softly and ask me if I wanted peanuts.

Several years passed. I received my master's degree in mathematics and came to the United States for postgraduate studies. Finally, I'd have an opportunity to observe women's lives in a modern Western society, a privilege, to be sure.

At first, I was totally awed by the vastness of the land, the openness of the society, and the freedom women enjoyed. A woman spoke her mind in mixed company, didn't conceal her body under layers of clothing, and didn't defer to her elders. On the surface, a woman had it all—heady stuff that filled the flimsy blue aerograms I mailed home. My relatives wrote back, wanting to hear more.

Then the Thanksgiving holiday came. Along with a few other foreign students who resided in my dormitory, I was invited to the home of a couple with several young children. On that cool November evening, we gathered around a large table draped in a rust-colored cloth in a warm, cozy dining room. The centerpiece, a bowl of shining green apples, winter squash, and grapes, stood as a reminder of the bountiful harvest season. Soon the hostess spread the meal on the table—a twenty-pound roast turkey with wild-rice stuffing and a garnish of rosemary springs; garlic-infused red potatoes; feather-light rolls; cranberry relish; and pumpkin chiffon pie. The host recounted for us the story of the Pilgrims and their plentiful first harvest, and of the native people who celebrated the blessings of the land. Then he led us in a few words of grace. I was enchanted.

But one thing was distracting me: The elderly grandmother who happened to be visiting had been relegated to a seat at a small kitchen table with the children.

As the second helpings were served, I heard happy shrieks from the kitchen and craned my neck through an open doorway for a view. The children were daubing the tablecloth with cranberry sauce, mangling the smooth orange top of the pumpkin pie, running around the backyard and tossing turkey bones on the lawn, having a great time of their own. The grandmother sat alone, stone-faced and forlorn, staring down at the floor.

Why was grandmother banished to the kitchen?

I wondered if I should swap seats with her, or perhaps offer her my company. As soon as the meal was over, I went out to the spacious kitchen. Grandmother stood up from her chair, smoothed her A-line charcoal dress, and greeted me, her eyes coming alive. Except for a smear of berry red lipstick, she wore no makeup, and only minimal jewelry. Her dinner plate was untouched, save for a bare turkey bone.

She pulled up a chair for me. "You've come this far to study?"

Enthusiastically, I narrated how much knowledge I had already gained, not just in classrooms, and how thankful I was for the opportunity. In turn, she told me of her life in a small town in Nebraska, the "three-mile radius" where she was born, schooled, and married, and where she still resided. She expressed regret that she hadn't traveled much. These days, her husband long since departed, she led a solitary existence. Her contacts with relatives were infrequent, limited mainly to holidays. Yet she insisted that she, too, had "a lot to be thankful for."

"You're so young," she said appreciatively as we parted, "but you have taken time to talk to an old lady like me."

I felt a sense of warmth and compassion tinged with sadness that she should consider my attempt at friendship so unusual. But that's the way I was raised, I wanted to say to her.

Silently, I expressed gratitude to my extended family and to Mother for her multigenerational get-togethers.

I completed my studies, entered the software field, married, and settled into life in America. In the decades that followed, I matured, and now my generation is experiencing what we had once thought of as "middle-age issues." Many women complain about being made to feel uncomfortable about their age wherever they go. In a magazine article, even Gloria Steinem laments about entering a crowded room and finding herself "invisible."

Aging, I realize, is considered a loss—of youth, beauty, and fertility. Aging well mainly consists of looking young. A woman acquaintance, not quite forty, undergoes a painful and risky plastic surgery procedure because, she says, "Men don't notice me anymore."

True to the exuberant American spirit, there is a stubborn determination to conquer the aging process. When I run into an old friend after many years and comment that she hasn't changed much, I mean that as a compliment. In return, she fairly bristles. "But I have changed. It's just that I've had so much done to try to conceal the years. Botox, liposuction, you name it."

Do you fight, or do you make a graceful transition? At first, I was torn between the beliefs with which I was raised and the norms of my adopted country. But soon I carved a path of my own, what one might call "the middle way." After a few attempts, I gave up coloring my hair. Nor would I try using other artifices touted in the marketplace to make one appear younger. Natural is best, I have concluded. A devotee of fitness most of my adult life, I keep up with my hikes, Nautilus routine, stretching, and other forms of exercise. For me, the body isn't a shell. A sound body just might keep my mind sound. And, as far as the mental realm is concerned, I believe in staying fully engaged—a consistent writing schedule, art-house films, gallery walks, books, and the company of bright friends.

Periodically, I return to India to visit my family, and I find the country metamorphosing before my eyes. The population clock ticks faster and faster. There are disturbing signs of encroaching materialism— more television channels, more designer shops, and denser traffic—but I can still take a few consolations. Beggars roam the streets less often. Though nuclear families are becoming somewhat more common, extended families still happily gather at every holiday, at every opportunity. Respect for the elderly, now that my mother and her generation have passed on, seems not to have fallen by the wayside. At a friend's house, I was heartened to see the oldest guest, a septuagenarian, being served first at dinner. A young girl proudly introduced her grandmother, who was ensconced in a wheelchair.

In my absence, my female relatives have grown older. During my last visit, I noticed Aunt Nivedita moved more slowly, wore only white saris, shopped less, if at all, and mostly confined herself to home. Her once-smooth forehead showed a few wrinkles. She served me a take-out Chinese dinner. The customary smells of soy sauce, toasted-sesame oil, and ginger were there, but not the bustle of the Chinese restaurant we used to frequent.

I desperately wanted to recapture the old conviviality. "Would you like to try one of the new Chinese places?" I ventured. "Maybe we could walk the Botanical Gardens afterward."

"Oh, my aching legs," she said, demurring. "Perhaps the next time you come for a visit."

I could see that she had ascended to the next stage of her life, that her mind had shifted gears. In the brief silence that followed, she seemed to be offering a word of advice: Slow down. Don't be so frenetic. Contemplate on the insights you have gained. Listen to the silence within.

For the remainder of my stay, I was happy simply to sit at home with her whenever I could, lulled by her luminous tranquillity. If her career and family life hadn't quite lived up to her expectation, she seemed unconcerned. She wasn't trying to make up for any losses.

Back home in the USA, a writer friend tells me of her essay, entitled "Don't Call Me a Hag." An activist informs me of her own support group of "forty-five and over." A career woman of fifty asserts, "I will continue my glorious material life even in my old age." A grandmother paints her lips redder, indulges in a second helping of sorbet, and exhorts others not to fade into the night silently.

The lipstick color I choose these days is more muted than in the past. I no longer crave the sensual pleasure of a rich ice-cream sundae. As I plot my next novel, I realize that it is the ordinary daily happenings that keep me joyously on course: the thud of the morning newspaper landing on the porch, the wind soughing in the pines, a car alarm going off in the distance, the clock's reminder that it's time to do a brisk walk.

And off I go to the tree-fringed trails of Green Lake, where the first sound I hear is that of water slapping against the shoreline in a gentle rhythm. A gust of wind swirls around me, making my skin tingle and sending a shower of yellowing leaves fluttering down around my graying curls.

On the sandy shore to my left, a flock of crows seems to be holding a conference. Wings fluttering and head bobbing up and down, they compete for some common source of nourishment. Oddly, they remind me of my upcoming dinner party this weekend. Unlike Mother's tea, I'll host a mixed group, mostly married couples, except for Margaret. Quiet, single, and elderly, she tends to gravitate to a corner. I'll take time to chat with her, introduce her to others, and hopefully draw her into conversations. When dinner is served, I'll be sure to seat her at the end of the table, in the position of guest of honor.

Like my mother, I'll devote the entire day to cooking, though it'll not be strictly Indian fare. My plan is to mix and match flavors from many cuisines: Mirin-glazed salmon, spicy peanut rice, garden vegetables splashed with marinara sauce, a plum-chocolate tart flavored with amaretto. It'll be labor-intensive, but then, I am not ready to slow down, to enter the *vanaprastha* or *sanyasi* phase quite yet.

As I easily complete the three-mile loop and take on the challenge of an uphill climb toward home, a young race-walker in an orange vest, coming from the opposite direction, approaches me.

She mentions attending one of my recent readings at a local bookstore. "I really enjoyed your novel. Thanks so much for writing it." Shyly, she confides how she fancies writing a memoir and asks me if I might give her a pointer or two.

"I'll be most happy to."

We exchange E-mail addresses, then continue on our respective paths. Her encouraging words have added bounce to my steps. I can hardly wait to return to my latest chapter, to the dilemmas of my protagonist, and to see where the words and images will lead me next. I also feel inspired to pass on my experiences to a young person like this race-walker, to bolster her confidence; it's a goal I see myself pursuing more in the years to come.

Not long after this walk, I receive a call from India. Aunt Nivedita has died.

During the course of a day, whether sitting at my desk, striding out for another vigorous walk, or leisurely shopping for a gift, I recall Aunt Nivedita's gentle eyes, the flutter of her white sari, and her message: Accept your passage through life's stages with equanimity. If you are at peace with yourself, you'll find that each stage offers its own satisfactions.

I am midway, between two worlds, balancing between youth and old age. I take another step and I am happy.

The *So What* Days of Moo and Big

BEVERLY LOWRY

When my mother was in her last years, she grew her hair out and, on most days, let it lie long and straight down her back, like Willie Nelson's. She was in her sixties then, but life had ground down on her pretty hard and she looked older. So the impression her hairdo gave was that of an old woman trying to look like a girl. In those days, she also sported a fuzzy red hat with a ball on top—a cheap, silly knitted thing, kind of a tam-o'-shanter golfer's cap with a bill—which she wore at a tilt and almost never took off, even in the high-summer heat of Texas.

So what hair? I remember thinking then and still think now. *So really what?*

I am, as I write this, three years older than my mother was when, late one Memorial Day afternoon following a family gathering, she sat down on the couch in my living room and, complaining of a headache, sank into herself and abruptly disappeared from time and thinking. I was right there; so were my father and my husband. Leaning into her, we called her name, thinking to bring her back. But she kept going, and even if she could hear us, she had no way to return. Her mind had been stilled by a massive stroke, which, by noon the next day, killed her.

Nobody thought she would go first. Daddy was older; his own father had keeled over in his mid-sixties: Daddy had hereditary diabetes and heart trouble. He'd been overweight his whole life; he was the one who had done—was still doing—all the drinking. Now I wonder why we were so surprised. Daddy brought a lot of life to the party all right, but he also took up more than his share of it, leaving Mama to do the nasty cleanup the next morning. Less than a year after her death, Daddy entered a thirty-day impatient treatment center for alcoholics, so debilitated from daily quarts of vodka that he could not walk, stand, or sign his name. At a meeting I went to there, a man with a chalkboard drew a quick picture of a crowned, bawling child. This was, he proclaimed, the chemical dependent among us, "His or Her Highness the Kid." And then he sketched the rest of us, smaller by far, gathered in a circle around the big one, and described the roles we'd been given to play. The spouse, he reckoned, tended to be either a do-gooder, making up for unending bad behavior, or a recluse. That was Mama, in later years, the recluse: Enough was enough; she flat opted out. And the man went on to describe the rest of our family, my two brothers and me, with such stunning accuracy, it was as if he he'd been reading our mail. The oldest child he named the standard-bearer, out front with the flag, perfectionist, straight A's, number one down the straight and narrow, drawing attention away from the chaos at home. My response was immediate: tears and utter acceptance (I knew he was right) accompanied by a quick shot of relief knowing I wasn't alone or to blame. The number-two child was usually the scapegoat. And he sketched a wild child, who did his best to distract attention from home life by causing trouble serious enough to do the job. David is three years younger than I and in high school had been labeled a juvenile delinquent—ducktail, hot rod, cigarette pack rolled up into his T-shirt sleeve—after consistently breaking the law. The third child was usually either a jokester—life of the party, lovable prankster—or the shy child who wanted only to withdraw into a corner and escape notice. One time, after I was married, I returned home from New York, where I was living then, and during one horrific night of drinks, flying bottles, and screaming fights, I found Eddy, the baby, twelve years old, hiding in the night beneath a bush, the chemical dependent's third child, the shy version. The shock for me at the meeting that night was not only to find out that somebody could key into my family life this way but that the man who did it was a Dale Carnegie kind of guy with chalkboard and jokes.

THE AMBULANCE TOOK Mama to the San Marcos, Texas, hospital, and the next morning, we—my father, brothers and I—gathered there. My father's doctor asked us to go into the ICU, where she lay, struggling for breath, still unconscious. Standing at her head, he told us that our mother's carotid arteries were completely clogged, to prove which, he put a stethoscope against her neck and asked us to take turns listening. Could we hear the whir? This, he said, didn't happen overnight; why hadn't she come to him? Later on, we remembered things. She'd been forgetful, a little off track, but Moo—as we called her in those days—was like that: She lived in her own time—Moo time and saw things the rest of us couldn't, heard what birds were saying, listened to the night. She'd had polio, a heart problem of her own, her gallbladder out. She'd smoked cigarettes for some forty-five years. Her own mother had died of a stroke. When we went through her stuff after her death, we found diaries that indicated that *she* knew something serious was up, even if we didn't. But she didn't like doctors anymore and she didn't say anything. And whether or not we should have had an inkling of it on our own, we didn't. The suddenness shocked us all and changed our family in ways we could never have predicted, the effects of which we still feel today, some twenty-odd years later.

Born Dora Lee Smith, she grew up in small-town Arkansas, the youngest of three and the only daughter. Her one baby picture shows her sitting in an enamel basin on the front porch of a shacky wooden house, flanked by brothers, her hair a froth of pale curls. She's holding on to the lip of the basin and smiling big, as if envisioning an exciting life ahead, no telling what good things to jump into. At seventeen, she'd been a beauty queen, crowned, dressed in lacy white, riding enthroned on a white float down the main street of Marvell, Arkansas. In those years she wore her hair curved in deep, tight waves down the sides of her face and, in pictures, affected a sultry expression, looking over her shoulder, blue eyes alive with fizz, taking the camera lens head-on. By then, in what may have been a lifelong rage against her own womanhood, Dora Lee's mother, Polly, had pretty much whipped the easy smile from her face and a lot of the bold joy from her heart. After Mama's death, I found a packet of folded Big Chief notebook pages she'd left for me to read ("For BEV ONLY" printed on the outside fold), telling of a time in high school when her menstrual period was late and she thought she was pregnant. Polly, she said, kept a calendar marking the twenty-eight-day cycle, and so there was no way to hide or keep her fears to herself. She had had a date with a boy, and in the car they'd kissed and he had moved against her, and when she got home, she discovered "messy stuff" on her skirt. Polly hit her daughter when she heard this news and gave her vile medicine to drink; Mama said she would sit in a classroom, looking out the window, thinking her life was over. Then her period arrived, which, she presumed, was because of the medicine. Soon after that, when she began dating Daddy, she told him this story. Shocked at how little she knew or had been taught, he told her she couldn't have been pregnant and was kind to her and took her side in the endless wars with her mother. She and David Fey ran off to Memphis to get married, the two of them and another couple, on a double date. Marriage to Daddy, Mama always said, saved her from Polly's mean streak and the peach-branch whalings she used to dole out. But Mama wasn't a pushover; she had a hot temper and she had her ways and she was a looker. In a talent show, she once sang a low-throated, blasé version of "You Turned the Tables on Me." When she was only nineteen, I was born.

She remained a blonde for most of her life, but in her last years she gave up dye jobs and let her hair take on whatever color age and nature decreed, which turned out to be muted shades of brown highlighted with the occasional strand of silvery gray. She had good hair, thick and heavy, the kind beauticians love to work with and style. When I was in high school, my friends and I especially admired her sleek pageboy—down one side of her face to her shoulders in a perfect roll—which we deemed more nearly perfect even than her golden French twist and the ethereal Gibson-girl upsweep she occasionally went for.

But by her last days, life had dripped slow and heavy on her for a long time, and in a kind of in-your-face response, which stemmed directly, if not completely, from her age, she'd given up artifice pretty much entirely. *My hair, my head, my life. I get to be the one to say.* No makeup, no curlers, no visits to the beauty parlor, and I don't remember the last time I saw her in a skirt. She was small, but her favorite outfit combined an oversized red-and-blue-striped rugby shirt handed on by one of her high school–age grandsons with cheap stretch pants and lace-up Rockports, providing support for her bad foot. She wore big-ass drugstore glasses, parted her hair in the middle, tucked it behind her ears, brushed it long down her back, and out she went, she and Daddy in that big Ford LTD of theirs, taking the world head-on . . . the world of the Wimberley, Texas, IGA, where they shopped for groceries, and the San Marcos Wal-Mart, where she bought her art supplies.

WHEN I PASSED my own sixty-third birthday, I made no particular note of it as the age my mother was when she died, the way some people do, thinking, From now on I am living on borrowed time. Not because I don't believe in fate or genetic disposition; I have just always felt so different . . . not just from her in particular, although there's that, but from her generation, from all the mothers of all the friends I had growing up. Every woman I know who's my age feels a great jag between our generation and the one before. But sometimes I think, *So what the jag and so what feelings of difference?* Genes catch up with us; people exercise, eat low-fat foods, drink in moderation, floss twice a day, only to keel over at the exact same age as a butter loving parent. These are irrefutable facts, yet I roll on, blinkered and perky, trained in the willed refusal to discount that which does not serve or advance by the master of the art, my father, whose grandchildren knew him first as, "Big Daddy" and then as plain "Big." He instilled in my brothers and me a belief in luck and the long shot that took hold in ways that I, for one, would never have expected, cannot justify, and have a hard time still acknowledging with a straight face.

But Big was a force more than a parent, and all of us felt his power. My mother lived under his sway and according to the direction of his whims and grand ideas, but we, my brothers and I, learned how to operate from him. To this day, whatever room we walk into, in whatever city or state, he is there, singing "Georgia," "Ain't Nobody Here But Us Chickens," or "Right String, Baby, But the Wrong Yo-Yo." Strumming his four-string banjo or pounding the piano with his fat fingers, looking back over his shoulder, giving us that MoonPie smile. *All night long!* I am a product of his songs and stories, the elegantly devised diversions and subterfuges he performed. And sometimes, looking over the life I have been leading for the past fifteen years, I wonder, *Am I becoming him? Am I turning into Big Daddy?*

When my family lived in Greenville, Mississippi, where I grew up, we went by the middle-class model of that time and place and left money-making up to Daddy. Disaster, therefore, cooked up a daily stew. But we *looked* prosperous enough, and no matter how low he tumbled, he always bounced back, shaved, perfumed, and ready. There was always a new dream of another fortune around the next corner, and besides, in the Mississippi Delta, nobody saved a penny that I knew. What counted was not how much money a man made or had; all that mattered—assuming his skin was white—was his line of credit. And because my father was a salesman to his bones and brought that much life to the party, he could talk his way into almost anything he wanted. The last time I was in Mississippi, a man in his fifties came up to me and said, "I used to sit on your daddy's lap when he played Santa Claus and came to our house. I still have a picture." And the next day, another man said, "Your daddy and I were in the 1956 Lions Club Womanless Wedding. He played the bride." This never fails to happen when I am there. *Aren't you David Fey's daughter?* And so he rolled on, singing his songs and borrowing more than he had a right to, riding the outside limit of his credit, gambling away whatever security we might have stored up, and we lived as if luck would never run out and money was never a problem, because who knew what big thing would happen next. In his fifties, Big began life as a commodities salesman, trading in pork bellies and cocoa beans. After some deals went sour (but before the pig meat was delivered to our door), investors from four states launched claims against him amounting to a quarter of a million dollars, at which point we took everything out of his and Mama's name—right down to his checking account—and with my husband Glenn's help, I became a guardian of my parents' financial life.

A careful girl throughout my elementary and high school years, I *hated* the uncertainty of that time, and the steady string of changes, the loss of furniture, cars, houses, and face, all of it. But there we were and there Daddy was, and my brothers and I learned quickly to adapt, to move on from yesterday's life into tomorrow's, to keep our feet light on the earth in order to move quickly when we needed to. And whenever we moved into the next new rent house, we cruised it together while the rooms were still empty, so that Daddy could ask his usual "Now, where will we put the Christmas tree?" Eddy, being the youngest, was of course the most hopeful and got the biggest kick out of this. Oh, Daddy's spirit was indeed large, and in many ways it fed us. And long after we all moved to Texas, following the tradition of people who tapped out in the Deep South, a banker wrote a book about rogues and rascals from the Delta who had played fast and loose with other people's money. In that book, Daddy was deemed a "rascal." My father got a big kick out of his new title and seeing his name in print. My mother tossed the book in the garbage.

And so by his example, our father taught us to ignore what we didn't want to think about or what could not be remedied or even helped by mental perambulation. As a commission salesman, he used to say, "If you have a bad day, it doesn't mean you'll have a bad week; if you have a bad week, it doesn't mean . . ." and so on. Like a stand-up comic after a dud performance, the commission salesman has to move on and make believe he has never had a failure in his life. All of this became part of my brothers and me, as firmly fixed as a stutter. We could put marbles in our mouth, learn tricks, talk around it, but the habit was as intransigently fixed as our brown eyes and high foreheads.

My mother, on the other hand, felt small to her heart, scared, even doomed perhaps. I believe that more than anything else, she wanted to have a nice home and to be a good middle-class mother and wife. Instead, we moved and moved and never knew what would happen next, from one morning to the next. But she and Daddy had a passionate, tumultuous relationship, which lasted. He bought her lavish gifts—the 1954 white T-bird with the detachable black roof and red leather interior, the Baldwin Acrosinc piano—and she held on to them as long as she could. For a long time, he made her laugh. They had their psychic arrangements, which neither of them could have expressed and which, I am convinced, neither of them understood or wanted to. They went on.

————

AND SO I said to myself when my mother grew out her hair and let it lie straight and long down her back like Alice in Wonderland's, *So what hair?* And anyway, who says someone else is too old to wear it which way and what these things matter and how much, if at all. Is there a natural order to all of this, or what?

Daddy was still drinking during those years, but the two of them were living a pretty secluded life by then, in a small stone house in the Texas Hill Country, and since my husband, Glenn, and I had not only bought the house for them but had also taken responsibility for their debts and much of their income, no one badgered her anymore about unpaid bills or threatened her with repossession and subpoenas. She'd kicked cigarettes and the prescription drugs she'd relied on for years. She'd given up on doctors, relying on a giveaway magazine she picked up at the health-food store. She used to pay on their huge remaining medical bills with small monthly checks, five dollars and under, having read that as long as you paid something, they couldn't sue. When she weaned herself off of pain pills, she wrote "I KICKED PERCODAN!" at the bottom of one Houston doctor's bill and swore that after that, she never got another.

My mother felt finally free then, I think, and the eccentric way she presented herself to the world showed it. She started taking art classes from a local woman who worked out of her house in Wimberley. She got a lot of work done during the years when she let her hair hang free, mostly watercolors—many of them, of the scrub oaks that emerge, gnarled and dark, from the stony ground of central Texas, some bright representations of sunsets in that landscape, and many, oh so very many, redbirds, which she fed and talked to. She talked also to her striped yellow cat—named Coletty, after the French writer Colette, whose bohemian life she admired, having read about it in a book I gave her—trying to convince her it was okay to kill mice but not birds.

Her work now hangs on my walls and in the homes of my brothers and son. She'd taken piano lessons as a girl but was too scared to play anywhere except at home, but the work of a visual artist suited her, and she had talent. She was working hard and she was getting better. Her sketchbook gives proof of her diligence, all those awkward drawings of her own hand and then her left foot—the good one—and, in the middle of the next page, a particularly appealing watercolor of a single pink-and-yellow-striped sock. And so at this late stage in the game, life was providing her with some new gifts. She was progressing, moving; she had a plan. I think if she'd had time, she might have become a town character in Wimberley, maybe doing tai chi on the Blanco or reading tarot cards at the outdoor market.

But then as writer Barry Hannah once said, "Life doesn't always curl out the way we expect it to, does it?"

Doesn't, hasn't, won't. We uncurl with it or knot up into ourselves in a permanent charley horse.

Sometimes, in fact, she pulled her hair back behind her ears and caught it in a low ponytail, especially when she drew.

In times of trouble, for comfort we look for the "at leasts." At least my mother did not live to experience the death of my son Peter, her grandson, in a hit-and-run incident in 1984, and I am grateful for that. She and Peter had a special relationship, and I frankly cannot imagine her getting through his funeral and the days—weeks, years—to come. She did not have to live through the amputation of both my father's legs, the failure of his body as his organs shut down one by one, or his death, in 1988. Those were hard years. It's good she missed them. Then in 1991, I left my marriage, an act that would have terrified her for my sake, and broken her heart, had she been alive then.

Since then, I have been steadily on the move, all over the country, and now the big question is, as it always has been, *What will happen next?*

In the thirteen years since my divorce, I have lived in fourteen different houses in six different states, alone for stretches, then not. Two weeks after meeting and falling for a British actor named Keith, I drove with him to Los Angeles, where he pursued Hollywood jobs and we lived in an apartment on the borderline between ritzy Hancock Park and the always-dicey southeast. At first, we had no furniture, not even a bed. From our small patio we could see the smoke from the riots there in 1992. A line of royal palms flanked a street just this side of the southeast area. From Los Angeles, we moved to Missoula, Montana, where I had a job. There, we lived in six houses in three and a half years, all of them temporary house-sits except one, a house I bought and sold in less than two years' time. In Montana, I learned to drive in snow and, after escaping summer by diving into a cool pool my entire life, learned what it was like to swim in natural hot springs surrounded by snow-laden evergreens; gained weight, lost weight; got a dog; adapted to a higher altitude; bought a four-wheel-drive SUV for the snow. During our three and a half years in Missoula, I held at chair at George Washington University in D.C., a yearlong job. Afterward, I went back to Montana, secured a tenure-track teaching job, but before I could sign the contracts, we left and went back to Washington, D.C., where I bought another house, even though neither of us had a job. We managed, somehow, Big Daddying along, thinking I'm not sure what, exactly.

IN 1998, THE year I turned sixty, life changed. I took another visiting job at the university in Tuscaloosa, Alabama, this one for one semester. Less than a month after I began teaching there, I went to Huntsville, Texas, for my last visit with my friend Karla Faye Tucker, who was under a death sentence for capital murder and then, in February, was executed by the state of Texas. Soon afterward, my relationship with Keith crashed. In May, we parted and I drove with Lucy, my beloved dog, to Austin—my most reliable refuge—to have my hip joints replaced. From my hospital bed, I sold the D.C. house and used the equity money from the sale to live on, alone, for a year in Austin in a sweet little house on Avenue D. Giving Lucy to a family broke my heart, but I had to. In the Avenue D house, I learned to walk straight again by doing a dance on crutches around and around the house. I cut my hair and, thinking I'd enjoyed my share of sex, made a vow and gave it up, then on Christmas Eve, after ingesting illegal mushrooms with a friend, decided I wanted a bigger share after all. In January of my sixty-first year, I became reacquainted with a man named Tom, whom I'd met in D.C. while teaching at GWU He was working as a strategic campaigner for the United Steelworkers of America, a job that involved constant travel. I was on the road a good bit myself, doing research for a biography I was writing. Our first meeting was in Indianapolis. And after that, we created a road-warrior kind of life, meeting up in various cities across the country—Des Moines, Chicago, Indianapolis, St. Louis, Pittsburgh, D.C., Clinton, Tennessee, Baton Rouge, Austin. For the past four years, he and I have been in what my students call a "committed relationship," which I hope will last from now on. After I lost my D.C. apartment and spent one summer house-sitting in Wimberley, Texas, and another writing the end of my book in Marfa, Texas, at Chinati, an Army base converted into an artists' colony, we finally moved into a place together, ten blocks from the U.S. Capitol in D.C. Then we moved again, and now we live in Buffalo, New York. As I write this, however, I am sitting in a furnished apartment in Fresno, California, where I am living alone and holding a one-semester visiting job at California State University in Fresno. Tom and I meet up in various cities where various members of our respective families live: Seattle, Stockton, Austin, Houston. Unlike us, our brothers, his and mine, and my son own homes and reside in them fairly permanently. I keep a yoga mat in my car, another in Austin, where my son Colin lives, and another in Buffalo. I have hair dryers in all three places, also bathing suits, swimming pools, gyms, hairdressers, coffee shops with Wi-Fi. My doctors are in D.C., and so if something happens in one of the other cities, I'll have to improvise. In a couple of months, Tom and I will drive from Fresno to Buffalo. Having traded in the SUV for a brand-new snappy city car, in a terrible financial deal, I then traded in the brand-new city car for a three-year old all-wheel-drive Buffalo kind of car. Having given away my snow gear upon my exit from Montana, I will purchase new on our way, somewhere between Austin, where we will spend Christmas (and swim in Stacy Pool, since it is heated), and Buffalo. In January, I will begin commuting from Buffalo to what has been my regular job for six years now, teaching in the MFA program at George Mason University in Fairfax, Virginia. I will leave my car in Washington, spend the two nights a week I am there with a friend. Medicare-eligible, I still remain on the university health-insurance rolls and have no plans to retire from my job.

Plans? Life curls out as it will, and sometimes I wonder, *So what plans?* Because in the end, who knows *what will happen next?* The big question, compared to which no other comes close in terms of size and possible blowback. What will happen next and how can I find the model to go by, and will somebody tell me when I need to change my hair, wear more makeup, lengthen my skirts, loosen my jeans, give up body-sculpt classes, live a different life, moderate, in other words, my passion for excess and change?

We go by signs, symbols, and fashion flashes, a world in which, as it turns out, nothing, in fact, is *so what* because everything matters: hair, hemline, gestures. Clueless how to deal with these questions rationally, I look instead for scenes, situations, the perfect story.

In my wedding album, there is a picture of the three mothers in the wedding party: my mother, my grandmother, my future mother-in-law. They are standing in the vestibule of the First Presbyterian Church chapel where Glenn and I were married, in Memphis, Tennessee. All three of the women are looking slightly askance off to the right, presumably at someone entering the church—I have no idea who—but if in nothing else, they are united in general disapproval at this moment. They are wearing slim dresses—sheaths, they were called then, I believe—small hats, gloves, and lipstick. It is June, and so their dresses have cap sleeves and reveal their meaty upper arms. But it is the way they are holding their purses that is so striking. Their elbows are crooked, forearms across their midsection as if either to hide their stomachs or to ward of purse snatchers. The purses bob against their bellies. It seems to me all women carried their purses in this way back then. Queen Elizabeth II still does. I do not, nor do my friends.

So what purses? We do not need to ask.

I began getting gray hairs in my early thirties, a few. Until I left the South, my hair had always been straw yellow, bleached by sun and chlorine-drenched springs, summers, and early falls. When Glenn and I married and moved to Manhattan, there being little chance for sunbathing or lifeguarding on the Upper West Side, where we lived, the blond grew out and my true dark color came through. The year Mayor Robert Wagner declared New York to be a Summer Festival, I did swim in a water ballet in the now-demolished Coliseum on Fifty-ninth Street, but that tiny bit of chlorine was not enough to taint my brown tresses, especially since the show closed after a week.

In my middle fifties, that sprinkling of gray hairs became a band of silver around my face. This happened all at once, if not quite overnight, the year of Peter's death. As in many other instances of change, I didn't notice until someone else did, in this case a Houston hairdresser, who, upon seeing me the first time, couldn't hide his shock. I saw his look and thought, Oh . . . I can date photographs of myself from those years by the color of my hair, whether before or after 1984, when it turned. Since then, the gray (I prefer to think of it as silver) has increased and turned almost white. I have considered coloring it, and have asked specialists to make the rest of my head match the front. But this, they say, is impossible; the only thing they can do is dye the whole thing blond, brown, black or red, and am I sure I really want to go to the trouble and expense and become a honey blonde like every other woman my age?

Silver so really what? I like it; other women say they do. But occasionally a child will call me grandma, and I know the hair is why. No one has ever questioned my request for a senior discount, and having a face-lift would not change this if I didn't dye my hair, because hair counts first and most indelibly. I am, however, relieved of any need or urge to lie about my age. One time, an ardent suitor significantly younger than I asked my age. I thought a minute and then told him the truth. What was I going to do, shave off five years?

Age is a puzzle. How to act, dress, what other people see. In Buffalo, a few months ago, I was in our favorite coffeehouse, alone, waiting for my cappuccino, when a man turned back and looked at me and wouldn't look away. "I'm looking, yes," he said. "I'm looking." And he told me he drove a dump truck but that the ground was too wet to drive in, so he was off. And what was I doing today? When I told him I lived with someone, he flashed a charming smile and said, "Well . . . is he at work?" He was probably in his forties, nice-looking. What was up? I left Spot shaking my head, flattered, amused, but mostly just plain flummoxed.

At a beer hall in Marfa, Texas, I once danced the fire out of "Mambo No. 5" with a Mexican-American macho guy, who afterward told me repeatedly that I'd danced him down, a fact that seemed to shock him and which he then turned against me by calling me Granny and asking what I was doing there. Up until which moment, I wasn't thinking about age at all.

In Austin last summer, on the Town Lake trail, I took a spill off a bicycle. Nothing serious, an ordinary spill, over the top and down on one arm. I came home to my son's house with what cyclists call "road rash," a sprinkle of bleeding bumps and scrapes across the outside of my forearm. Nothing really. But by the next week, the blood had pooled and become a blue-red splotch the entire length of the meaty side of my arm. The bumps were not healing; if anything, they looked even worse. Weeks later, I could still feel the wounds, like small pebbles lodged beneath my skin. And I remembered my grandmother Polly, my mother's mother, picking bits of glass from her shins years after a car accident she'd had in the central California valley where she lived, not far from where I am now teaching. She used to hold up a sliver for me to see. I could see nothing but didn't much want to look anyway. I was a young girl and all I could think was, When is she ever going to stop talking about her legs? She's *fine*." I remember Polly now because now I know how long the smallest scratch takes to heal when you have lived this many years. I also remember those same blue-red splotches on my mother's arms, which she said came from the cortisone she took, but they didn't. Skin thins; blood pools. Time creates splotches. The first week I was in Fresno, the temperature reached 105 degrees. My arm was ugly and not like my own. My choice was either to cover up like Martha Graham when, declaring herself too old to be looked at anymore, she swathed herself in yards of cloth or wear my same sleeveless shirts and, like Big the morning after, just go on. Fashion counts; pride counts. But I like my arms out, so—went on and wore sleeveless and made no comment.

There is no way to figure it except as it comes.

The last Christmas my mother was alive, she had me take a picture of Daddy and her standing before a huge pyracantha bush in the side yard of their little stone house. She wanted to use the picture for a Christmas card, something I don't believe she had ever done in her life. I was a little startled. It was odd, after all these years, to be sending people your picture, especially when you didn't know that many people anymore and you knew you look so much older. But she wanted to do it, "A picture of Daddy and me," she said. "By the berries." Maybe she knew it was her last Christmas and she wanted it recorded. I don't know, but I think she wanted to see what she looked like in her new getup and look. They stood there. I snapped a couple of shots. She took the film to the drugstore and had the photos made into cards and sent them around.

The pyracantha is laden with red-orange berries, the limbs bent down with their weight. Mama has half-draped a limb over her shoulder and is gently pinching a stem of green and red between her thumb and forefinger. She's pulled her long hair back in a low ponytail for the occasion, and she's wearing her red hat, the red-and-blue rugby shirt, and her big-ass glasses. Daddy is standing beside her, his big belly pushed against her. They are pressed closely together in a way that I think indicates some warm feelings for each other, perhaps even love, after all those years and so many troubles. He is smiling a camera-conscious, fakey smile, but she is just standing there looking really, I think, happy.

I look at that picture now and see a woman who in a life of chaos and trouble has finally found a measure of calm, and things of natural beauty not only to look at but to paint. In those last days, I believe, she simply *loved* that long hair streaming down her back like Willie Nelson's, no matter what happened next. And like a girl, she was proud to have grown it.

The Reluctant Bedouin

DIANA ABU-JABER

There is something wanton above a move, a great laying waste, deliberately tearing up connections and familiar rhythms, shredding your daily reality in exchange for who knows what. Moving rates up there with all the great forms of loss, staggers you in your tracks, makes you wake up wondering where you are, makes you wake up thinking, I just want to go on back home. It is a small death, a rift in reality, to physically remove yourself from friends and family. And perversely, it seems that this is something we choose to do.

I was forty-two years old and had already settled into what I'd assumed was meant to be my "real life"—working on my novels; teaching writing at Portland State University; sharing a lovely bungalow with my husband, Scott—when I heard about a faculty opening at the University of Miami. Why not? I thought. Miami had long been one of our fantasy destinations. My parents had purchased a winter home in South Florida and my husband and I had visited several times and loved it. After a decade of relentless steel-gray Oregon drizzle (the five-day forecast featuring the same graphic of a cloud dropping rain, as repetitive as a Warhol print), after switching all our lightbulbs for full-spectrum happiness bulbs, we'd started talking about a getaway bungalow on a sunny beach.

Still, that was fantasy. I hadn't really planned to leave my home in Portland. Scott and I had good jobs, a house, no kids, but a shivery little Italian greyhound who tries to impersonate a child. I had a new novel coming out, we had great friends, neighbors, a community. Even—do I dare to say this?—happiness. In the past, I'd moved around a lot, and it had always been a pleasurable chaos, but then I managed to stay put for ten years. It was long enough to sense the dark side of moving.

When the University of Miami called me back for an on-campus interview, Scott and I got caught up in the pleasure of the pursuit, of being pursued, of imagining a whole new life for ourselves. I flew down for the interview and then received the job offer a few days later. We deliberated; made lists of pros and cons; monopolized dinner-party discussions with the question of the move. Was it right? Were we crazy? Would we like it? No one really knew—very few of our friends had ever actually been to Miami—but everyone had an opinion anyway. "Miami isn't a place that normal people go to live," our friend Andrew proclaimed. Mavis said, "Well, you can always come back."

We began to learn more about what Portlanders thought of Portland. It's not easy to get to Portland overland—it's surrounded with mountain ranges, ocean, and desert. Like a mountain kingdom, it glories in its seclusion, its views of Mount Hood, the Willamette River, its rose gardens, coffeehouses, and farmers markets. It seems enchanted, a world apart, special and remote. People were incredulous that anyone would ever want to leave once they actually got there. Certainly not someone in the middle of her life and career, and certainly not to a place like Miami! "That's like something you do when you're twenty years old and want to go live on the beach in your bikini," one of my twenty-year-old students (in a polar-fleece jacket) observed—not quite finishing her thought that no one past thirty-five has any business in a bikini.

If there was one generalization that finally seemed to come clear for me, it's that every place is different for every person. And it finally dawned on me that the way each individual feels about places changes, as well—from year to year or from day to day. I know this is true for myself: I can go from worshiping a glorious sunrise to grousing over a bad morning in traffic. For all the friends who told us not to go, there were plenty of people who'd admitted that occasionally—sometimes frequently—they felt prompted by the same urgings, the drive to explore, to break free and reinvent themselves. So many of us, wading into our forties, felt something that might have once been called a midlife crisis but what might also be considered a resurgence of curiosity: something I'd rather refer to as "the call of the wild."

I remember talking on the phone with one of my closest friends, once again discussing the idea of moving; my friend was saying how it requires a sort of audacity to leave not only everything but everyone and sail into the unknown. I'd first come to Oregon when I was thirty years old and had felt, at the time, like I was traveling to the ends of the earth. Everyone back in New York certainly thought so. But when I was thirty, I could live on the pure distilled juices of adventure. Over a decade later, though, I thought it was time for me to be through with adventure. I had a good life, an easy, comfortable life—wasn't that something to relax into and enjoy?

My friend considered this and said, "Yes, you're comfortable there, but even so, you've always seemed a bit restless in Portland. You know, maybe if you go, you'll get to be even happier."

I WAS WELL acquainted with the notion of moving in search of happiness. My father, a Jordanian immigrant to America, is descended from Bedouins. Genetically nomadic, he moved our family between Jordan and America several times, both literally and metaphysically. I was raised on my father's nostalgic recollections of the old country, to which all other places paled in comparison. Of course, the key to this sort of nostalgia is that you must never actually attempt to return.

So we would move back to Jordan. My friends and languages switched overnight, nothing smelled the same or looked the same. And as soon as we got there, the family, the people, the entire country would fail to live up to my father's expectations. Suddenly—almost magically—the country we'd just left would turn into the country behind the looking glass—the place where all good things and good people were. It seemed that the harder he tried to pursue the good place, the true home, the further it slipped from his grasp.

But this was all a part of the pleasure, as well. Because would you ever really want to come to that perfect resting place, like the heaven where nothing ever happens? One of the possible side effects of being chronically dissatisfied with where you are is the perpetual pleasure of anticipation for the next place. And, of course, as long as there is something unsatisfactory with the place where you are, you don't have to worry too much about whatever it might be that's making you feel so dissatisfied with things in general.

This observation is meant affectionately. Especially now that I feel I've inherited the same condition and know how strange it is—how estranging—and that there is no easy path for a person who lives in a state of chronic longing.

We moved households nearly every year when I was growing up. People thought my father was in the military. I was constantly asked, "Why does your family move so much?" I truly didn't know the answer, I just thought this was natural, that movement, flight, and restlessness was a natural state of being.

As a young child, I accepted this state of affairs—I was easy! I had great appreciation for the way Jordanian kids got to run around loose in the streets and alleyways, their facility for openness, curiosity, and affection. In America, I openly admired the gleaming lunch boxes, bicycles, and hip-hugger slacks that the kids wore, their cool, sophisticated style. But as I got older, all the moving wore on me: I began to be dimly aware that there were other ways of doing things. I learned, to my suddenly intense envy, that not everyone moved to a different place every year. And I discovered that the new kid in school was always at a distinct disadvantage.

And so now Scott and I focused on advantages and began writing our lists of good reasons to move—like being closer to our families, a hankering for sunshine and great Cuban food. But then there were also the intangibles, like a deliberate contrariness, the impulse to try to bookmark life, create chapters, so perhaps there would be something contained, a set piece to contemplate. There was my sense that I'd come to the point of wanting more—personally and professionally—I wanted to create more space for my writing. And in this last reason I saw that happiness or the lack of it didn't necessarily reside in finding that one Good Place, but rather in the freshness that could come of starting over, in a different angle of light, in the blank page that allows a person to write a new sort of book

"IT'S THE SEASON!" Our realtor proclaimed as she bustled in with a stack of brochures. "Everyone loves to move when it gets warm!"

The brochures extolled the virtues of our home in that laudatory lingo peculiar to real estate fliers and personal ads: "Gorgeous view! Landscaped lot! Three fireplaces!" I stared at it and thought, Gosh, now why are we leaving again?

Packing felt like violence, every book I slipped off the shelves a dismemberment—I was hacking up my own home and hiding the pieces in boxes like a serial killer. Much of the move was translated through belongings—these, it seemed, were the only proof of our time in this place. Objects and shared memories—the only real artifacts we had of having lived anywhere.

We decided it might make the move easier, more cleanly efficient, to have a garage sale. But we were already exhausted with packing and open houses by that point. The only price-tag amounts that either of us had enough energy to come up with were for one dollar or twenty-five cents, so that's what we sold everything for. After the early-bird collectors swept through, our friends and neighbors started to arrive. My friend Whitney bought a little plastic horse, Chelsea bought a pair of moccasins, and Nanny bought a CD of bad experimental music. "I'll think of you every time I wear this," my friend Janine said, fingering a small glass necklace.

Yet even as we were divesting ourselves of possessions, friends started bringing us all sorts of good-luck charms—pieces of jewelry, colored beads, a silver bell, a carved bit of jade. People pressed amulets on me, as if I were about to cast off to the ends of the earth with Christopher Columbus. Or join a Bedouin caravan.

I hugged people over and over and spent half that day in tears. Afterward, Scotty and I collapsed at the one remaining card table that hadn't gotten carted away. We looked at each other in bewilderment: Why were we doing this? We tried to recollect the reasons, the menu that we'd recited for people so many times: family, sunshine, white sand. But ultimately there was the one most difficult and prickly reason—that I was in my forties now and change wasn't getting any easier. It was the thought that if we didn't go now, I would always wonder, What if? If I didn't go now, at midlife, would I ever?

THE YEAR I turned twelve, we were living in New York State, and my thirty-five-year-old father decided for the third or fourth time that he wanted to move back to Jordan again. This time, he said, it was definite. He'd made up his mind, no second thoughts—he knew beyond a doubt that we were all meant to live in Jordan. By that point, we'd lived in the same upstate neighborhood for two consecutive years and I'd tasted the sweetness of being an old-timer. I had an established confederacy of friends, new Levi's, and I had decided that I was definitely an American girl.

I pleaded with my parents to let me stay behind in the States. I was ready to offer my services as a slave girl to our neighbors. Anything, just so I could luxuriate in stasis, the sweet state of staying put. I wanted to run away, but there was no place to go. Running away, I realized to my dismay, was just another way of moving.

My parents sold the house. Mom quit her job as a reading teacher with the school district. They sold all the furniture, packed up what little was left, and shipped it to Jordan in a couple of steamer trunks with big brass padlocks. Dad flew back to Jordan a few weeks ahead of us, to look for a job and a new place to live.

For the next week, I wandered around our empty house like a ghost, trying to make sense of everything. But things most certainly did not make sense. How can anything make sense—how can anyone tie her thoughts together or consider her own state of being if she keeps moving her household year after year, with no hope of stopping? But then again, that's probably the whole point.

Don't misunderstand me. My parents are charming, delightful people, great fun, socialities, sybarites, party throwers, and iconoclasts. But I've sometimes suspected that the mixed-up, multicultural, and interreligious nature of their relationship had something to do with the way they drove themselves—and our family—outward in such a relentless search for home. In the seventies and eighties, there were still few images of an interracial family (and even fewer of an Arab-American family) in the popular culture. Their marriage kicked up great controversy in my mother's small Catholic Jersey hometown. Upstate New York was their first refuge from gossip and family disapproval.

So I think that part of their flight was not only about going to the Good Place; it was also about safety, acceptance, and wholeness. Dad was frequently the victim of racist comments; some of them were blatant, some committed in the pure, terrible innocence of ignorance, like the time one of Dad's coworkers told him that she wouldn't like to visit Jordan because she liked to bathe regularly.

A few weeks after my father had flown to Jordan, three days before we were due to join him, my mother, sisters, and I received a mysterious telegram. It was from Dad and it informed us in one curt sentence that he was coming home. I was astounded; I demanded that Mom explain what it meant. All she could say was, "I really don't know."

Of course, at some level, we all knew. Dad was coming back for the same reason that he always came back—because you can never arrive at the Good Place. Because it will eternally evade your best efforts, dodging and feinting as you reach for it, slipping back one step for every step you take toward it. It's just that, in his fourth decade, he'd gotten better at recognizing that.

THE BLESSING AND the curse of moving is that it takes a person over. The process is so arduous and involved that once you commit to it, it's very difficult to really look at what you're doing.

Scott and I made the cross-country drive to Miami while in a state of shock. Each night when we pulled off the highway to find a hotel, we'd pass cozy neighborhoods lined with little houses, fences, flower beds, and I'd wonder, Who lives here? Are they happy? I saw women around my age toting their groceries and herding their children. Was that supposed to be my life? I wondered. We'd eat the gray food served at franchise truck stops and watch the swirl of travelers around us—frenetic, scrambling, buying, everyone rushing to get somewhere: Where were we all going? Would we ever stop?

Over and over, Scott and I would say to each other, "I can't wait till we get there and we can just start our lives." As if we hadn't started them already.

We set out without a house, a map of Miami, or any address at all to speak of—just the warning of a Florida realtor we'd contacted over the phone before we left, who'd predicted (accurately) impending sticker shock. But part of our excitement came from exactly that sense of strangeness and possibility. It was like turning back the clock. As we get older, such possibilities seem more rare and precious. How often does life hand us such a completely blank slate?

Once we crossed the border from Georgia into Florida, the sky turned the color of bruised eggplant. Lightning lashed the sky from Tallahassee all the way down the length of the Sunshine State. And it poured so hard, we had to pull over several times, waiting until we could see the road. It would rain and rain for the rest of the summer.

"SO YOU'RE HERE? You really came!" my new colleagues in the English Department kept saying, as if they couldn't believe their eyes.

One of the (occasionally) great things about moving to a new academic post is that each new school presents you with a ready-made family, a cadre of individuals with similar ideas, pursuits, and passions. But at UM, they weren't entirely certain about us. We learned that during my contract negotiations, one of my new colleagues had told the others in the department that, in his opinion, we'd never really make the move. He'd spent a lot of time vacationing in the Northwest and felt strongly that no one in their right mind would ever leave Portland for Miami.

A week after we'd arrived, another colleague walked me around campus, pointing out the splendid outdoor pool. "Students like to sunbathe here to show off their work," he said, chuckling. I thought this seemed like an odd forum for reading work out loud; then, looking over at the scantily clad and well-augmented students, I realized he was referring to *body* work.

I wasn't sure I'd be able to keep up with this place after all.

My students wore bikinis and fishnet skirts to class; even the professional writers I met—the sort who wore Birkenstocks and knitted cardigans back in Oregon—exuded a hot Miami chic, glittering on stiletto heels. Once I put away my polar-fleece jackets, flannel-lined jeans, and hiking shoes, I discovered I had no clothes at all. I was starting from absolute zero.

And yet I wasn't—which is one of the benefits of starting over a little later in life. I didn't schedule appointments with plastic surgeons or buy any death-defying heels—I purchased sandals that looked a little like my hiking boots. I discovered I didn't want, or need, to tear everything down, just expand on what had come before.

Still, the first year was hard. I was stunned by the heat, disoriented with fear of the Miami drivers, who were just as aggressive, free-form, and unpredictable as the ones in Jordan. Our house—selected for its proximity to campus—hummed with a low-level traffic drone from the nearby highway. Scotty's bicycle was stolen, our car was broken into, ants swarmed the kitchen, house inspectors asked for bribes, possums and rats roamed the attic, termites roamed the walls, and three hurricanes rolled through, one of which knocked the bougainvillea bush onto our car, and we had to cut it out with hedge clippers. Both of us got socked with an achy, low-grade, lingering illness that seemed to rise straight out of the humidity.

And there was hardly anyone to talk to. My colleagues were busy with their own work and families—they were older, more professionally and socially established folks, not as receptive to adopting itinerant newcomers like ourselves. And I, in turn, felt overwhelmed by the roller coaster of my own writing career. Everyone was perfectly cordial, and one or two colleagues even invited us over for dinner, but I longed for the established bonds of my old friendships. And, of course, we had moved away from all our old friends. I was living my father's life: I had turned into the reluctant Bedouin.

SO HOW DOES it all turn out? That's what I want to know. How far along in time do you need to be before you know what "the end" to an open question is? Or is that, finally, what moving turns out to be—a way of trying to stay two steps ahead of the end?

A year after moving to Miami, I received a surprising counteroffer from my old school, Portland State. They wanted to lure me back: In exchange for teaching part of the year, they offered me the rest of the year off to travel, research, and write. I would be, in essence, a writer at large. It seemed like the perfect solution, as it turned out to be a reflection of my own life, "at large." My husband, a Bedouin at heart, said he'd also be glad to try working freelance. We had several long, intricate debates over Miami café tables, made a series of impossible lists of pros and cons, and then one day we started packing our bags again.

Another way of looking at such a decision is that it is simply a way not to decide anything. Like my father, I've selected an existence suspended between hemispheres. We kept our house in Coral Gables and returned to Portland for the fall semester. As I write this, our Florida house waits for us, distant yet tantalizing as a dream. We will return when the semester is over. And I have discovered, to my delight, that I feel homesick for Florida.

Not that it isn't fun to be back. Here in the Northwest, I have pulled out my woolly sweaters and heavy shoes, revisiting them happily as my old friends. We are subletting the condo of an elderly couple who are traveling across the country in an RV. I walk around in the condo carefully—it has been elaborately decorated with the artifacts of their travels: ceramic figurines, embroidered pillows, silk-screened wall hangings. These living arrangements are all a bit more provisional than I'd planned on. I think about my fantasy other life: a house that I was born in, that my ancestors have lived in for generations, well-established orchards filled with apple trees, a tree swing, the sounds of my children at play, the windows open and a breeze lifting the old lace curtains. In this fantasy, I know exactly who I am and where I belong—I am not terribly curious about other places because I am home.

When I was a child, this seemed like the truest sort of life I could imagine. It is a cozy fantasy and I like to visit it from time to time, imagining what such a life would feel like, though it calls to me less frequently as I get older.

And these days, I wonder if the idea of permanence isn't the greater illusion. I'd never expected the life it turns out I have—skimming over the earth like bubbles of sea foam; my husband talks about learning to fly, about the enticements of space travel. Perhaps it is natural to want to entwine our minds and imaginations with those of other places—we belong to the whole world and the world to the universe. But if there's one thing that years of moving has taught me, it's that I have to learn how to live comfortably within myself first.

I suppose it's reassuring to discover that growing older doesn't necessarily mean you feel any differently than you did when you were twelve. I still chase dreams, just like my father does. My parents don't move back and forth between Jordan and America anymore; now it's just between Syracuse and Pompano Beach. Early every fall, my father rushes back to Florida, eager to get to the sunny weather. He proclaims Florida the best place in the world and swears he'd move there year-round if only he could convince my mother to sell their house in New York. Come spring, he develops amnesia and is rearing to return up north. It's a permanent state of impermanence, built-in homesickness and eternal longing for another place. I watch him carefully as he moves—first to this place, now to that one. I shake my head; sometimes I feel a sort of joyful despair. It's good to watch him in action. After all, it's a little like watching myself.

Moving My Mother

ANDREA CHAPIN

y eighty-three-year-old mother sits very straight in one of her oval-backed Victorian chairs and says, "Why do you think Natasha has no memory of her childhood?"

We recently moved my mother from her large house in New Hampshire, where she lived for over fifty years, into an apartment complex for old people. It's a nice place—brand-new; there's lots of natural light, and even a small washer and dryer. My father died of lung cancer in 1990, so my mother's been on her own for fifteen years. She's ten minutes away from my sister Natasha now, an hour from me, and six hours south of our old hometown. I've come up from the city to spend the day with her.

My mother has always had a good memory and a sharp mind. She kicked butt in games like Trivial Pursuit, she seems to know every piece of classical music ever written, and she can still recite, in German, poetry she learned over sixty-five years ago. But lately, I've noticed her short-term memory is beginning to go: little things—she sometimes forgets that I've called her or she thinks she's called for a refill of her prescriptions when she hasn't.

My mother's question about Natasha's memory comes out of nowhere. I've been helping my mother arrange her kitchen—her eyesight is failing and she has trouble getting around. And now I'm taking a break, sitting on the couch, flipping through an L. L. Bean catalog. It's not the sort of question my mother usually asks. But every decade or so, she'll come out with a statement that makes me stop breathing. I'm in my forties, so I have, maybe, four or five such statements in my memory bank. Unlike Natasha, who is in her fifties, I have no trouble remembering. There are five of us: I am the youngest and Natasha is the eldest, and the pendulum has swung in one direction with her and another with me.

My mother was never tall—five one in her prime, and now she's under five feet. She has short, wavy white hair, sparkling blue eyes, dimples in both cheeks, and a strong, angular jaw. She's as patrician as they come. Her ancestors came over early on boats like the *Mayflower*—my father's did, too. Apparently, somewhere back in their family genealogies, hopefully very far back, they are actually related. My father had a clef chin. My mother says that when she was growing up, she put a clothespin on the end of her chin in an attempt to make a clef, but it never stuck.

I got my father's clef chin and my mother's two dimples. Today, I'm purposely not wearing all black, because even though my mother is losing her eyesight, she never fails to comment on it if I do. She likes to see me in "happy" colors, as she calls them: hot pink, mint green, baby blue.

"IT'S NOT BRAIN damage that makes Natasha have no memory," I say to my mother from the couch. "She didn't get hit in the head."

My sister's "no memory" thing is her mantra. She repeats it over and over and over again. If I ask her about something that happened thirty years ago or three years ago or even three months ago, she looks at me with the same puzzled expression and says, "Andrea, why are you asking me? You know I have no memory." I used to think she actively hid behind that phrase—that it was easier for her to say that even if she did remember—but now I know that when she answers that way, she's being completely honest. At the moment I ask her, she actually can't remember.

Sometimes I experiment with Natasha: I push and prod her a little. At first, she responds with her "no memory" mantra, and she often holds to that, but occasionally interesting things emerge. It never lasts long—once a spec of the past appears, she immediately brushes it away. Maybe there's a connection between her memory and why she's compulsively clean. She has a big house with scads of bedrooms and bathrooms, and even though she has a housekeeper, my sister has been known to vacuum the same rug several times in one day. Maybe that's why I'm such a slob; all those memories hang around me like dirty clothes and old mail, and as much as I try, I can't seem to organize them or throw them out.

"It's trauma," I say to my mother. "She's blocking her memories."

My mother's brother was a famous scientist, whose groundbreaking research on the brain put his name in all the psychology textbooks. But my mother is not particularly interested in how the brain works, or at least how the parts that I'm fascinated with work. Normally, my mother would change the subject after a response like the one I just gave. Ten years ago, I called my mother one winter afternoon to tell her that I had a tumor, the biopsy was inconclusive, and I had to have surgery. My mother paused and then, without commenting on what I'd just said, she started to describe the birds at the feeder. She was at the kitchen sink in the big house, looking out the window.

TODAY, MY MOTHER doesn't change the subject; she sits on the chair that was her grandmother's—her feet barely touching the floor—and stares off into space. She has large clear-rimmed glasses and the lenses magnify her eyes and make them look larger than they actually are. So it's hard to escape her stare—it takes over the room for a minute.

"A couple of years ago," I continue, "I asked Natasha about Dad's accident, and at first she said she couldn't remember a thing. But then I said I remembered hearing that the kid he picked up, the hitchhiker, had heroin in his knapsack, heroin and needles. And then Natasha actually said, 'I don't remember the heroin part, but he had a dagger, I think, some sort of a knife in his knapsack.'"

My mother glares at me, her eyes even bigger now. "I never knew you knew," she says.

"About what?" I say.

"The accident. I'm sure I never told any of you about it."

There is a history of accidents in my family. My father's father died in plane crash in 1931, flying his own plane. My father was four, and for almost a year his mother didn't tell my father or his older sister, my aunt Helen, that their father was dead. One year. Grammy created her own type of mourning by sending her children to her mother's in Maine and spending whatever money was left on a trip around the world in a luxury liner. It's not too different, I realize, than my parents never telling us about my father's accident. Of course we all knew about it, just like my father knew his father was dead. Children know these things—they can translate air if they have to.

"That was the worst day of my life," my mother continues.

I can tell we're hovering over a breath-stopping moment, and I'm intrigued.

"Why?" I ask.

And as it happens with my mother when she actually, once in a blue moon, confronts a disturbing memory, she recounts it as though it has just happened or is actually still happening. Perhaps she never has any distance from a painful event because she never consciously mulls it over. So when she actually looks at it, decades later, there's an uncanny feeling of immediacy.

"Your father had been on the wagon for several weeks. I was really hopeful this time, and he was, too. There was an annual dinner for the National Association of Elevator Contractors in Boston, and I drove down from work and met him. As soon as he walked in, he went to the bar and ordered a drink. He didn't stop. As soon as his drink was finished, he got another and another and another, as though he'd been crawling on the desert for days without a drop of liquid."

My mother sips from a glass of white wine and takes a bite from a Wheat Thin. "Usually, at events like this, your father showed some restraint, because he was a salesman and these people were his clients, but that night something in him just went off and he decided he was going to drink. Since he hadn't had a drink in awhile, maybe he thought he could have just one, but of course he couldn't. He was usually pretty good at holding his liquor. But he drank so much so quickly and he didn't eat a thing; toward the end of the dinner, he began acting drunk. His boss was there, and when your father started being sarcastic, I was afraid of what might happen, so I tried to get him out of there.

"It had begun to snow while we were at the dinner, and I wanted to get home before it turned into a full-fledged blizzard, so I had a good excuse. Both of our cars were in the parking lot. I had expected we would each drive our own car—or maybe even that he'd drive back to the little attic apartment he rented in Dorchester and I would drive home. But by the time we got outside, I knew he couldn't drive. He was already angry that I had hurried him out, and now he refused to let me drive, refused. So I let him drive. But the minute we drove out of the parking lot, I knew I had made a mistake, that I should have refused to get into the car, but I'd had a few drinks myself. And so we drove, and the snow started coming down harder, and I tried to convince him to let me drive, and finally we were on 95 heading north, and he said he would let me drive, so he stopped the car and I got out and he came over to where I was and hit me so hard I fell over the rail and rolled down the embankment. I was wearing my brown fur coat—you know, the fake fur coat. And before I could even make it back up the hill, I heard him slam the door and drive off."

"Then what did you do?"

"I flagged down a truck driver, who picked me up and drove me to a gas station in Portsmouth, and then I called a taxi. And a few minutes after your father left me, he picked up a hitchhiker, and a few minutes after that, his car spun out of control."

I'M THE OPPOSITE of my mother. Instead of remembering a painful event once in awhile, my mind often feels like it's working overtime, retrieving one memory after another or going over the same bad memory like a cat licking the same sad wet patch of fur over and over and over again.

As I listen to my mother recount my father's accident, I'm surprised by how similar my imagined version of the accident is to my mother's account some thirty-five years after the event. I had remembered it was my father's office Christmas party that served as the prelude to the event, not a dinner for an elevator association. Maybe it's because I missed those parties—I looked forward to getting dressed up and eating white caked rolled with raspberry filling, but after a few years we stopped going. I saw my parents in that bright orange VW Beetle, the snow coming down hard, my father refusing to let my mother drive, my mother finally persuading him to stop and then her getting out and watching him pull out into the blizzard, the little orange car disappearing quickly into an abyss of white.

And then I envisioned a kid, no more than seventeen, with shaggy dirty-blond hair and a green canvas knapsack, hitching on the side of the road. I always imagined he wasn't properly dressed for a blizzard, no hat or mittens, only a plaid wool jacket—not more than a shirt really—over a hooded sweatshirt. And then there was my father's orange VW Bug swerving to a stop and the kid getting in, and after a few minutes the car hitting a stretch of ice and smacking into a guardrail at a high speed and the teenager flying through the windshield to his death. Because he did die—we kids all knew that; though we were never told, we knew.

Now, as I ride back down from Westchester on the train, the event as my mother has just described it plays over and over again in my head. I can't let go of the image of my father hitting my mother hard enough for her to flip over a guardrail and roll down the hill. I know the coat she was wearing. It was her dress-up coat. It had a shawl collar and swung out from the top with a fifties car-coat flare. And even though it wasn't real fur, it was an expensive coat with a thick satin lining. I wonder if I would have been able to wear that coat again, the way my mother did, for decades after that night.

The sun has gone down, and though there's still light in the sky, most of the houses we pass have lights on. I often wonder what brings people together and what makes them stick. Once, at a lovelorn time in my adolescence, I asked my mother if she had been in love with my father when she married him. She didn't answer me then, but she came back that evening and sat on the end of my bed and said, "No, I wasn't in love with your father when I married him. I learned to love him, but when I

married him, I loved his last name—Chapin. I wanted it. It was a name
I'd grown up with, an important name. It meant so much to me."

Then she went on to rhapsodize about how her college had a building with that name and the college where her grandfather was president
(the college where my father, his grandfather, my mother's brothers, her
father, and my brother-in-laws all went and where I went when they accepted women) had a building with that name, our name. Those buildings weren't named for any direct relatives of my father's family, but it
didn't matter to my mother: It was the name that counted. Her words
have haunted me since. I realize now she was trying to be honest, something that has always been hard for her to do, and I guess I have to give
her credit for that.

I TAKE THE subway from Grand Central Station to the West Side
and then transfer to a train going downtown. Ever since I moved to New
York over twenty years ago, I've loved the subways. The fact that
strangers, people from completely different walks of life, with their own
histories and their own memories, spend a moment together in a
brightly lit space never fails to impress me. When I moved to the city
from college, my brother Teddy and my sister Natasha were living in the
same building on the Upper West Side. Natasha was a newlywed; she
went to work in midtown, returned to her apartment every night, and
rarely veered from that course. She hated the city—it was too dirty, too
chaotic—and moved to the suburbs with her husband as soon as they
had their first child. Teddy came to New York years before, in the early
seventies, to be a model. He was a pretty blond boy who hung out with
the Warhol crowd at the Factory and Studio 54; he always had rich
lovers and fabulous friends.

But Teddy moved to L.A. seven years ago, and I'm the only one in my
family left here.

When I get out of the subway station, I walk down Seventh Avenue.
I pull up the collar on my black leather jacket. Halloween has passed
and the air is cool. The city streets have that Saturday-night buzz: The
pace quickens, lights in restaurants dim, candles flicker. For years I was
right there, washing my hair about now, deciding what I was going to

wear. But I'm walking back to my apartment, where my husband and my two boys are waiting for me.

As I walk, I think about my mother in her new digs. She likes the people she's met—they are intellectual enough for her, and that's important: They know who Thorstein Veblen was and what Zoroastrianism is; this woman was the first female chair of the economics department at Cornell, that man was the head of OBGYN at Columbia-Presbyterian, and the woman down the hall was the president of a small college in North Carolina. It is a pretty heady crowd. And they are all Democrats, which my mother also likes. My mother's heart is not in great shape. She had a heart attack a few years back and a pacemaker put in. I hope she is well enough to enjoy her new neighbors.

UNTIL RECENTLY, MY sister Vanessa, or Nessa as we call her, the middle child, had a memory like a balance, with scales that shifted between romance and reality. Once she called me up and said that a new friend had asked her what her childhood was like and that she'd responded quite simply with one word: *wonderful*. Later, Nessa mentioned this conversation to her husband, Dan, and he had snorted, and that bothered her, so she called me.

"Wasn't it?" she asked me.

"Wasn't it what?" I said.

"Wonderful?"

I paused before answering. In those days, sometimes when I spoke to Nessa, I felt as if I were speaking to a very young, very naïve girl. "Parts of our childhood were wonderful," I began slowly. She sighed on the other end of the phone. "And parts of our childhood were not wonderful. Parts of our childhood were extremely painful, terrifying, and sad."

"Oh," she said. There was a moment of silence on the other end of the phone, and then, as if what I'd said had allowed Pandora's box to open, she launched into a recent memory: Teddy was about ten years old, "and you, Andrea, were too young to remember." The whole family was sitting having dinner at the kitchen table and Dad and Teddy got into an argument over something small that our father had turned into something large. Dad ordered Teddy from the table and Teddy wouldn't leave. Nessa said Teddy held on to the chair and sat there with his knuckles turning white. The more Dad screamed, the tighter Teddy held on to the chair, and all the other kids knew that Dad was being irrational and that Teddy was the rational one, but my sister said, "We were so scared, we sat there in silence and didn't stick up for Teddy." Finally, when Teddy wouldn't budge, our father picked Teddy and the chair up and threw them both out the kitchen door. Teddy got up off the lawn and, without turning around, without looking back at Dad or the rest of the family, walked slowly down the length or our long, sloping lawn and then out into the street. Nessa was sobbing by the end of her tale.

But Nessa has changed over the last few years. As she's progressed into middle age, she's become less tolerant. Where she used to call me up and use me as a sounding board, she's now become quite zealous in her rallying against memories—telling me not to bring up the past anymore. A few years ago, she said, "I don't want to hear or read about it anymore. That's why I moved three thousand miles away so many years ago—to get away from all that!" I found letters from the sixties and seventies while going through things in the house in New Hampshire before its sale; one letter was typed by Natasha, who was fifteen at the time, and signed by all five of us, me barely old enough to write. It started with the line "Alcohol is destroying our family."

Nessa scolded me for keeping those letters. "You're pathetic," she said. "It's time to forget about the past and move on."

I'm not happy about my obsession. Sometimes I think my addiction to the past is chemical, that it's not learned behavior, but that my brain is actually made differently than everyone else's—in my family at least. I'm sure, in this era of medications, there's the perfect drug out there to take my memories away. I often wonder if that is why Teddy got hooked on heroin when he was already in his forties, that as he grew older, it became more difficult to forget history and with that history came a pain that was too great.

MY MOTHER CALLS me the day after my visit. Now that she is in her eighties, she sleeps much later than she used to—she used to call me at seven o'clock in the morning on the weekends. But today my husband has already taken the boys to the park, and I've started to clean their room when she calls. She's chatty and pleasant, and I feel hopeful.

"I had such a nice time with you yesterday," I say.

After my father's death, I didn't visit my mother in New Hampshire very often. My work got in the way, I started going out to Long Island in the summer, and then I had one child and, four years later, another. The time never seemed quite right, I rationalized. But I've been thinking that, perhaps, with my mother's move, we'll enter a new stage in our lives. She's closer geographically, and we'll see each other more.

Much to my surprise, she brings up Natasha and her lack of memory again. As I've said, my mother doesn't usually worry about these types of things—we used to call her "Queen of Denial." She's always had a good mind, and over the years I've come to realize that, unlike Natasha, my mother remembers and acknowledges things but chooses not to think about them. It dawns on me that something is truly bothering her. I put a pile of dirty clothes down and sit on my couch.

"Why are you wondering about Natasha's 'no memory' thing?" I ask.

There's a silence; then my mother says, "Because I've read things that say people with no memory might have been sexually abused."

"You think Natasha might have been abused?"

"I wonder," my mother says.

"Why?"

My mother takes a deep breath and I realize that we never actually got to the breath-stopping statement yesterday and that right now we're on the verge of it. And off she goes. "I wonder if your father—"

"Dad? Why would you think that?"

"Because once when Teddy was about ten, I came into our room one night and Teddy jumped out of our bed and shouted, 'Dad was touching me!'"

"What was Teddy doing in your bed?"

"He'd crawled into our bed—maybe he'd had a nightmare."

"Where were you?"

"I must have been cleaning up the kitchen, washing the dishes or something."

"What did you do?"

"You father was very drunk and he must have thought Teddy was me."

"Mom, a ten-year-old boy feels different from a woman."

"But he was so drunk, I don't think he knew the difference."

I THOUGHT WHAT I knew about the past was static—events occurred in chronological time: This was the year my father committed sixteen-year-old Teddy to the state mental hospital for being caught smoking pot a second time; that was the year my drunken father wrapped his VW Bug around a tree after picking up a seventeen-year-old kid with a knapsack, who's final mistake was hitchhiking home for Christmas; this was the year my mother passed out from pills and alcohol and forgot to wrap the Christmas presents; that was the year Teddy, barely nineteen years old, was taken to Bellevue after overdosing on angel dust and using the ledge of a Manhattan apartment building as a balance beam while spouting that he had seen Christ and Christ had talked to him; this was the year, when I was fourteen, when my father lost thirty pounds, started smoking again, sobbed all the time, refused to go to work, and wouldn't leave the living room couch; that was the year my father was dying and he told me his stepfather had molested him; this was the year my father died and Teddy was drunk the whole weekend of the memorial service; that was the year Teddy admitted to me he wasn't just going to the dry-out clinic for alcohol, but heroin, too.

I thought by now, by middle age, I knew our history. I am the self-proclaimed family archaeologist after all, the one to whom everyone tells their secrets, but I'm not ready for newly discovered events to be added to the time line. After I hang up the phone, I pull my feet up on the couch and lie supine, staring at the ceiling as though I am in a coffin, waiting for the lid to close.

THERE'S SOMETHING ABOUT my mother's revelation that reminds me of a good ending to a short story—good in the sense of well crafted—an ending that makes the reader rethink the whole narrative. What my mother has told me immediately becomes part of my inventory. I hear Teddy's words that night and see my mother's face at the bedroom door, and I think of Teddy at fifty, forever looking for love. He shoots himself up with testosterone now, and his once beautifully sculpted body has been transformed into a tan hulk with a thick neck, huge shoulders, and arms the size of my thighs.

I start the endless revisiting of events, of Teddy's whole life, of my father's. I think of my father when he was dying of cancer, telling me, and no one else, about his stepfather. It was July Fourth weekend and I was in my late twenties. We were in the kitchen in New Hampshire, Mom was racing around preparing a large breakfast, and there was something on the radio about sexual abuse. My father turned to me and said, "I've always thought that's why Helen [his sister] ran away from home, because Daddy Apgar was molesting her." And then he continued: "One night I woke up when I was about ten, and Daddy Apgar was in my bed, holding my thing." My father couldn't say *penis*. At that moment, my mother burst through the swinging door from the dining room and the subject was changed.

And then days before my father's death, while the TV was blaring something about sexual abuse at a nursery school, my father, in a morphine stupor, eyes closed and as if dreaming, brought it up again. I was alone with him and I hadn't been sure that day if he even knew I was next to him—his eyes had been closed most of the day and he'd been slipping in and out of consciousness. When the news came on about the abuse, he started tossing and turning and mumbling about Daddy Apgar, his Waspy bespectacled stepfather, and I leaned in close to my father and tried to decipher what he was saying. I can't remember his words now; I'm not even sure if I knew them then—but I gathered he was connecting the words on television with his stepfather.

AND THEN THERE'S Teddy, who lies to shock and, when he's drunk, will launch into an unbridled list of all the sadistic things Dad did to him as a child. But he has never mentioned the bedroom scene my mother just laid before me. And I can't help but wonder, Is there more? Was that it?

Let me fly into the future for a moment. Shortly after the phone call

with my mother, I mention what she said to my sister Nessa—in defense, really, when she calls me up to berate me for my financial insta-
bility (a direct quote: ". . . and therapy . . . you're such a New Yorker, you
have to go to therapy. It's only made you worse. If you hadn't spent so
much money on therapy, you'd be able to pay your tax bill!"). I counter
with how I need therapy coming from a family like ours, and then I tell
her the Teddy/Daddy story. She scoffs at me: "I can't believe you believe
everything Mom says." Then she doesn't bring it up again.

So, I keep this information to myself for months. Even when Teddy
tells me he went on a gay cruise with the goal of taking a bottle of sleeping pills and jumping into the water, but that when, pills in hand, he
stood at the railing of the ship under the moonlight, staring at the water, it looked too dark and too cold, and he changed his mind.

My mother's health starts to decline: There are several falls with cuts
and bruises and swollen legs, and her cardiologist diagnoses stage-four
congestive heart failure. Sometimes when I go up there to sort through
her myriad medications and organize them for the month, her breathing
is so short, I worry that the visit will me my last. I want to ask her more,
but I'm afraid my questions will disturb her so much that her heart will
give way.

Then one day, Teddy and I, who haven't spoken in several months,
are on the phone. "This move has rocked us more than anyone wants to
admit," I say. "I think everyone is having a hard time." My two older sisters have been acting out—Nessa calls me up and finds fault with every
aspect of my life; Tasha is mad at everyone and, seething, recounts how
she stayed at home with her kids for twenty years, and now with Mom
nearby and failing, she has to take care of her, when what she really
wants is time for herself.

"I suppose we have all been acting out in our own ways," I continue.
I think of Teddy on the deck of the cruise ship with a bottle full of pills
and of our brother James, who has spent much of his adolescence and
adulthood disengaging from our family. James runs a high-tech company
out west and stays away from it all, checking in—efficiently but sporadically. And about myself, distracted, depressed, bursting into tears easily.

I go on: "I dream about that large, rambling house almost every night.

I am back in there again and again and again—every piece of furniture where it was for so many years." It was a house spilling with rooms, and it was like a boardinghouse; my parents rented rooms and an apartment above the garage and one in the basement to students and graduate students at the local university.

"I dream about it all the time, too," Teddy says. "But my dreams are more like nightmares, really."

And then, in what seems at first a digression, Teddy blurts out, "Why do you think when I was about six Mom and Dad took me down to the Children's Hospital in Boston because I was bleeding from my rectum? It's so strange."

I've never heard this story. Bleeding from the rectum? I can't believe we're talking about this. "Was it bleeding like you were constipated or—"

"It was gushing out. That's why they took me all the way down to Boston."

"Well, that usually means, I think, that, well"—I fill my lungs with air and then let it out—"sexual abuse."

Then I tell Teddy what Mother told me. At first, there is a silence on the other end of the phone, and then Teddy says, his voice shaking, "No, no, not Dad. I don't remember anything. I don't remember that."

"Why would Mom say it, then?"

"Maybe someone else did it to me, but not Dad. Maybe one of the tenants." Then Teddy says that all the psychiatrists he's seen say he seems to fit the profile of a victim of sexual abuse. "But no, I have no memory of that; Dad was cruel, but not that." And there is silence and then weeping on the other end of the phone. "I've got to go," he says, and hangs up.

The following day, I get an E-mail from Teddy with the subject line "It was good to talk with you":

> Andrea, I was thinking about our discussion and feel the need to clarify the portion in which we talked about my strange visit to Children's Hospital in Boston, when I was a young child, because of fresh blood in my stool. If I was sexually abused, I am very sure

it had nothing to do with Dad. I don't believe he sexually abused any child. As cruel as he could be, I just don't think that was part of his nature. Love You, Teddy

I send a long E-mail in reply, saying how it seems so confusing—the scene Mother described and then the visit to the Boston hospital Teddy brought up—out of the blue. "Why," I ask him, "didn't they take you to one of the three local hospitals?" I tell Teddy the Daddy Apgar story and wonder if it's abuse repeating itself. "I just don't know what to think about all of this; it haunts me and makes me question everything. . . . This is all so very upsetting, down to my very core. I wish I had answers. I love you."

Teddy responds:

Andrea, There was not lots of blood, as I remember, and Boston Children's Hospital, I believe, was recommended by the doctor because it has always been considered one of the best Pediatric Hospitals in the World. I was certainly much younger than when the other incident occurred. I remember it because staying at the hospital and the anesthesia were terrifying to me. I do not remember anything directly before that.

The other incident, I remember more clearly now. I had had a nightmare and asked Mom if I could snuggle in bed with her, but she evidentially couldn't sleep and went to sleep in another room. While sleeping, Dad started to snuggle me with his arms around me in the spooning position and I was pleasantly shocked in receiving love from a man who never showed any to me. Then he started to remove my underwear. I don't think he got it all the way off, saying something like, "What's this?"—meaning the underwear that Mom didn't wear to bed with him. I bolted and ran back to my room. In his probably drunken, half-asleep state, I think he had mistaken me for Mom. Love, you, Teddy

By the spring, my mother hasn't made it up to the dinners she so enjoyed when she first arrived; she cannot walk without a walker but mostly uses a wheelchair now; also, her eyesight and hearing have gotten worse. In June, on my forty-fifth birthday, Natasha and I spend the day moving my mother to a one-bedroom apartment in the assisted-living section. There's a full-time nurse on her floor, who checks up on each resident every four hours, and instead of just dinner, there are three meals a day. Only seven other residents are in this part of the facility, compared to the eighty or so in the independent-living area. I have sleepless nights, worrying about moving her away from her newfound friends, about how she'll be in two small rooms, compared to the large twenty-room house in New Hampshire.

A week later, I call my mother, and the phone is busy for over an hour. I finally call the nurse on her floor to see what the problem is, and she tells me my brother Teddy is there. She takes her phone into my mother's room, and I speak to my mother briefly: She says she didn't know Teddy was arriving. When I speak to Teddy, I can tell by his voice that he is on something, or several somethings.

"I've been on the phone, trying to track down all my luggage," he slurs. "The airline lost it all."

I call Tasha after I hang up, and she tells me Teddy called two nights before and asked her to pick him up the next morning at the airport. The next morning when she was on her way out the door, Tasha got a call from Teddy, who said that he had missed his original flight, then flew to Washington, D.C., spent the night in the airport, and was now on his way to New York. When he finally arrived, he had scrapes and bruises on his face and a bump on the back of his head, and he was acting strangely, but Tasha let him take her car. Within ten minutes, he had an accident. No one was hurt, but her new Volvo was badly damaged. She finally dropped him at Mother's. She didn't hear from him that night and assumed he'd decided to spend the night on the couch in The Mother's living room. When she spoke to him the next morning, he had no idea how he got to Mother's or what he'd done the previous day. Tasha sounds befuddled and distant.

"Did you ask him where the scrapes came from?" I ask her.

"No," she says.

"Did you ask him why he ended up in D.C.?"

Again, no.

"How could you let him take your car when he was so fucked up?"

"I don't know. Tim [her husband] asked me the same thing."

"He's been on the phone for the last hour, trying to track down his luggage," I say.

"His six suitcases and his computer are right here," she says. "In my house. He had them with him when he arrived. His little dog is with him, or at least he was when I dropped him off."

"He's on some sort of a binge, Natasha; he's blacking out. We have to do something."

"I know," she answers quietly.

I call him back at my mother's. "Teddy, what's going on? Tasha told me about the scrapes on your face and the car accident, and now you can't remember what happened yesterday."

"I'm okay," Teddy says.

"You are not okay. You need help. I'm here. Natasha's here. You are surrounded by people who love you. We can find a place for you to go nearby."

Then it comes out. He tells me he took a bottle of pills, but not enough, maybe, drank most of a bottle of vodka, put a plastic bag over his head, and then lay down on my mother's couch. "I must have pulled the plastic bag off my head at the last minute. I can't find the bag, though. I don't know what happened to it."

"Where was Mother?"

"Sleeping in the next room, I think."

As the day unfolds, with me on the phone, Teddy swings from saying I'm overreacting to telling me I've betrayed him by letting Tasha know about his suicide attempt. I talk to psychiatrists, who advise me to alert the authorities at my mother's place—all I can imagine is my mother dying of a heart attack as the police drag my hugely pumped-up six-foot-two brother out the door. I ask Natasha if my mother said anything about the night before.

"Mother said it was scary."

"Did you ask her what 'scary' meant?" I ask.

"No," she says.

Teddy is still at my mother's. I go to bed not knowing what is going to happen to either of them.

———

I CALL MY mother the next morning. Tasha has already picked Teddy up and taken him to the train to visit his friend Michael in the city—business as usual. I ask my mother what she meant when she said Teddy's first night was "scary." She says she got up once during the night because my brother's little dog woke her up, and when she went into the other room, Teddy was babbling incoherently. She tried to wake him up, but she couldn't. Then she went back to bed. My mother can't see well, and she tells me no more than that. I wonder what she saw or if she really even looked.

By the time I hang up, I'm frantic. Once again, my family is acting as though nothing has happened. Teddy is on his way into the city to spend the weekend. I can tell by Tasha's inability to ask questions or make phone calls that she can not deal with any of it. I call Teddy's friend Michael, tell him the story, and we arrange an intervention; Michael, Sam (Teddy's ex-boyfriend), and I meet at Michael's and try to convince Teddy to check into Bellevue; Teddy, sweating profusely, pulls prescription bottle after prescription bottle out of his shaving kit, saying, "I'll throw this out and this out and this out. I'm fine now. I really am. . . ." He has no health insurance, is afraid of the costs, and refuses to go the hospital.

When I put my brother in a cab later that afternoon, he says he's going to the airport to get on a flight back to California, and he promises to seek help, but I don't know if that is the case or if he's going to check into the nearest hotel—with me being the last person to see him alive. I start walking south. It's a beautiful June day, but I hardly see it. There are times, as I walk the seventy blocks home, when my eyes are so blurred with tears, I can't even see the sidewalk. I chant, "You did what you could, you did what you could, you did what you could," all the while wondering if I did—now, before, ever.

TEDDY DOES GET on a plane to California that night, and he goes to AA the next day. The first time I return to my mother's rooms after Teddy's visit, I get down on my hands and knees and look under the sofa. I don't find the plastic bag, but I find one of the pills and flush it down the toilet. In the following months, every time I go my mother's, the time never seems right to ask her any more questions. She sleeps much of the day. I dole out her daily doses of medications for the month, and then we talk for a few minutes and I leave. But I make a date with myself to ask her about what she told me that day. The date arrives, and, as usual, she sleeps for most of my visit. When she wakes, she has to be wheeled into a monthly meeting for the assisted-living residents. My window of opportunity is closing. She's gotten up from her nap and I'm helping her get dressed. I force myself to speak.

"Did the nurse ever say anything about the night Teddy was here?" I've always wondered how much the nurse on duty that night saw; Did she find the plastic bag? Did she revive him?

"She came to me and said, 'Your son needs help.' "

In keeping with my family, I've never talked directly to my mother about Teddy's suicide attempt. We've talked around it.

"Mom, remember what you told me last year about that night when . . . you know, with Dad and Teddy?"

She pulls herself up and is balancing her small, frail body on her walker. "Yes, I remember."

"Do you think, Teddy's . . . some of Teddy's troubles . . ."

"I've wondered that," she says.

"Teddy once told me that he had to go down to Boston Children's Hospital because he was bleeding in his butt. Why was that?"

"Yes . . ."

"Why?"

"I can't remember. He was sick, too. I think he had the mumps."

"But why not a local hospital?" I say. I had mumps, too, as a child, but I certainly didn't go to the hospital.

"I can't remember." Her voice fades.

"Mom . . ."

"We're already late," she says. "Can you get my blazer?"

"But why go down to Boston Children's Hospital?"

"I don't know. Bring me my blazer, please," she says.

I pull the blazer from the hanger and carefully help her on with it. And then I wheel her out.

———

THOSE FIRST FEW weeks in 1970, after my father's accident, he limped around the house with his arm in a sling. He never mentioned what had happened, nor did my mother. After a month's hiatus, my father resumed drinking, and after six months he was driving again. At first, that terrible night was whispered about by my brothers and sisters. One if us said the hitchhiker had a dagger in his backpack. Another said he was carrying needles and heroin. Slowly, among the five of us, the seventeen-year-old kid who had gone through the windshield to his instant death turned into a bad kid, a monster, and then he receded into our collective silence and life went on. And the following year, three of my siblings all had minor car accidents, and then when I was the same age as the kid, I ran through a sliding glass door, thinking a child was drowning in a pool on the other side. Until I was older, much older, until recently really, I'd never linked these accidents with my father's before, nor had I understood how contagious guilt can be; it was as if, after that winter night, it had spread through my family like a disease.

My mother is still alive, sleeping most of the day, moving very little. Sometimes as I watch her sleep, I wonder if her method of denial is what's killing her or if it has kept her alive all these years. She is not someone who is riddled with regret, and when she brings up the past, she never voices how she should have done things differently.

Teddy has passed 150 days of sobriety. He's tried AA before but never felt he had anything in common with other members. This time, he's made friends, and he sounds different in his E-mails; there is a tone of acknowledging, or the long process of beginning to acknowledge. We don't speak or send E-mails often, but when we do, he sounds upbeat, and I'm full of support for him.

And so the story continues. When memories are kept secret, I realize as I write this essay, they can age you in many different ways. It took me almost a decade to tell my husband how my father's drunk driving caused someone else's death, and he was the first person I told. I don't think my siblings have ever told anyone. Denial runs so deep in my family, it's almost a genetic trait by this point, and I, too, fall victim to it. Yet when I don't—when I react, when I push, prod, and needle, when I try to force memory onto my family—I get very little satisfaction. Maybe that's the lesson for me—as I find myself midway between childhood and old age, between memory and forgetfulness, between my family's denial and my recognition: I can't will others to remember, but I can remember, and, no matter how sad, ugly, and painful it is, I can write it down. There is, I admit, some satisfaction in that.

What We Keep

MARY CLEARMAN BLEW

From a distance—from the window of my youngest sister's cabin, for example—the stone ranch house looks unchanged from when, as a teenager in the 1950s, I lived there with my mother, father, grandmother, and two younger sisters. The house looks much as it has since the turn of the last century, when its massive sandstone blocks were chiseled and mortared by immigrant stonemasons. Two-storied and enduring, it turns its back to the Snowy Mountains of central Montana and looks out of its deep-set windows at the creek and the pole gate that opens to the county road.

I left home when I was seventeen and returned only for visits, but I remember the rooms of the stone house the way I remember rooms I have dreamed, one opening into another that unfolds restlessly into another. Perhaps because I first saw the stone house in winter, in my memory those rooms are always winter rooms, the heat pipes hissing, the linoleum freezing under my bare feet, the cracked windowpanes filled with white light after a fresh snowfall—and always with that stark radiance, I feel the involuntary shiver at the back of my neck. In fact, it was July when I last visited the stone house. My youngest sister, Jackie, the only one of us three sisters to stay on the ranch, had suggested that we look through the old house and see whether there was anything we might want to keep. There was a chance that the house was going to be sold, and if that happened, it would have to be emptied.

"Sold?" I asked thinking of its ruined furnace, its outdated wiring and plumbing, its cracked masonry. "Who'd want it?"

Jackie explained. "Rich people do. They'll dismantle it and recycle the stones as architectural detail on their new houses."

No one has been living in the stone house for over twenty years. After my father died, my mother fled the ranch for a one-bedroom apartment in town, where she could see the lights of neighbors and hear the sounds of traffic. She took only what she needed to live from day to day: a few clothes, a few pots and pans. She was closely pursued by Jackie, who brought her her sewing machine and ironing board and a dining room table and chairs—"Why would I want those?"—and put up pictures of her grandchildren—"Why would I want those?" When it became necessary for her to move from her apartment into an assisted-living residence, it was Jackie who brought hammer and nails and rehung the pictures; it was Jackie who brought the quilt I had made for her and spread it on her bed. Now it is Jackie who will oversee her next-to-final move, into the Alzheimer's wing of the assisted-living residence.

My mother never wanted the clutter of keepsakes. "Why would I want that?" I remember her asking when offered—what?—a laminated invitation to my first wedding, perhaps. While the rest of her family saved the letters and souvenirs that connected them with their past, what my mother seemed to want was an absence of reminders. In my garage today is a large box that I inherited from one of my mother's sisters. It is filled with letters my aunt saved—letters that her mother had written to her, letters from her sisters, even letters from me and my sisters and our children. My mother, however, kept no letters. She kept, so far as I know, no samples of her daughters' schoolwork, no report cards, no clumsy elementary school artwork. No newspaper clippings of our small high school triumphs, no wedding announcements, no announcements of the births of grandchildren. Any such keepsakes that I possess today are those I saved myself or were passed on to me by my aunts.

Keepsakes are a shadow of what has been lost or abandoned. I think of all the artifacts that have had to be dumped along my family's restless trails across oceans and continents and centuries. My forebears, setting out in their flimsy seventeenth-century ships from England and the Netherlands, must have had to lighten their loads, must have left the heavy baggage behind, and what they kept became an image of absence. I imagine that absence like a negative impression of the piano, perhaps, set out by the wagon ruts along the Oregon Trail, where its strings vibrate in the wind for no one to hear; or perhaps the carved rocking chair, a few miles farther down the road, rocking gently by itself in that same wind. How can anyone endure that breath of space in which the piano still hums, the chair rocks? Better not to look back.

It was the backward glance, the involuntary shiver at the knife blade between past and present, I believed, that my mother resisted. Her life had been difficult. Growing up as a homestead child during the terrible drought years of the 1920s, coming to young womanhood during the years of the Depression, she worked as a ranch wife over a woodstove and a washboard, the water carried in a pail from a pump. She bore four daughters and lost one of those daughters at birth. Looking back, collecting reminders, I thought, must have been for my mother an unendurable source of pain.

I, on the other hand, seem to have become the family curator of keepsakes, many of which have lost their power for pleasure or pain by disconnection. On my desk, as I write, sits a black pasteboard ring box, and in the box is a gold wedding ring, too small for my finger. It arrived in a recent consignment from one of my two surviving aunts, who is cleaning out her house in anticipation of what we don't speak of. (I, who once had plenty of aunts, over a dozen living aunts and great-aunts, even a living great-great aunt, am now down to Aunt Sylva and Aunt Florence.)

Aunt Florence thinks the ring may have been my grandmother's, or possibly my great-grandmother's. I don't think it was my grandmother's, because I already possess a gold wedding ring with a narrow matching band set with a tiny turquoise, both of which were said to be hers. So, my great-grandmother's. Who knows? There are few clues. The ring is eighteen-karat gold. It fit a smaller hand than mine. I hear my mother's voice: "Why would I want that?"

My youngest grandson, two-year-old Tayler, loves the ring. The first time he saw it, he immediately tried it on. Now he looks for it every time he visits. He likes to twirl it on his finger. The last time he played with it, he lost it, but eventually I found it again, under my desk, and I put it back in its box.

So now that the stone ranch house may be sold for its chiseled sandstone, now that the gritty Montana I grew up in has become glamorous and the antiquated has become chic, it occurs to me that the chic carries no significance. Stripped of its story, the artifact loses its power. The backward glance inflicts no pain when there is nothing to be seen; the ring twirls harmlessly on a little boy's finger; the past spins out.

"What a story that could tell!" I hear people exclaim, and I wonder if they really would want to hear it.

Last July when I visited Jackie on the ranch, the air was warm, even in the foothills. Above the dark points of the pines on the ridges around the cabin, the sky arched blue and endless, as though the summer itself were immortal. I was twelve and Jackie only two years old when our family moved to this ranch. Now I was sixty-four and Jackie was fifty-four, and we were walking along the same bleached gravel on the road down from the cabin to the stone house, breathing the same faint scent of turpentine from sun-warmed pine bark, ripening grass, and cold creek water. Time at such moments seems a transparency. What is it? Where does it go?

Oblivious of deep thoughts, Jackie's dogs frisked along with us, stopping to sniff, then running ahead. We were aware, though, that as we neared the stone house, illusions began to fade. The two front-yard firs had reached the roof, the old willow tree had grown over the porch, and cracked and clouded windows looked out at us with the vacant stare of the deserted. Jackie opened the gate in the ruined picket fence, and I followed her up the old boardwalk to the back door. The grass of what once had been a lawn had grown knee-high, and she had turned in a pair of her young horses to graze it down. The horses were beautiful crossbred Arabs, their bay coats shining with health and dappled with sunlight falling through the willow leaves. They had been dozing in the shade, switching at flies, but their heads jerked up when they heard us, and they came trotting, full of curiosity at what we were so interested in.

Jackie opened the back door on a stench of mice and decay. The dogs dived in ahead of us as she shut the door on the noses of the horses, who would have followed.

My first impression, after the odor and the heat, was of the familiar overlaid by a coating of dust and clutter. I was finding it hard to breathe. We found our narrow way through the crowded little utility room, which we had always called "the out-kitchen," hung with old coats and stacked with stuff—boxes, tools—into the real kitchen, which took up the length of the house. There was the refrigerator, standing open. There was the stove with a pot holder crumpled on top of it. Plates had been left on the countertops, cans of food in the little pantry behind the sink, all under a film of grime. Cracked kitchen chairs stood around, pulled out from the old chrome table as though by ghosts.

"She just walked away and left everything," said Jackie.

The deep window ledges were drifted with dead flies, the floors scattered with mice dung. I remembered how my mother had fought the flies and the mice in this house, how she had set traps, laid poison, swatted and sprayed and sworn. Nothing she did was enough. The mice came in from the fields through the cracks in the stonework and built their nests, and the flies crawled into the deep crevices to lay their eggs, which hatched in the warm rooms in the wintertime. And then those flies buzzed and swarmed and died. My mother also fought the bedbugs, which she believed were carried in by the bats that roosted in the attic. She boiled bedding, she swabbed down the bedsprings with disinfectant, she stood the legs of the beds in cans of kerosene, and still we girls woke with rings of red bites around our wrists and waists. Now I wondered whether whatever rich people might buy the house would get the mice and flies and bedbugs along with the sandstone masonry.

We wandered from room to room, with the dogs exploring busily behind us and then diving between our legs to get ahead. A dark hallway led into the ramshackle frame addition my father had built on the stone house for his mother to live in. Here was the house's only bathroom; here was the room where that grandmother once had watered her houseplants and sat in her oak rocker and knitted. The floors out here had never been finished, and the rough boards sloped dangerously. Nobody is likely to buy these boards for their architectural detail, I thought, and I had a brief vision of bulldozed wreckage, splintered and smoking.

Through a curtain was what had been my grandmother's bedroom, until a series of small strokes had riddled her senses, and my parents had moved her to the same nursing facility that my mother would soon be moved into. They had then moved into her bedroom, because it was closer to the bathroom, and I, in my ignorant twenties, had seen both moves as a betrayal: How could they?

Now I moved the curtain aside. The bed was made up, and my father's old red bathrobe hung on a nail. Clothes hung in closets; clothes were folded in drawers. Dust. Dead flies. Mice droppings.

Jackie had paused, tipping her head to read the titles of some of my father's paperback western novels crammed into bookshelves, and for just a moment her face was caught in a shaft of dirty sunlight. Fifty-four winters on her head. Where had the little girl gone, with her blue eyes and blond braids? Where had my grandmother gone? Briefly, I saw my grandmother's face, tanned and lined from years of ranch work in all kinds of weather, superimposed upon my sister's. It was almost enough to set the old rocking chair in motion on the warped floor. But if there was a ghost in this house, it should have been my mother's ghost. This had been her house, after all, especially after my grandmother's presence faded. These had been my mother's rooms, which she had painted and hung with wallpaper and arranged to her satisfaction. For some reason, she disliked doors. Her idea of a doorway was to hang a curtain in it. And she never wanted more than one way in or out of a room or a house. She wallpapered over unwanted exits, or she nailed them shut. To this day, the front door to the stone house is nailed shut.

She disdained knickknacks and cared nothing for niceties. I never knew her to use a tablecloth or napkins, and she welcomed coffee mugs as a way to dispense with saucers. Sometimes she took a violent dislike to inanimate objects. My grandmother's solid oak table, for example, which had served as our kitchen table as far back as I could remember. One winter, with a force that could only have been fueled by a fit of rage, my mother wrestled that heavy five-legged table past the obstacles of stove and refrigerator, through the congested out-kitchen, and out the back door, where she heaved it into a snowbank.

There the table spent the rest of the winter, on its back, with its legs in the air, where it reminded me of a dead animal when I visited in the spring. I tried to imagine the rage that must have flared in my mother and could only imagine the animus that must have risen from the solid oak to meet hers.

She herself would give no clues. "I never liked that table" was all she would say. "It wasn't high enough."

So could I have it, if nobody else wanted it? Yes, sniffed my mother. She had already replaced it with the chrome-legged table with the Formica top.

After a winter in the snowbank, the oaken top had warped from moisture, and it had to be planed and sanded and refinished, and my plates and cups always tended to rock on it. Still, it was my kitchen table for years, until I moved to another state and, with the persistence of things, the table found its way back to the ranch to wait in my sister's shed for its next incarnation. As a child, I supposed I was the cause of my mother's anger, although I was never sure of the hairline crack, the spark in the tinder that would set her off, flaring and contemptuous. More and more, I turned from my mother to the company of my aunts, which in part accounts for why my house, on the outskirts of this university town in northern Idaho, contains so many objects my mother would never have given houseroom. Sometimes I consider a massive donation to the Goodwill; often I wonder which of my daughters would willingly take on the task of family curator. None of the keepsakes I preserve are valuable, and some are downright strange, like the eight or nine locks of curling goldbrown hair, tied separately with white yarn and wrapped in a sheet of newspaper dated Tuesday, March 9, 1915. I keep coming upon the locks of hair by accident and recoiling as if I've touched something alive.

"What are you doing?" asks my twenty-two-year-old daughter, Rachel, reading the computer screen over my shoulder.

"I'm trying to write an essay."

"Oh. Good. I was afraid you were making out your will and leaving the hair to me."

Whose was the hair? I've never known, nor can I recall how the hair came into my keeping, although I speculate it was bundled, newspaper wrapping and all, among my aunt Imogene's belongings, which my daughters and I gathered together and stored after her death. One thing is certain, the Goodwill won't want it.

Neither will the Goodwill want the strip of what looks like dirty string but really is several yards of lace knitted by my grandmother after her mind deteriorated past the point where she could count stitches. The strip of lace lives in the tray of my blanket chest, with its irregularities, its humps and lumps and holes like a map of what my mind may come to. I should throw it away, along with the locks of hair, but I don't.

Nor have I thrown away the black fur hat, which also lives in my blanket chest. The hat belonged to one of my great-grandfathers; I have no idea which one, and only the ghosts could tell me the reason why someone so carefully preserved it. Old fur is like the outer husk of the undead. My great-grandfather's hat has lost its leather odor but not its texture or its aura, and when I open its box, the fur reaches for my hands, as though it is awakening from its long sleep in the dark.

Some of the things I've inherited do contain some intrinsic value. There are the four white Havilland dessert plates, rimmed in gold. Their porcelain is so translucent that when I hold one of the plates up to the light, I can see the shadow of my hand through it. The plates were a wedding present to my grandmother, and she carried them from Iowa to the Montana homestead frontier in 1910 and cherished them through all the hard years. "Mother never had a very good place to keep them," my aunt Sylva told me when, cleaning out her house for her own next-to-final move, she gave them to me, and I imagined the Havilland plates wrapped in newspaper and stored in a box to be moved from shack to shanty, then packed under a bed or in a dirt cellar, collecting layers of spiderwebs. I imagined gray cellar dust smearing my grandmother's bosom when she carried the box up the steep wood stairs and unpacked the plates for a special occasion, someone's birthday perhaps, and I saw her corded hands, familiar in memory, as she washed cake crumbs from the plates and carefully rewrapped them.

There were five plates when Aunt Sylva gave them to me. I washed them and put them in a china cabinet, but one day my cat saw her chance to explore by sneaking through a glass door I had left open, and she kicked out one of the Havilland plates, which shattered. As I gathered up the pieces, I berated myself for my carelessness after all the years my grandmother had cherished her tiny collection of Havilland, under such difficult circumstances, when all I had had to do was remember to shut the cat out of the china cabinet, and it was not until much later that it occurred to me to wonder whether, in fact, there had been only five plates in the beginning. Five seems an odd number for a wedding present. Say six, then, or even eight—or could there have been as many as a dozen dessert plates in the set?—and now I scent a faint trail of smashed Havilland through the years. A plate broken during the endless, dusty train ride out from Iowa, another during the rough buggy ride over the ruts on the way to the Montana homestead. Another plate broken when the wind blew down the shed, still another dropped from a child's hands or knocked off a table by the cat. The set ever dwindling, until those remaining five translucent white plates, emblems of the persistence of things and also of their transience, came into my keeping.

Is there intrinsic value in the collection of antique fabrics that has found its way to me? The eighteenth-century linen mattress covers, for example, that do not fit modern mattresses. Probably they began as flax grown on the family farm in upper New York State, retted and beaten and spun before the work at the loom began. I have no idea whose were the woman-hours it took to create them.

Or the pair of handwoven linen pillowcases that do not fit modern pillows, fringed and numbered "12" in cross-stitch that has faded from green to pale brown. The number may indicate that they were the twelfth pair of pillowcases that Eliza Bunn spun, wove, and embroidered in upper New York State. Eliza Bunn was my grandmother's grandmother. Perhaps as she worked on her pillowcases, she thought about her daughter Amelia, who had married one of the Bennett boys and moved with him to the wilds of Iowa. Amelia's first baby had died, and she wrote home that her second baby, Mary, seemed spindly and unlikely to thrive. Would either woman have been comforted, I wonder, to have foreseen Mary's growing up, her marrying and moving to the Montana homestead frontier, her suffering there from drought and deprivation, her loss of a child of her own, and her death at the age of ninety-six in furious silence at the daughters who had forced her out of her own home and into nursing care?

Or the quilts. One is hand-pieced and quilted from dark woolen hexagons arranged in a simple circular pattern. I don't know who pieced and quilted it, but it is in very good condition, which suggests that it was

cherished and little used. My aunts thought it came along with some of
the other family possessions from New York State. My oldest grandson,
when he spends the night with me, likes to drag down the hexagon quilt
and roll up in it.

The other quilt is white-on-white stitching in a petal pattern on cotton fabric. It is a little newer than the hexagon quilt. My grandmother
and her three younger sisters made it as a present for their mother,
Amelia. Although she never showed me how, my grandmother knew
how to trace the petal quilting on fabric, using a dinner plate as a guide.
Her stitches and her sisters' stitches are as even and tiny as though set
by mice, and I think of the four Bennett girls in the last years of the
nineteenth century, working secretly in their bedroom through the hot
Iowa afternoons, and how their needles and thimbles must have grown
slippery, and how they must have longed for cool air and relief from the
aches in their backs. So far I've kept the white-on-white quilt out of the
hands of my grandson and the other children, but the fabric is so thin
that I can see through it in places, and I know it won't last forever.

There can be no intrinsic value in the shoe box of snapshots, newspaper clippings, and land deeds, Civil War militia rolls, letters, and
recipes, some of them dating back to the eighteenth century. The box
was passed down to me by my great-aunt Mable, who, for reasons having to do with her spinster status, acted as the family curator before me.
During her long life, Mable added a few keepsakes of her own to the
cache and, childless, left the box to me. I keep the box on a bookshelf,
a rubber band around it, and occasionally I get it down, sort through the
ancient documents, try to read the copperplate on paper worn to velvet,
and wonder what to do with them. If the papers contain a code, I'm too
far removed to read it. And yet they exude their own power; I can feel
them pulsing on my desk, warm enough to darken the edges and fray
the creases, blur the pencil lines and fade the ink to gold. By some un-
spoken process, I've been designated the servant of the shoe box, the
guardian of this shabby little ark full of papers passed down from folk
who apparently worshiped anything written down, and so I stack the papers back, snap the rubber band in place, set the shoe box back on its
shelf, and try to imagine one of my daughters lifting the lid one day, un-

folding papers I have unfolded, breathing the dust of five or six generations, closing the lid again.

And then what? Sometimes I imagine the box of papers riding the crest of some landfill in the future, briefly glimpsed over the jetsam of plastic bags and broken furniture and rotting fruit, its power blotted out by rising plumes of dust before it disappears forever beneath the treads of the Caterpillar.

Just as, last July, my sister and I wandered the rooms of a house that, after its massive sandstone blocks are hauled away, is likely to disappear into dust and splinters beneath the treads of a Caterpillar. On that day, however, the house and its contents seemed like a grimy capsule of the past, as indestructible as memory. I kept thinking I could see through the dust to the time when my father sat in his chair at the head of the chrome-legged table, brooding over his mug of stewed coffee; when my mother bent to take her roast of venison out of the oven; when a small blond sister ran through the kitchen with her cat in her arms. These were the walls that had witnessed my teenaged angst, my longing to be pretty, to be popular, to be elsewhere. That was one wish that had come true for me, to be elsewhere. For a part of my life, I wondered whether my mother would have been less angry with me if I had stayed home. If I had chosen, like Jackie, to stay on the ranch. If I hadn't gone off to a profession that, to my mother, seemed absurd—"Mary would make a good absentminded professor," she used to say about me, little dreaming how prophetic her words would be.

Now I recognize such thoughts as little more than a child's imagining herself to be the center of all things: It was my fault; it was my doing. The task of my later years, it turns out, has been to unlearn what I thought I knew.

Jackie had climbed the stairs behind the kitchen to the second floor, where our bedroom had been, and I followed. Halfway up those familiar wood treads, hollowed by several generations of feet before mine, I had a memory as sharp as a lightning bolt splitting my skull: a screaming child, a furious woman, and a rhapsody of blows. Some last straw, some spark into smoldering tinder, and a rage that blazed until it burned itself out.

Until the arms exhausted themselves, until the fists could open.

The two older girls huddling together in the kitchen, listening.

Jackie has said that she doesn't remember those episodes. Neither the beating on the stairs or the worse beating outdoors, by the old picket fence. What had happened—something to do with the pony, some last straw, some spark into the smoldering tinder—until the furious woman finally picked up the pony's leather bridle and lashed the child with it, lashed the screaming child over and over with the weight of the bridle until her arm wore out. And the two older girls had watched, silenced and stilled in the flaming red heat of their mother's rage. What Jackie says she remembers is the telling of it—her older sisters telling her about it over the years. Sometimes I think that if there hadn't been two of us to witness, I wouldn't have remembered.

If I was ever a last straw myself, I don't remember that, either.

In that dim upper story, filled with everything my mother walked away from, Jackie and I found a few things we would carry away. My pressure cooker and canning jars, stored from the days when I cultivated a large vegetable garden, I would take those. My oldest daughter, Elizabeth, plants a large garden every summer, and she can use the cooker and jars. The thought was almost enough to lift me out of that stale, overheated atmosphere under the attic. But it wasn't until we came to the big closet at the end of the hall, the closet that probably had been planned as a bathroom but never plumbed, the closet that had held the chamber pot and the overflow of clothes and the boxes of dress goods and some of the books, that we came upon what my mother had kept.

Had kept carefully. Meticulously. Folded precisely and reinserted, each in its own envelope. Rows and rows of pattern envelopes crammed tightly together on a shelf. Here was every dress pattern, every shirt pattern, for every garment my mother had ever sewn. I touched one. From the illustration on the front of the envelope, I could see it was a pattern for a western shirt with a bib front, a shirt my mother had probably sewn for my father or possibly for my brother-in-law. She had refolded the pattern pieces and put them carefully away, so that if she ever wanted to make a shirt like that again, she would have every yoke and cuff and facing. For a moment, the content of all those pattern envelopes rose and danced, each a simulacrum of the bodies that had worn the clothes those patterns had traced, skirts and blouses for little girls and shirts for my father and housedresses and aprons for that ranch wife, my mother, each a ghost of itself in gray pattern paper. And I had the mad impulse to take all those patterns and lay them out on fabric and sew the clothes, to give shape and substance to all that has passed, all that has been lost.

Instead, I turned and, with my sister, walked down those strangely familiar stairs and through the haunted kitchen, out the door, with the dogs bursting ahead of us into the sunlight, where the young horses raised their heads from grazing.

Beginning Dialogues

TOI DERRICOTTE

On the way he said, "When you visit the cemetery, you do it for yourself. They don't know you're there." But maybe some part of me believes she will know, that she brought many good things to me after her death, that she's taking care. Maybe I visit her grave because she would have visited the grave of her mother, because she taught me to send thank-you notes and be a good girl. Maybe I'm going to find signs of whether she's still there, that she hasn't blown open the ground and we find an angel lounging on her gravestone, saying, She's not here. Go and find her elsewhere.

I DON'T SEEM to suffer the pains of anguish that many women feel whose mothers have died. Last night, a group about my age, all in that midlife past midlife, late fifties or early sixties, ate dinner and talked about our mothers' deaths. It's not a new conversation—women whose mothers die always talk about it; they did even when I was in my twenties. Yet, here, no one is hearing these stories with expectancy; everyone has faced that which at one time was unthinkable. It's as if we're all in the same club, as if we have all finally arrived, as if we could all look back at those women on the other side and know we are totally new.

———————

O N E   W O M A N   T A L K E D about that inconsolable stabbing in the heart when she realized she wouldn't buy a Christmas present for her mother again this year. I've wondered about it, about perhaps having grieved the separation between my mother and myself in my early child-hood, for, in a way, I truly do not miss her like that, do not feel that ir-reversible moment of no return as I did when she would go into the bathroom and shut the door, the ache that breaks the heart and has no answer. I felt the goneness of her then as if the center of me was gone, and I tried to bring it back by peering under the crack at the bottom of the door, trying to see anything, her feet.

I said this to the women who talked last night about their mothers. One woman said that her mother had died a few days after she was born, a woman who had always struck me before as cold, contained, and now, as she spoke, I noticed she was squeezing the fleshy part of her check, near her mouth, making a little fat bubble of flesh between her ring and baby finger. I have seen that before, a kind of clumsy uncon-scious pinching of the self, and it makes me feel great pity; her fingers seemed squat, doing an act whose purpose I couldn't imagine—perhaps a partial holding to signify that she could not hold the whole of what she needed held; now, clumsily, here was her body—was it her clumsy body that had killed her mother, ungracefully slipping out?—her liveliness as if covered by a dreary cape, her hair dreary, her face unmade, as if no-body would care, speaking about her mother's death—we had never heard of this, though we had known her years!—without tears, just those two fingers clenching and opening, pinching a clump of cheek, letting go and clenching again, moving slightly, as if she couldn't find the right spot, and since the cheek is larger than what those two fingers can grasp, and since the two fingers form a small vise and take in only a slot of flesh, it seemed she was stopping the flesh from moving, clamping it in place. It seemed inadequate, incomplete, and ill-chosen; in literature, the small thing signifies the whole of something we can imagine from the reference to the small thing, but here, the small reference did not convey. Perhaps it was a clumsy effort, as a child might pinch the breast, or an effort to make another mouth, to pucker the face, as the lips of the child might pucker for its mother's breast.

———————

AT MY MOTHER'S grave, I tried to imagine what I should do. My partner had taken my picture at the grave, and had taken a picture of the inscription. He was sitting in the car. How long should I stay? My mind didn't know what to settle on. No particular feeling or idea carried me. I became lost in nothing. Just me stuttering over an immensity that I couldn't absorb, the way I used to feel guilty for not feeling enough happiness at Christmas, after my mother's great efforts. I guess I felt that I was incompetent, too broken to hold. I sang her favorite song, "This Little Light of Mine." I wanted to give her a promise; I wanted to change my life because of her, just the way I had before.

I am struck with my own inability to feel that grief. It feels like a refusal to face an end. I know I have great trouble facing boundaries, my own and other people's. So, instead, perhaps there is this magical thinking built on my own inadequacy to face the truth: I say I get messages from my mother that she is still in my life, and now, perhaps even more, she is reaching me, now that her destruction is out of my way.

ONCE, WHEN I called a friend to say I couldn't go on teaching at the prestigious workshop I was visiting because I could not stand the torturing voices in my head, twenty-four hours a day, saying that I'm no good, stupid, not as smart as the others, not as respected or loved, that I have no value, that I am only there because I am black, that I have done or said the wrong thing, that I am not really a poet, my friend said, "Why not ask the torturing voices from where they get their information." I did and, without hesitation, they answered, From your mother. Things had changed by then, so I flipped back: You haven't got the latest news!

Just a few months before she died, my mother turned the universe of an unloved daughter around with one sentence. Instead of screaming at me when I asked her not to come to one of my readings because I might read things that would make her uncomfortable, she said, "Oh dear, would you be uncomfortable? I don't want you to be uncomfortable. Then I won't come."

I've written a lot about messages from her, so I won't repeat them here, except to say my conversation with my mother isn't over, and I think it isn't over for her, either.

IN THE MANUSCRIPT of her book, I read about the women in her childhood, her mother, aunts and grandmother, who helped one another beyond the bounds of the imaginable. Because of their hard labor, our family succeeded. I read this manuscript, which she put into my hands to publish only two days before her death, and I think, My mother began writing after I did, after I was published, and yet she was a writer before she began writing. Though she is dead, our stories are in dialogue—my writing has been against her writing, as if there was a war between us. It is more than our writing that is in dialogue; it is our lives.

WHEN I WAS seven, she told me how, when she left the house of the rich white people her mother worked for, the white kids were waiting to beat her up on her way to school, and as soon as she crossed the line to the black part of town, the black kids were there to beat her up, too. Why would she tell me that story? Why would a mother tell a seven-year-old such a sad story, such a defeating one? I thought it was her way of saying, Trust no one but your mother, a way of binding me to her by making me fear.

It's a question, what she said and did that I didn't understand, what she did to hurt me. It is not over; it is still a riddle being solved. I do not need to be held and so, therefore, isn't my mother, too, free? Is that why she told me those stories? Was I to be the mother who freed her?

MY PARTNER AND I have just spent a delightful weekend together, a sunny, windy fall weekend with the trees half-shredded, the bright blue sky both miraculous and unavoidable through the nude branches and their silence. On the drive home, my mind comes to how my life has changed since my mother's death; how, slowly, I have been unloosed from those heavy, nearly inconsolable fears like Houdini from his chains, lock by lock; as if some magician part of me occasionally appears from some unseen and undetectable room with one more chain gone. Finally, I am gloriously undrowned.

Everyone says that I changed for the better, as if, when my mother's slight body, not even one hundred pounds, slipped into the earth, the whole world suddenly belonged to me. The first year, I stopped jogging. People said it was grief, but whatever grief felt like—except for the first few days after her death, especially the burial day, heavy lodestar—it was too indistinct for me to grab on to. Two years later, I bought a house and found a man in my life, like finding a spectacular hat pin in just the right hat. The simple explanation would have been my mother's narcissism, the way she pushed me toward independence, screaming, "You're weighing me down," and yet when I came in late one night when I was sixteen and slammed the door behind me, she was behind it in the shadows, like a burglar, and her hand went around my neck while she screamed, "I'll kill you." Who hasn't wanted to kill the one she loved?

But there was so much unaccounted for, so much in my mother's past that I couldn't fix, not ever, or make up for. Maybe my mother never had such a weekend of happiness with a man as I have just had. Though once a man whom she had had an affair with told me, when I asked about it, how much she had loved to make love to him—perhaps because he loved me and thought I should know that aspect of my mother; perhaps he thought knowing might help me put a necessary piece in the puzzle. Perhaps he had sympathy for me—in spite of the fact he had loved my mother—and didn't feel he needed to protect her. And perhaps he was bragging a bit when he said it.

My mother had slept alone, in another room, in another bed, for eighteen years of her marriage, until she and my father were divorced. I never saw her kiss my father, and the only touch was that time I heard him smash her against the table. My mother always gave abundantly with one hand and pushed you away with the other. The mystery of a beautiful woman. Perhaps in some reciprocal way, my unhappy, angry, guilt-producing mother had been the planter, had been planting the seeds of my happiness with an invisible hand, the hand I didn't see. She left me enough money to buy a house. She told me all my life she loved me, as if she had completely forgotten the hundred slights, humiliations, threats, and insinuations. Of course she loved me—why would I doubt it? She'd scream at me as if my doubts were another evil, another proof of my unworthiness. How exasperating it must have been to be planting those seeds all along with that invisible hand.

The women of that generation, my mother and aunts, counted their blessings: Chinese food and beer on Friday nights after work; a sunday early-afternoon dinner of fried chicken breasts, twice-baked potatoes, and broccoli; parties with a bounteous table, polished glasses and silver, a chandelier, ammonia shiny, every bauble, heat's seven coolnesses, the little cups of rice turned over and decorated, each small white breast with a nipple of parsley. Polished floors, shopping trips, lunch at Hudson's, these were the good things, the punctuation marks that held back despondence, that danced away despair. No hardship was unredeemable to women who had one endless belief: Bread on the water always comes home. I am eating bread from hands that are no longer there. I cannot reach back to touch their actual bodies. It is good that they are gone.

MY MOTHER HELPS me. She sends me signs. Her African violet, which bloomed for the first time on my windowsill three years after her death, on the first day of her death month. She says, Remember me; my miracles are still there for you, still becoming apparent, as you have eyes to see.

I love my mother now in ways I could not have loved her when she was alive, fierce, terrifying, unpredictable, mad, shame-inducing, self-involved, relentless, and determined by any means necessary. When she was a child, she could hold her breath until she was blue and then passed out to get what she wanted from her mother. Even if she had to inflict the greatest pain on me, of making me see her suffer, making me fear her death and feel that I had caused it, she would do it without thinking, without hesitation; that worst threat was always between us, that she could take herself away, that she could hurt herself in my eyes, and it was out of my control to stop it. She was the hostage of an insane government, her own body. And so I revoked my love; I took away, as much as I could, the only real currency between us. I would not count on her to save me from her death. And, therefore, I saved myself by cutting the part of my heart that was in her heart. I cut it off like snipping a pig's tail.

It is only now, now when I am at a safe distance, that my heart begins to grow again, like a little gray balloon that the surgeon puts a valve in to open it up to blood. I listen to the women grouped around me, speaking their mother-grief, and there begins to be an invisible cell, chamber, a thumping like the thump inside the embryo shell, tissues paper-thin, of hardly any substance, except that somewhere within it, still knows what it is, what it will grow up to be used for.

Outport Shadows

MEREDITH HALL

I forget that I am fifty-five years old until I look in the mirror. An average, lumpy, middle-aged woman, I move in the world in another body, my younger body, a body I lived in sometime in the past. I haven't forgotten that home. I know it and love it. It is fluid and agile and smooth. Busy. Graceful, I remember. Strong. It loves work. It loves to heap the wheelbarrow with steaming sheep manure and wheel it down the hill to the garden. To dump the load, which requires all its strength. To grab the spade and spread the manure, load after load, over the soil in the hot sun. This body I know loves to lie stretched on its side, reading, my hand—this hand, if I don't look down—absentmindedly stroking up and over its tight ribs, its bony hip, its long, smooth thigh. This body I live inside loves to burst into a sprint to retrieve my wallet from the car. To tease the dog with a romp. To dance when no one is home, the childhood ballet poses—arabesques, pirouettes, fifth position. To make love in the light of winter sun, goose-fleshed and generous. This body catches the eye. Its clothes hang easily, comfortably. Its skin is stretched tight. Its hair swishes heavily in a long blond ponytail. This remembered body I live inside moves large in the world, visible, watched, wanted.

But the mirror reminds me I am a middle-aged woman. I have grown invisible in the world. I am shocked by this shift every single day. I walk from table to table at a bookstore, moving around other shoppers, picking up books, reading back covers, authors' introductions. A young man with soft black curls and gentle eyes steps in tight beside me and reaches across for a best-selling novel. I smile, move farther down, and say, "Sorry, I'm in your way." He glances at me, through me, and goes on reading. No one looks up.

I stand in front of my college class, a room packed full of hormones and smooth flesh. We are talking about Tim O'Brien, Vietnam. I tell them that, when I was their age, we marched against the war in the streets of Cambridge, that we were chased by cops in riot gear, that we believed we were changing the world. Jessica, a favorite student I know from other classes, says, "It's just so hard for us to imagine you our age. I mean, that you were young and did all these things. That you were ever like us." Twenty young faces nod.

I resist this invisibility. Sometimes the protest is silly: I resent the confident young clerk at the grocery store, her shine and elasticity, her belief that she is here, like this, forever. Sometimes I pity her, her failure to foresee her own inevitable fading. Sometimes I foolishly compete, counting calories and walking extra miles, pretending I'm regaining a few years. Mostly, I'm careful not to look at my reflection in the store window as I walk back out to my car.

But I understand that what I am resisting is not just the inevitability of becoming no longer seen, no longer watched, a giving up of that physicality the world once noticed. What I fight is this certainty: I am slipping along toward erasure, toward no-body. I will die. Once, I was young and vibrant; now, I am in the middle and eclipsed; soon, I will be old, and then I will be gone. Every time I walk unnoted among people, every time I glance in the mirror, every time I look down and see the ropy veins of my hands, I have to tangle, in a quiet, stunned moment, with this underlying truth: I am far along the path.

MY MOTHER DIED before she was old. The mother I remember from my childhood was a miracle of perpetual motion. On two pots of percolated coffee and a pack of Winstons, my mother went to work and came home and cleaned and gardened and cooked her way through each day and long into the night, singing George Gershwin and Ella Fitzgerald tunes. She waxed the floors on her hands and knees with Butcher's wax, then put her old wool socks on my feet and told me to skate until the floors shined. She changed the wallpaper or made new curtains on a bored Saturday. Sometimes we would come out of our rooms early in the morning and find the couch reupholstered in red or green or gold. "Do you like it?" She would beam at us. She stripped and refinished chairs and dressers and beds. She sewed clothes for herself and my sister and me, pleated wool skirts and jumpers and sundresses from curtains she had taken down the month before. She cleaned the chimney and kept red paint on the clapboards and replaced wiring in old lamps and helped Sandy build pens in the garage for her sheep. We wore her knitted mittens and sweaters when it snowed. An insomniac, she read in the long quiet of the sleeping house. The next morning, we would hear her singing as she met the new day head-on.

She was diagnosed with multiple sclerosis when she was fifty-two, close to the age I am now. Multiple sclerosis, we read again and again as we searched for hope, is an incurable progressive disease of the central nervous system. It is an autoimmune disease in which the body itself attacks the myelin sheath that surrounds and protects the nerves in the brain and spinal cord. My mother's body did not recognize itself, and we were faced with the horror that, cell by cell, it was eating itself to death.

Multiple sclerosis is not a kind disease. What we did not yet understand was that, before she could die, my mother would have to say good-bye to her hands, her feet, her arms, her legs; to living her days without pain; to her sight, her bladder, her bowels; to her speech. She was blessed, in the end, because the nerves in her brain outlasted the rest of her and she did not, as she feared, go crazy.

She was brave. She figured out how to get hand controls in her car, how to cook sitting down, how to visit her mother as if she were still the child, second in line to die, how to call me when she needed bread or milk or my voice to calm the panic, how to think about her past without crying, how to think about her future without crying, how to hold grandchildren in her lap and read quietly when she was tired, how to dress without falling over, how to find clothes with no buttons, how to make it to the bathroom on time, how to wash out her panties when she didn't and hang them out of sight to dry, how to allow us to empty the urine bag once she was permanently catheterized. Worst of all the rapid changes was the wheelchair, emblem of an end, of losing the fight, of complete and irreversible helplessness. Mum started to have bad dreams: Fallen beside her wheelchair, screaming, she was helpless while the house burned down around her. I carry those dreams with me still, her dreams of fiery erasure.

I remember her two bodies. One is young, thin and strong, tanned. In pictures of her when she was about the age of my own remembered self, my imagined body, my mother is at ease, confident, graceful. She is leaning against the kitchen door frame, her gabardine slacks and blouse draping loosely on her strong, thin arms and legs. Her eyes flash. She smiles. Her other body is just as vivid: white, her spine collapsed, her hands heavy lumps in her lap, her eyes masked. A long skirt drapes her heavy, shiny legs and hides the urine bag strapped to her calf. Backless, the skirt allows us to change her diapers more easily. This body lies as it is put, a stiff, swollen case that holds my mother.

But there is actually a third body I carry with me every day, still: her perfectly beautiful, translucent body transformed in death. She died on a starry December night. I sat with her for many hours after she died, stroking her face, her arms, her hands. I expected to be stunned with grief. I was not. Instead, as my mother's body cooled, I watched a great and mysterious transformation. The devastation from the illness receded, as if time were in rapid reverse. Her skin smoothed. Her arms and legs and hands thinned, as if muscle again held flesh to bone. Her paunchy belly flattened. The etchings of courage against such fear, of effort and grit, left her face. As her body receded into death, I watched its return to the remembered body, to the life she imagined, to the promise and hope, slipping back and back, an erasing of all the years of struggle. And then she was gone. On the bed lay a pure and perfect—sublime— casting of a woman's form, my mother's body.

Each glance in the mirror startles me not only because I am suddenly a middle-aged woman, but because I am so much my mother, before the disease started to claim her body. Here is her smile, lines creasing her cheeks. Thick hair going gray. The sloping nose with the little ball at the end. Mostly the eyes, my mother's eyes, which stare back out at me from a life lived and ended.

Sometimes when I laugh, I hear my mother's soft, ready laugh. When I sit, curling one foot under me on the chair, I am settling my mother's strong legs. I read, my thumb and little finger holding the book open in my lap, and I am my mother reading. My mother's body is remembered in me, like an echo rising from the past and carrying toward the future. In the mirror, her eyes speak to me from before those years of illness. She is a shadow moving just ahead of me, calling back with the news.

I AM MEMORY. Everything I have been is carried here in my body. I am written, the pain and the great love, the surprises, the losses and the findings. The young woman's body I live inside still, that unforgotten home, is a text. It is engraved with memory, my life. Psychologists believe that grief and trauma are taken up by our bodies and held, that we envelope the memory and build it into ourselves, make it part of us, write it into our cells. We think we have mostly forgotten, but our bodies do not. And we remember love. I have often wished that my children could remember all the tender, floating hours of being nursed, of being held into my heart, stroked and safe. I believe now that they do remember, that their bodies know love and safety. If this is true, then I, also, must carry my mother's love, my father's. Whatever else may have gone wrong, whatever of grief and loss is carried by each of us, so, too, is love. Nothing is lost.

THE WIND WHIPS in from the southwest across the icy water of the Strait of Belle Isle. My tent leans and thunders like a sail. Surf crashes on the shore just below. The stars are out, millions of them, silent and calm in their dome, and a quarter-moon silvers the wave crests. This is not a storm. It is always windy in Newfoundland.

I am fifty-four, seeking solitude on this wild and haunting coast. My tent is crouched up against one of the old houses, where I have tried to find protection from the ceaseless southwest wind. There is no one here but me. There are six houses, all of them abandoned. They cling to the steep rocky hill rising from the bay, as if they themselves are boulders that are slipping into the sea. The bright and cheerful paints of the old Newfoundland—red, blue, yellow, ocher, turquoise—have been worn away over the years; the narrow clapboards are soft gray, black where water has entered the wood and started the slow process of rotting. The houses are square, two-storied, practical cubes of hard work and determination. Their hip roofs, nearly flat, are designed to take as little wind as possible. They needn't carry a snow load; the wind whips it off as it flies. Three of the houses list heavily downhill, like stooped old women. The doors have popped out of their frames from the pressure. Outhouses stand askew. Below, along the shore, several fish sheds ride just above the high water, tilting seaward on rotting pilings. Meadow grass grows high between the houses, but the old paths show clearly still, purposeful paths winding house to house, house to stream, fish store to cod stage, cod stage to shore. In the luminous glow of the night, I can see white lace curtains in the windows, tidy remnants of the lives once lived here.

This is Upward Cove, an outport on Baie Verte on the northern coast. It was abandoned in 1967 when the Canadian government "resettled" Newfoundland's population, forcibly moving families and clans from their ancestral homes in dozens of remote outports into population centers where the benefits of modern life—schools, electricity, medical care, plowed roads—could be delivered more economically. This is a ghostly place. I am drawn here. I sit awake in the night, watching the sea roil, listening to the stones roll in the surf, longing to move into one of these lonely houses. The sadness of the place rides on the wind, heavy and unanswerable. All across Newfoundland, the empty outports cling stoically to their mountainsides, resisting the inevitable.

The beauty is so large and so lonely—the green rocky mountains dropping into the sea, the incessant wind, the hushed village—I am content to sit in the lee and watch, all day, all night. Mostly, I listen for the voices that murmur from so many years ago, asking for borrowed butter, reminding about auntie's bulkhead door, calling the child to her afternoon chores. Someone laughs. Then an answering laugh. Men call up from the fish stage. A boy sings as he stretches a net on the hillside to dry. I remember things I never knew.

The sun rises sharp and clear and warm. The wind dies down; the sea flattens. I sit in the sun in front of one of the old houses, listening to the rich everyday murmur of life, to its thread back in time to other voices that haunt this village. Shadows of its inhabitants slip through the grass, coming and going. The curtains hang white in the morning sun.

In the early afternoon, a woman comes in a rumbling old Ford sedan. I am happy for the company. I smile my greeting as she stops in front of one of the houses that still stand fairly straight. She waves and calls out hello as she stretches. She is about my age, middle-aged. Like most Newfoundland women, she is sturdy, strong-shouldered and short-legged. There is a perfect practicality to her body and her clothing—a cotton skirt and blouse, sneakers.

"Hello, I'm Carolyn," she says easily, barely looking at me. "I'm coming to check on me mother's house." She pulls a dry mop and plastic bucket filled with rags and sponges from the backseat. "Would you like to come in?"

I am always astonished at the matter-of-fact welcome in Newfoundland. "Okay," I say, "if it's all right. I'd like that. My name is Meredith. I'm camping below that lower house. I hope that's okay."

"Oh, yes," she says, "yes." There is a soft, drawn-out patience to her vowels. "No one here to complain anyway, is there now? You're not hurting anything."

Carolyn carries her cleaning supplies to the old door, fishes for a key in her pocket, and pushes the door open. I'm curious but don't want Carolyn to know that. I have tried to peer in the windows of all the houses, but the curtains let me see just shadowy shapes. I have imagined broken furniture and boxes, discarded shoes and worn-down hairbrushes—what was too old or too useless to make the move to the modern world nearly forty years before—lying about on crumbling linoleum rugs, the molding newspaper underlayment showing at the edges. We enter a front hall with steep stairs rising to the bedrooms above. It is surprisingly bright inside, the afternoon sun filtering through the thin curtains in a pleasant glow. The wallpaper, soft pink roses on trellises, is faded but in perfect condition. The banister and newel post are shiny dark wood, polished smooth and bright. The air is musty. That is the only part of this I expected. I am stunned by the homeyness of this decrepit old house. It feels as if its family has been away for a few weeks and is home now to air it out and get back to the rhythms of their daily life. Carolyn stops still, her hands hanging at her sides. I understand in a rush that she stops like this every time she comes here, shocked herself at the life that still breathes in her childhood home.

"Yes," she finally says quietly. "Yes, lovely. This is always harder than I think it's going to be." She looks to her right into a front room, to the left, lifts her eyes up the stairs, then walks toward the back. "Want to see the kitchen, then? Me mother kept a beautiful kitchen, she did. Seven of us kids, five boys, and my mother kept a beautiful home. I wanted her to come out today from town, but she says she can't do it anymore. Me sister doesn't want to come, so it's me."

I follow Carolyn into the square kitchen. The chrome trim on the green cookstove gleams. The table and chairs and sag-bottomed rocking chair and tin-covered kitchen counter are spotless. Glasses and flowered plates lie on the pantry shelves. A young man in uniform gazes softly from a framed photograph hanging over the wood box. The door to the icebox is held open with a wooden spoon. Carolyn bursts into tears. I touch her arm and look away.

The dining room and parlor and four low-ceilinged bedrooms upstairs are time capsules of an old-fashioned life still working in 1967. A sweater hangs on a hook beside a crucifix. The beds are made. Small rugs, braided and hooked, cover the painted floors. "Grammy made these for Mum," Carolyn says. "She made so many rugs, we all have them in our houses." Water stains course down the corners of several rooms. Except for those terrible reminders that this house is sinking into the ground, that its roof is rotting, its sills, its window frames, the house seems ready for a homecoming. Carolyn moves slowly from room to room, opening windows, fingering curtains and bedspreads. "This was my parents' room," she says. She opens a drawer in a small table and pulls out a sewing kit bound in frayed pink ribbon. She opens it, lays it on the bed, then closes it again and ties the ribbon carefully. She shuts the drawer slowly. "It took the longest time for us to believe we were never coming back," she says. "We packed as if we were going for a month. I was seventeen. I thought someday I would live here, just like me mother did. I thought I was going to get married here and dry the fish and have me children here. Some people tried to stay. But the government cut the electric and closed the school. They stopped plowing the road and sending in the nurse once a month, and people got scared. That was it. Everyone's scattered now. It's not like it was. That's all gone forever."

Carolyn sits down on her mother's old bed and stares out the window. She looks older now, as if memory is a weight. As if these sun-filled rooms, waiting for an impossible future, tick along in time, vessels carrying Carolyn toward her own mortality. I think I hear a voice below, and an answer. The white curtains flutter in the summer breeze. I walk back down the stairs and out the front door. Below me, stretching to the shores of Ireland and Scotland and England and France, the sea sparkles in the dispassionate sun. The houses lean toward their own disappearance. They will become heaps of the past, archaeological relics of lives erased. Carolyn picks up her dust mop and bucket, resisting. Someone laughs next door. Shadows slip along the paths in the overgrown grass. I sit by the shore, tossing rocks into the water. The sun creeps across the afternoon, and my shadow follows it. A shadow-arm lifts, throws. Carolyn's mother calls from her kitchen. Carolyn answers, "I'm coming."

As night comes, the wind rises again. I sit in the door of my tent, watching the sea slip from blue to purple to black. The shadows fade. The forms of the houses disappear, and I feel a sudden moment of fear, as if I, too, am being erased. I touch my fingers to my face. I am here. I still have time.

THE LARVAE OF some insects carry "imaginal cells," which hold the blueprint of certain organs in the mature insect. We know that blueprints are carried in DNA. It has been a surprise that cells themselves can carry as memory their future form, separate from DNA. Only a very few of these cells, sometimes called "imaginal primordia," initially live among the larval cells. They are quiet during most of the larva's life, patient repositories of eons of evolution, nests of memory of what the insect will become. When the larva has matured and is ready to transform into its adult state, the imaginal cells start to cluster, and then to organ-

ize into strings of potential. Head structures, legs, internal organs arise
from these masses of imaginal cells. For members of the *Papilio* genus
of butterflies, this means that the imaginal cells abide quietly in the
soup of the chrysalis, knowing all along just what they will become:
fluted wings, legs, haired antennae. The mystery of this metamorphosis
becomes more astonishing. Memory of the very form itself is carried in
these cells, memory of all past generations, transmitters into the future.
Clusters of reassurance binding past and future.

I AM TWENTY. I am somewhere in southern Turkey. It is late summer. It is warm, and very dry. I am thirsty. My bare feet are strong and
calloused. I am thin. I am a girl wandering, searching in solitude for a
way to belong in the world, to carry the past and imagine the future. The
land is beautiful, rolling, arid, and silent. This is an enormous place. I
lose myself in it.

For several days, I have been following a dusty track winding south.
The track has been getting smaller and smaller, an animal trail, or
maybe a shepherd's path. It winds up and over the dry brown hills. I
have not seen a house or shepherd's hut for two days. I am not lonely. I
hear my steps muffled in the stone dust, and the pulse of blood in my
ears. I hum a fragment from one of Bach's Partitas, the same bit over
and over.

Night comes quickly here. In the near dark, I feel the clinking of pot-
tery under my feet; I am walking on tiny mosaic tiles. Fragments, brilliant blue and yellow even in this diminishing light, stretch for hundreds
of feet in the sparse grass. I know nothing. I know no history. Who laid
these bits of clay, this plaza that feels too beautiful even now to walk on?
Other women have walked here. Other women, I know, have been
alone. I feel a momentary jolt of connection, of steadying order.

A small stone building, round and low, rises in the dark. I feel my way
to a door. I have to step down three feet to the floor, where more tiles
crackle each time I step. It is damp and smells green inside. I feel for
the roof—it is a low dome, and tiles clap to the floor when I touch them.
There is a raised platform in the middle, an oblong, covered in tiles. I

listen, but I hear no rats. Pleased with my find for the night, I spread my blanket on the platform and wrap myself up as well as I can against the coming cold.

I wake abruptly in the night, knowing suddenly that this is an ancient tomb. I am a trespasser. I am in over my head. Glued to that altar all night, I stare straight into the pitch-black dome. At dawn, I crawl up into the faint light, the air, the patterns of lives etched for millennia in the soil. On my hands and knees, I study the mosaic design, searching for clues, a map for how a life gets lived, how it all can be contained, how the boundaries can hold the past to the future. Women, mothers and their daughters, walked here once, splashed water on these tiles, laid clothes to dry in this morning sun, called out to one another. I am a girl, a daughter, linked to my mother and my grandmothers. Since birth, I have carried the eggs that will someday become my children. I hear my mother's voice echoing across the brown hills. I answer her: "I am here." These are her hands at the ends of my arms, lifting the small tiles and placing them again, one by one, in the ancient patterns.

THE HUMAN BODY absorbs minerals from the soil in whatever area we grow up in. These minerals bind with our teeth and bones, and bind us to the earth itself. Otzi, the Neolithic "Iceman" found mummified in the permafrost of Austria's mountains, actually grew up in a valley in northern Italy. We know this because his teeth carry molecules of specific minerals—lead and strontium—in a chemical signature unique to that valley. My teeth and bones must carry isotopes—iron? magnesium? selenium?—from the soils of southern New Hampshire, from a small town on the beautiful rich marshes of the coastal plain. I will die somewhere else. When I die, the minerals that have become me will be released into the soil—in Maine or Newfoundland or maybe even Turkey—and will rebind with indigenous minerals in the soil, microscopic testaments to a life. Another girl, there, will eat her carrots, drink her milk, absorb the minerals of her native soil, and carry me in her teeth and in her bones.

———

AMONG MY MOTHER'S old papers, I find a small photograph of a young child. She is wearing a red corduroy jacket with a peaked hood. Her small fingers hold the end of the hood's cord in her mouth. Nearly white hair slips from under the hood. Her head is tilted and she stares straight at the camera with a wide, soft, trusting gaze. Her irises are so large, they make her eyes look black, with a thin halo of deep, deep blue. Her eyes catch me: a child so ready, unmasked, unguarded. I am this child. There is my hand, my chin, one ear.

There is another photograph: an eleven-year-old girl in a yellow dress she has sewn herself, with buttons from the hem to the throat, a softly gathered skirt, and a narrow belt. She is barefoot, leaning against a tree. Her arms and legs are smooth and boneless like a young child's, but small breasts press at the buttoned dress. Her hands are clasped around the tree behind her, leaving her exposed to the camera, but her eyes are shadowed in the bright summer light. I am this girl, these eyes, these legs and arms, this thick hair in the same ponytail I wear now. I remember this day, this time of coming to my new body, of the dawning awareness that I lived in the world, that I had a past, and that a future was coming which I could not imagine.

I am this child. Sometimes I glance in the mirror as I brush my hair back in an elastic band, and there I am: still those girls gazing back at the world with the same blue eyes. We all recognize each other, the child and the woman we could not yet imagine.

THE STREAM ROARS its steady rhythms as I paint my cabin. A family of otters, two adults and a baby, fish at the old beaver dam where the stream leaves my little pond. The only sounds I have heard since I arrived three days ago are the eagle screaming from the sentinel pines ringing the pond and a pair of loons who fly over at dawn, calling in their wild, warbling voice. I am in the middle of Maine's northern wilderness, seven miles from the nearest electric pole and three from the closest hunting camp.

My sons helped me build the cabin two years ago. I was fifty-three. It's small, sixteen feet by twenty. It was hard, hard work. Every single piece of lumber had to be carried three hundred yards down a steep hill on a very rough moose path. I lost weight, became muscle again, slept deeply in the old square tent we lived in for the summer.

I got to know the land. Just behind where the cabin was going, I found the remnants of an old logging camp where a few men had worked the forest with horses and waited for the spring melt to run their winter's work down the stream to the lakes. The bunkhouse, small barn, and cook camp are piles of rotten logs and broken windows; mature trees are rooted in the rich humus of the decaying logs. The old cook-stove, rusted, its parts strewn over ten feet, lies hidden under a stand of moose maple. Orange and red and brilliant yellow mushrooms erupt each summer in the camp remains. When the six or seven feet of standing snow melts in the late- spring, I find more bottles—whiskey, liniment, vinegar—thrust up through the moss by the frost.

We cleared just enough of the white cedar and hemlock trees to tuck the little building into the woods at the edge of the pond. After emptying the new load of lumber and materials from the trailer and lugging it down the path on our shoulders, we spent long days making our way through the piles of new lumber. We laid the ribbons and joists, insulated the box, and stapled hardware cloth and screening to keep mice and burrowing insects out of the insulation. Then we raised the first-floor walls, the upper and lower plates and studs, framing out the rough openings looking out on the pond. We decked the second floor and raised the bedroom walls. Then hair-raising days of setting the ridge and rafters, and sheathing and shingling the steep roof. Windows next, a lot of them because I love the light. Then the doors. Outside trim and clapboards. Insulation. We nailed pine boards horizontally on the inside walls, laid the floors, and built a little kitchen that has an old slate sink and gas stove. My sons managed to bring an old iron bathtub and a new woodstove down the path, and winter came. In the end, it took seventeen trailerloads of tools, lumber, shingles, nails, insulation, windows, and doors, brought from home four hours away and then carried down the moose path on our shoulders, to put together this little cabin. We built it to last. My sons and their children will come to this wild place, listen to the loons on the pond in the night, and eat good food at the table we built.

Today I am giving the clapboards a second coat of stain. The late-summer day is cool and breezy. The pond shimmers with sunlight. A kingfisher sits in her favorite cedar snag at the edge of the pond and cackles. Below me, a wild garden of ferns and bunchberry and bead lily spreads in the moss. One spring of brilliant red maple leaves, the herald of winter coming, catches the light like a gem. I climb down the ladder and move it over four feet, climb back up and work under the eaves with my brush. The wind soughs in the pines and spruces over my head.

The world outside feels chaotic to me. Here, in short respites, I find myself. I remember a slow-motion calm. There is a perfect system here of evolution, the universe silently revolving, expanding. Rhythms of light and dark, warmth and cold, abundance and need, growth and decay. I enter and feel the reassurance that I am part of that perfect order. Invisible in the busy world, an aging woman beyond the pulse of making and doing, here I participate in the fecundity and beneficence of earth and water. I come back to myself. I am beautiful, strong, bursting with life.

I catch my reflection in the window as I paint: the middle-aged face, mine, stretching back to that gazing child, and my mother's—fading blue eyes, squint lines, jowls forming. My hands as I paint are my mother's, the extra skin and thickened knuckles. Signs of arthritis, I'm sure, an old woman's condition. But here, my small life is measured against such an enormity of time, I don't panic. I will die. Mystery and no mystery. The pond will reflect sunlight and ice over and melt and rush the two hundred miles to sea. The moss will die in drought summers and glow like jewels in wet seasons. The bear who leaves muddy paw prints on my outhouse will be another bear. Venus will dominate the evening and predawn skies. No need to panic.

This is a sturdy cabin. It will hold. Carolyn's house in Upward Cove, the ancient tomb in Turkey, the remains of the bunkhouse rotting back to soil behind my cabin keep me from the conceit that it is forever. But as I stain the clapboards and sashes, laid up by my hands in lovely square and true, I am at ease. The day is long. I have a lot of work to do. Then ripe tomatoes for my supper. Later, I will sit by the shore as the light seeps slowly from the pond. My shadow will float among those lengthening on the water. I will rise and make my way back into the cabin's soft glow, part of the world.

CONTRIBUTORS

DIANA ABU-JABER'S new novel, *Crescent*, which won the PEN-USA Award for Literary nonfiction, was published by W. W. Norton in April 2003, has been published in six countries to date, and was included in the top five for the national BookSense list of new spring fiction. Her newest book, a food memoir entitled *The Language of Baklava*, was published in 2005 by Pantheon/Visule Vintage Books. Her work has appeared in such publications *as Good Housekeeping, Ms., Salon, Gourmet,* the *New York Times,* and *The Nation,* and she is frequently featured on NPR. Her first novel, *Arabian Jazz,* won the Oregon Book Award and was republished by W.W. Norton. She is an associate professor in the creative writing program at the University of Miami.

MARY CLEARMAN BLEW is author of the acclaimed essay collection *All But the Waltz*; a memoir, *Balsamroot*; and three books of short stories, most recently *Sister Coyote* (2001). She has also edited *Written on Water: Essays on Idaho Rivers by Idaho Writers.* Her own most recent book of essays is *Bone Deep in Landscape* (2001). Her stories have been reprinted in both the *Best American Short Stories* and the O'Henry Prize Collection. She has won a Pacific Northwest Booksellers Award twice, once for fiction and once for nonfiction.

JUDY BLUNT is the author of *Breaking Clean,* her memoir of life on a Montana ranch. Published in 2002, the book became a national bestseller, garnering extensive reviews and both the 2003 Mountains and Plains Booksellers award and a Willa Literary Award. Blunt is also the recipient of a PEN/Jerard Fund Award, a 2002 Whiting Writers' Award for nonfiction, and a 2004 National Endowment for the Arts fellowship. Her short work has appeared recently in *Oprah Magazine* and the *New York Times.* She teaches creative nonfiction at the University of Montana, Missoula.

ANDREA CHAPIN studied in Spain, worked in Mexico, and acted professionally in Germany in a thirty-city tour of Edward Albee's *Seascape.* She has been an editor at art, movie, theater, and literary magazines, including *The Paris Review, Conjunctions,* and *The New Theater Review,* of which she was the editor. Her fiction has appeared in journals such as *Frank* and *Icarus,* and her articles and essays have been published most recently in *Redbook, Self, Martha Stewart Living,* and the anthology *The Day My Father Died.* She is an editor in New York City and teaches creative writing at NYU.

TOI DERRICOTTE is the author of *The Black Notebooks* (1998), *Tender* (1998), *Captivity* (1990), *Natural Birth* (1983 and 2000), and *Empress of the Death House* (1978). She has received numerous awards, including a Guggenheim Fellowship, two fellowships in poetry from the National Endowment for the Arts, and two Pushcart Prizes. She is the recipient of the Paterson Poetry Prize, the Anisfield-Wolf Book Award, the Black Caucus of the American Library Association Award in nonfiction, and was nominated for the PEN Martha Albrand Award for the Art of the Memoir. *The Black Notebooks* was on the *New York Times* Notable Books of the Year list. She is co-founder of Cave Canem, a historic first workshop retreat for African American poets.

LYNN FREED was born and grew up in Durban, South Africa. Her first novel, *Heart Change* (New American Library, 1982), was republished by Story Line Press in 2000 as *Friends of the Family.* Since then, she has published four more novels, all of which have been on the *New York Times* "Notable Books of the Year" list, and also its "New and Noteworthy Paperbacks" list. *The Curse of the Appropriate Man and Other Stories* was published by Harcourt in 2004, and *Reading, Writing & Leaving Home,* also by Harcourt, will appear in the fall 2005. Ms. Freed's short fiction and essays have appeared *in The New Yorker, Harper's, The Atlantic Monthly, Southwest Review, the Michigan Quarterly Review, The Georgia Review,* the *Santa Monica Review,* the *New York Times,* the *Washington Post, Newsday, Mirabella, Elle, House Beautiful, House & Garden,* and *Vogue,* among others. In 1986, Ms. Freed won the Bay Area Book Reviewers Association Award for fiction for *Home Ground.* Her short fiction has been named in *Best American Short Stories* and *The O'Henry Prize Stories,* as well as reprinted in a number of anthologies. In 2002, Ms. Freed was awarded the inaugural Katherine Anne Porter Award by the American Academy of Arts and Letters. She has also received grants from the National Endowment for the Arts and the Guggenheim Foundation. She is professor of English at the University of California at Davis.

JULIA GLASS'S first novel, *Three Junes,* was awarded the 2002 National Book Award for Fiction. In 2004, Glass was awarded an NEA literature grant and a Radcliffe Institute for Advanced Study fellowship. In 2000, she received a New York Foundation for the Arts fellowship in fiction writing. She has won several prizes for her short stories, including three Nelson Algren Awards and the Tobias Wolff Award. "Collies," the first part of *Three Junes,* won the 1999 Pirate's Alley Faulkner Society Medal for Best Novella. Her second novel, *A Piece of Cake,* is forthcoming from Pantheon Books. Glass lives with her family in Massachusetts.

MEREDITH HALL is the 2004 recipient of the Gift of Freedom Award, a two year writing grant from A Room of Her Own Foundation. She received the 2004 *Pushcart* Prize, and was named in "Notable Essays" in *Best American Essays 2005.* Her work has appeared in *The New York Times* and *Creative Nonfiction.* She lives in Maine and teaches writing at the University of New Hampshire. She is completing her first collection of essays, entitled *Without a Map.*

PAM HOUSTON is the author of two collections of short stories, *Cowboys Are My Weakness* and *Waltzing the Cat,* as well as a collection of essays, *A Little More About Me.* Her work as appeared in many magazines and anthologies, most recently *O* magazine, and most notably *The O'Henry Prize Stories* and *Best American Short Stories of the Century.* She recently finished her first stage play, *Tracking the Pleiades,* and her novel, *Sight Hound,* was published by W. W. Norton in January 2005. She is director of creative writing at the University of California at Davis.

KAREN KARBO is the author of three novels, all of which were named in the *New York Times* "Notable Books of the Year" list. Her most recent book, *The Stuff of Life,* a memoir about caring for her father during the last year of his life, was a People Magazine Critic's Choice and winner of the Oregon Book Award for creative nonfiction. She is a past winner of the General Electric Young Writer Award and the recipient of an NEA grant. Her essays and journalism have appeared in *Outside, Elle, Vogue, Esquire, The New Republic,* and the *New York Times.* She lives in Portland, Oregon, with her daughter and her younger man.

BHARTI KIRCHNER is a prolific author who has published eight books since 1992, including the critically acclaimed novel *Pastries: A Novel of Desserts and Discoveries,* which was released in 2004; *Darjeeling; Sharmila's Book;* and *Shiva Dancing.* Her books have been translated into German, Dutch, Spanish, and other foreign languages. Winner of two Seattle Arts Commission literature grants and a GAP grant by Seattle's Artist Trust, Bharti also writes articles and essays for many national publications and anthologies, including book reviews for the *Seattle Times.* An award-winning cook, she is the author of four popular cookbooks, including the best-selling *The Bold Vegetarian.*

BEVERLY LOWRY is the author of six novels and two books of nonfiction—*Crossed Over: A Murder, A Memoir,* about her friendship with Karla Faye Tucker, and, most recently, *Her Dream of Dreams: The Rise and Triumph of Madam C. J. Walker.* Her essays, feature journalism, and book reviews have appeared in various periodicals, including *The New Yorker,* the *New York Times, Vanity Fair,* and *Granta.* She teaches in the MFA program of creative writing at George Mason University.

JOYCE MAYNARD began her career at the age of eighteen with the publication of a cover story in the *New York Times Magazine,* "An Eighteen-Year-Old Looks Back on Life." Since then, she has been a reporter and "Hers" columnist for the *New York Times,* a syndicated newspaper columnist, a frequent commentator on National Public Radio, performer with the Moth in New York City, and a longtime magazine journalist. She is the author of five novels, including *To Die For.* Her best-selling memoir, *At Home in the World,* has been translated into five languages. Mother of three grown children, she makes her home in Mill Valley, California. Her most recent novel, *The Cloud Chamber,* was published in 2005. She maintains an interactive Web site, JoyceMaynard.com.

REBECCA MCCLANAHAN'S most recent book is a collection of essays, *The Riddle Song and Other Rememberings* (University of Georgia Press, 2002). She's also published four volumes of poetry, most recently *Naked as Eve* (Copper Beech Press), and three books about writing, including *Word Painting: A Guide to Writing More Descriptively.* Her work has appeared in *The Best American Essays* and *The Best American Poetry,* and she has received a Pushcart Prize, the Wood Prize from *Poetry,* and has twice received the Carter Prize for the Essay from *Shenandoah.* McClanahan teaches in the MFA program at Queens University in Charlotte, *North Carolina, The Kenyon Review* writing program, and the Hudson Valley Writers' Center. She lives with her husband in New York City.

BRENDA MILLER is the author of *Season of the Body: Essays* (Sarabande Books, 2002). She is associate professor of English at Western Washington University and has received four Pushcart Prizes for her work in creative nonfiction. Her essays have been published in many periodicals, including *The Sun, Utne Reader, Prairie Schooner, Shenandoah, The Georgia Review,* and *Seneca Review.* With Suzanne Paola, she coauthored the textbook *Tell It Slant: Writing and Shaping Creative Nonfiction* (McGraw-Hill, 2003), and she is the editor in chief of the *Bellingham Review.*

ANTONYA NELSON is the author of four short story collections, including *Female Trouble* (Scribner's, 2002), and three novels, *Talking in Bed, Nobody's Girl, and Living to Tell.* Her work has appeared in *The New Yorker, Esquire, Harper's, Redbook,* and many other magazines, as well as in anthologies such as. *The O. Henry Prize Stones, The Pushcart Prize, and Best American Short Stories.* Her books have been included in the *New York Times* "Notable Books of the Year" list for 1992, 1996, 1998, 2000, and 2002, and she was named in 1999 by *The New Yorker* as one of the "twenty young fiction writers for the new millennium." She is the recipient of the 2003 Rea Award for Short Fiction, as well as NEA and Guggenheim fellowships.

LISA NORRIS'S book of short stories, *Toy Guns,* won the 1999 Willa Cather Fiction Prize and was published by Helicon Nine Press. She won a 2004 Virginia Commission for the Arts fellowship for work on a new book of fiction, *Women Who Sleep with Animals.* Her stories, essays, and poems have been published *in Southern Poetry Review, Notre Dame Review, Ascent,* and other journals. She teaches creative writing at Virginia Tech in Blacksburg, Virginia.

JOY PASSANANTE'S poems, essays, and stories have appeared in numerous magazines, including *The Gettysburg Review, Short Story, College English, Xavier Review,* and *Alaska Quarterly Review.* She has won several awards for fiction, poetry, and scriptwriting, including two fellowships and a grant from the Idaho Commission on the Arts. A fine-press collection of her poems, *Sinning in Italy,* was published by Limberlost Press in 1999, and her novel, *My Mother's Lovers* (University of Nevada Press), was a finalist for the *ForeWord Magazine* award for best fiction in 2002. Her story collection, *The Art of Absence,* was published by Lost Horse Press in May 2004. She is associate director of creative writing at the University of Idaho.

JOAN SILBER is the author of the story collection *Ideas of Heaven*, a finalist for the National Book Award, and four other books of fiction—*Lucky Us, In My Other Life, In the City,* and *Household Words,* winner of a PEN/Hemingway Award. Her stories have appeared in *The New Yorker, Ploughshares,* and *The Paris Review,* and in the *O'Henry Prize Stories* and *The Pushcart Prize.* She has received awards from the Guggenheim Foundation, the NEA, and the New York Foundation for the Arts. She lives in New York City and teaches at Sarah Lawrence College.

LAUREN SLATER'S latest book is *Opening Skinner's Box: Great Psychological Experiments of the Twentieth Century.* She is the author of *Welcome to My Country; Prozac Diary; Lying: A Metaphorical Memoir; Love Works Like This: Travels Through a Pregnant Year;* and *Love Works Like This: Moving from One Kind of Life to Another.* Her work has been chosen for inclusion in *Best American Essays, Best American Science Writing,* and *Best American Magazine Writing.* She is a psychologist and lives in Somerville, Massachusetts.

ANNICK SMITH is an independent filmmaker and producer, arts administrator, and freelance writer whose projects include work on the films *A River Runs Through It* and *Heartlands.* She has received both the Western Heritage Award from the National Cowboy Hall of Fame and the Montana Humanities Award from the Montana Committee for the Humanities. Her books include her memoir, *In This We Are Native; Big Bluestem: Journey into the Tall Grass;* and *Homestead.* With William Kittredge, she coedited Montana's centennial literary anthology *The Last Best Place.*

ELLEN SUSSMAN'S novel, *On a Night Like This,* was published by Warner Books in 2004 and became a *San Francisco Chronicle* best-seller. It has been translated into German, French, Italian, Dutch, Danish, and Hebrew. She has published a dozen short stories in literary and commercial magazines, in addition to winning *Redbook's* short story contest and *Paris Transcontinental's* story contest, as well as a Writers at Work fellowship. She recently published a "My Turn" column in *Newsweek.* She has taught at Rutgers University, UCLA, and Johns Hopkins University. Since returning from five years in Paris, she has taught through UC Berkeley Extension. She lives in Northern California with her husband and two daughters. Her Web site is www.ellen sussman.com.

LOLLY WINSTON'S essays and stories have appeared in *Redbook, Family Circle, Working Mother, New Woman, Sunset, Lifetime, The Sun,* and other magazines. Her first novel, *Good Grief,* was published by Warner Books in 2004. It was a BookSense number-one pick for March/April 2004 and hit the *New York Times* best-seller list. The film rights for *Good Grief* have been optioned by Universal Studios.

THE EDITORS

KIM BARNES is the author of *In the Wilderness: Coming of Age in Unknown Country,* for which she received the PEN/Jerard Fund Award for an emerging woman writer of nonfiction. *In the Wilderness* has been honored with a Pacific Northwest Booksellers Award and was a finalist for the 1997 Pulitzer Prize. *Hungry for the World,* her second memoir, was published by Villard in 2000. Together, she and Mary Clearman Blew edited *Circle of Women: An Anthology of Contemporary Western Women Writers.* Barnes's poems, stories, and essays have appeared in numerous journals and anthologies, including *Shenandoah, Manoa, The Georgia Review,* and *The Pushcart Prize: Best of the Small Presses* anthology. Her first novel, *Finding Caruso,* was published by Marian Wood Books/Putnam in 2003. She teaches creative writing at the University of Idaho and lives with her husband, the poet Robert Wrigley, and their children on Moscow Mountain.

CLAIRE DAVIS'S work has been published in numerous literary journals, including The *Gettysburg Review, Southern Review,* and *Shenandoah.* Her short fiction has been included in *The Pushcart Prize: Best of the Small Presses* anthology as well as in *Best American Short Stories.* Her first novel, *Winter Range,* published by Picador USA, received the MPBA and PNBA awards for fiction. Her second novel, *Skin of the Snake,* was published in 2005 by St. Martin's Press, which will also publish her collection of short stories, *Labors of the Heart,* in 2006. She lives in Lewiston, Idaho, where she teaches creative writing at Lewis-Clark State College.

ACKNOWLEDGMENTS

The stories gathered here represent only a small fraction of the midlife tales and truths that have been passed on to us by female friends and family. We'd like to thank all of those who have shared their joys and their laments in person, over the phone, via E-mail, and over wine at the café.

Thanks to our visionary agent, Sally Wofford-Girand, who encouraged us into action, and to our editor, Deb Futter, who believed in this project from the beginning and became our ideal reader. Robert Wrigley offered his support and sympathies. Our children and siblings offered insight and perspective.

Mothers, aunts, sisters, daughters, grandmothers, cousins, nieces—thank you all for being a part of the continuous community of women who offer empathy, encouragement, wisdom, and grace.